Creating Safe Schools
for All Children

Daniel L. Duke
University of Virginia

Allyn and Bacon

Boston ■ London ■ Toronto ■ Sydney ■ Tokyo ■ Singapore

Series Editor: *Paul A. Smith*
Editorial Assistant: *Lauren Finn*
Marketing Manager: *Brad Parkins*
Editorial-Production Service: *Omegatype Typography, Inc.*
Manufacturing Buyer: *Julie McNeill*
Cover Administrator: *Kristina Mose-Libon*
Electronic Composition: *Omegatype Typography, Inc.*

Library of Congress Cataloging-in-Publication Data

Duke, Daniel Linden.
    Creating safe schools for all children / Daniel L. Duke.
      p. cm.
    Includes bibliographical references and index.
    ISBN 0-205-32018-X (alk. paper)
    1. Schools—United States—Safety measures. I. Title.

  LB2864.5 .D85 2002
  363.11'9371—dc21

                            2001018227

This book is dedicated to all the individuals who have contributed to the success of the Thomas Jefferson Center for Educational Design. Special thanks go to Monica, Jacqui, Dan, Lisa, and Rebecca for contributions above and beyond the call of duty.

It is also dedicated to my mother, Gale Linden Duke, whose caring and sacrifice enabled a little "discipline problem" to mature into a big "discipline problem."

CONTENTS

PREFACE

Creating Safe Schools for All Children is divided into three sections. Following this introduction, readers are given an opportunity to reflect on the issue of school safety and how it has developed in recent years. The first chapter provides an overview of the past half-century, a time that has seen school safety move from the level of a modest local concern to a high-profile state and national priority. Various themes that characterize this dramatic shift are identified and discussed. Chapter 2 examines six perspectives on, or ways to think about, school safety—ranging from the educational and psychological to the organizational, political, cultural, and design-based. It is important for educators and concerned citizens to appreciate the contributions to school safety of each perspective.

The second section of the book is devoted to in-depth discussions of each of the seven standards of school safety. The chapters in this section review contemporary scholarship and "best practice" related to various aspects of school safety, from proactive and preventive measures to effective ways to handle misconduct and criminal activity when they do arise.

Although much is known about how to create and maintain safe schools for all students, considerable controversy and disagreement also characterize the topic. Consequently, the chapters in Section II also investigate a number of unresolved issues concerning the seven standards of school safety. The issues include the costs and benefits of behavioral incentives, the disciplining of students in special education, the merits of zero tolerance policies, and the proper locus of accountability regarding school safety. Matters such as these generate strong feelings on all sides and present educators with a number of challenges. The book avoids taking sides on school safety controversies, opting instead to lay out the strengths and weaknesses of various positions.

The last section of the book contains two chapters. The first raises a variety of questions regarding school safety that educators and citizens in general might ask. Questions concern matters of law and policy, specific safety problems, and school safety in general. The concluding chapter examines some of the lessons that have been learned from the last half century's efforts to safeguard schools.

The appendix contains a comprehensive list of the seven school safety standards and specific recommendations related to each standard. This list can be helpful in auditing the status of school safety efforts in a particular school.

School safety is not the result of luck or magic. It is a consequence of reflection, careful planning, systematic feedback from all those with a stake in schools, training, data analysis, and continuing evaluation. In other words, school safety is a function of thought and effort. Those searching for shortcuts are likely to be disappointed. It is, however, hard to imagine a cause more deserving of our thought and effort than the safety and well-being of our children.

Acknowledgments

Lastly, I would like to thank my colleagues who reviewed this work, offering their professional insight, experience, criticism, and encouragement: William J. Bailey, retired and formerly of the University of Delaware; Judith H. Berg of Rhode Island College; and C. Elizabeth Campbell of the Ontario Institute for Studies in Education of the University of Toronto.

INTRODUCTION

Amanda's mother has heard it all before. The "I'm not feeling wells" and "We're not doing anything todays" are just another sign of adolescent laziness. So, Amanda is pushed toward the school bus as her mother prepares for her own journey across town to the department store where she works as a clerk. Amanda knows what is in store for her, and it has nothing to do with laziness. The eighth-grade boys will taunt her and the other girls on the bus ride to Proctor Middle School. If she's lucky, she won't get hit by a projectile, grabbed, or pushed aside as she tries to exit the bus. Once she arrives at Proctor, she'll have to run the gauntlet of kids from Broadmoor, a tough neighborhood adjacent to Amanda's, in order to reach her locker. More taunts, grabbing, and pushing. Amanda used to breathe a sigh of relief when she finally reached class, but ever since her favorite teacher retired, first block has been taught by a long-term substitute. The woman looks little older than Amanda, and she cannot control the class. Every day Amanda expects a fight to break out. She no longer brings anything to class because she's had two books, a sweater, and a pen stolen. When the teacher's back is turned, the boy behind her tries to touch her in places he shouldn't.

Megan, as usual, is anxious to get to school. She wants to meet with the students in her study group before first period. "Will you *please* hurry up, Mom? We've got a quiz today, and I'm supposed to share my notes with my study group." Megan's mother is pleased that her daughter wants to go to school and that she takes her studies so seriously, but sometimes she'd like to have another few minutes to sip her coffee and read the paper. When Megan is dropped off at school, she typically finds some of her friends and shares any juicy gossip from the previous day. On days when quizzes are scheduled, though, she meets in homeroom with her study group to review. Ever since she started seventh grade at Wilson Middle School, Megan has enjoyed going to school. She likes most of her teachers and finds time to work on the school newspaper and play basketball. So far, to her mother's relief, Megan has shown little interest in boys or dating.

Two seventh-grade girls. One cannot wait to get to school in the morning. The other would welcome any excuse not to leave home. Megan rarely gives a second thought to matters of personal safety. Her teachers provide orderly learning environments in which students like Megan are free to develop academically and socially. Amanda, on the other hand, has trouble concentrating on her studies because she is preoccupied with worries about getting to and from school safely. Her day consists of various maneuvers designed to avoid confrontations. She dare not look too long at a boy for fear of attracting unwanted attention or, worse, upsetting his girlfriend. At Proctor a day does not go by without at least one serious fight requiring the intervention of the principal or the school resource officer. Megan, on the other hand, has witnessed only a few shoving matches outside the gym at Wilson, and the boys who were involved clearly wanted adults to break it up before someone was compelled to throw a punch.

Much of the recent history of public education in the United States is a chronicle of efforts to extend to students like Amanda the opportunities and benefits available to students like Megan. These opportunities and benefits are not limited to quality instruction. They also include matters related to school safety. Amanda should have the opportunity to travel to and from school without fear of being heckled or picked on. She should be able to go to her locker without trepidation. She should have access to the same orderly learning environment that Megan enjoys. Amanda, after all, does not choose to attend school. The state requires her to do so. To compel a young person to attend a school where she is subject to verbal, and possibly physical, abuse is unconscionable.

Although no school, however privileged, is completely safe, the fact is that some schools, such as Wilson, are far more orderly and disciplined environments than other schools, such as Proctor. As concerns over school safety have grown, educators, researchers, and policy makers have tried to understand why some schools experience far more disruption and dangerous conduct than others. As a result of these efforts, knowledge about the conditions that support and sustain school safety has increased substantially. *Creating Safe Schools for All Children* is a consequence of this expanding knowledge base.

Why This Book?

A trip to any library or bookstore reveals a number of helpful resources that deal with how to handle individual behavior problems and manage classrooms effectively. Fewer books, however, provide a comprehensive, schoolwide perspective on safety and related matters. Many threats to school safety do not occur in classrooms, nor are they limited to individual students. This book is intended for any person or group committed to ensuring a safe environment for all students, whether they are in class, walking the halls, eating lunch, or riding the school bus. It should be of value to those involved in creating safe schools from scratch, those charged with reversing a downward spiral of disorder and disruption, and those committed to maintaining productive and orderly learning environments.

Given national concern over raising student achievement, it would be tempting to justify the book's focus in terms of the connection between order and learning. Although such a connection is well established, it is unnecessary to treat school safety instrumentally—as a means to the end of higher test scores. Every student has a right to attend safe schools. The primary justification for school safety is ethical and moral in nature. Were no link to exist between student learning and school safety, parents still would insist that their children attend safe schools.

Many parents unfortunately cannot assure their children that they will be safe at school. When the U.S. Departments of Education and Justice sponsored a compilation of data on school crime and safety, they found that during the period from 1992 through 1994, 76 young people were murdered or committed suicide at school (Kaufman et al., 1998, p. 20). In 1996, students between 12 and 18 years of age experienced approximately 255,000 incidents of violence (rape, sexual assault, robbery, and aggravated assault) at school (p. 2). This same cohort of students was more likely to be victims of theft at school than away from school (p. 2). About 2.1 million thefts occurred in the nation's schools during 1996. The students who were most vulnerable to violent crime were those living in urban areas, but the chances of being victimized by theft were roughly the same in urban, suburban, and rural schools (p. 2).

It would be a mistake to see school safety as an issue solely for adolescents. As the residents of Mount Morris Township, Michigan, can sadly testify, violence knows no boundaries. On February 29, 2000, 6-year-old Kayla Rowland was shot point-blank in the chest and killed. Her killer—a 6-year-old classmate who, himself, was a victim. The young boy lived in a rundown crack house without even a bed to sleep on (Claiborne, 2000, p. A1). Drugs and weapons were easily available. Fences and doors cannot always prevent problems in the community from coming to school.

The challenge of creating and maintaining safe schools is to help people understand that safety is a process as well as a condition. The absence of violence does not necessarily mean that a school is safe. If students and teachers worry that harm may come to them, then school safety is still an issue. School safety is best regarded as a continuing process demanding constant awareness and initiative. School safety entails not only the prevention of inappropriate behavior, but also the promotion of appropriate behavior.

It is possible, on the other hand, to overreact to concerns about safety and, in so doing, create prisonlike environments that repel young people, deny them their rights, inspire disruption, and subvert the academic mission of the school. The fact is that most students most of the time observe school rules. Depriving everyone of an inviting and caring environment because of the transgressions of a small number of students is not the answer to school safety.

Four "Commandments" of School Safety

Efforts to create and maintain safe schools must:

1. Support the academic mission of the school
2. Recognize that students have rights guaranteed by the Constitution
3. Avoid producing hostile and uninviting environments in which students feel alienated and distrusted
4. Inspire students to see the value of order and authority

This book regards efforts to create and maintain safe schools in the same way that a good basketball coach thinks about the fundamental skills of the game. No matter how talented a group of players is, the team must continue to practice and refine the fundamentals—dribbling, passing, and ball movement. Similarly, veteran educators should never assume that they have mastered the fundamentals of school safety. Nor should they decide that they have discovered the perfect plan for school safety. No such plan exists. Just as an expensive automobile must be tuned up periodically, so too the best and most carefully constructed plan for school safety must be reviewed and revised from time to time. Schools and communities are not static entities. Students and communities change. Norms and expectations shift. Resources increase or decrease.

If the approach to school safety advocated in this book had to be given a label, it might be called *pragmatic idealism.* Ideals such as the Golden Rule and safe learning environments are important to identify and pursue. Without ideals, it is too easy for people to settle for the status quo, and with it conditions that are far from desirable. So where does pragmatism fit in? As important as are ideals, their pursuit must not obscure the fact that the world is characterized by inequities, self-interest, misunderstanding, and stress. Such factors mean that people are not always prepared to pursue ideals. People who are jealous or fearful of the motives of others may behave in ways that jeopardize their welfare and the welfare of those around them. Pragmatism dictates readiness for such contingencies.

What Is a Safe School?

Because this book is devoted to creating safe schools for all students, it is important to consider what is meant by a safe school. First of all, school safety is regarded in broad, rather than narrow, terms. A narrow view of safety focuses only on physical harm and encompasses such serious problems as assault, armed robbery, and homicide. A broad view of safety, on the other hand, addresses psychological as well as physical safety. Any threat to an individual's well-being, self-inflicted or otherwise, is regarded as a safety issue. Adopting a broad view means that a school should not be regarded as safe if students are subject to verbal abuse, intimidation, hazing, and sexual harassment, or if they engage in acts that jeopardize their own health and peace of mind.

Though the book takes a broad view of school safety, it refrains from trying to cover every conceivable threat to an individual's well-being. Environmental hazards such as asbestos and poor air quality are not addressed. Nor are threats related to mechanical failures and transportation accidents. Safety issues involving infections and diseases are not discussed. *Creating Safe Schools for All Children* focuses on threats to individual well-being that result from human action. The action may be aimed at one's self, as in the case of drug abuse or a suicidal gesture, or at others. Although some behavior that harms people is inadvertent, this book deals primarily with intentional behavior.

Safety, it should be noted, is more than a set of statistics. It is also a matter of perception. Data tables can reveal declining rates of assault or disciplinary referrals, but students may continue to come to school fearful and anxious because they perceive that the possibility of harm continues to exist. Those who try to understand and respond to the challenge of school safety consequently should never rely solely on school crime and discipline statistics.

A safe school can be considered a place where students and staff not only are physically and psychologically safe, but where they believe themselves to be safe. In addition, a safe school is a secure and disciplined environment. Personal property and school property are not subject to theft, destruction, or defacement. Instruction and other school business transpires without disruption or disturbance. Students and staff respect each other and behave in ways that contribute to effective teaching and learning.

This idealization is based on a dichotomous view of school safety. Such a view holds that a school either is safe or unsafe. Unfortunately, the practical value of a dichotomous view of school safety is limited. No school is likely to be completely safe.

The preferred view, for present purposes, considers school safety to be a continuous variable. In other words, safety exists along a continuum from unsafe to safe. No school is totally unsafe or totally safe. This book strives to help educators and communities create and maintain schools that are relatively safe—as safe as they possibly can be, in other words, given available resources, expertise, and circumstances beyond the school's control.

What is a school, then, that is *relatively* safe? A relatively safe school is one in which *every reasonable effort* has been made to ensure that

- Students and staff are not fearful, anxious, or preoccupied with self-protection.
- Students and staff are free to focus their time and energy on academic achievement and healthy psycho-social development.
- Daily instruction and other activities are not disrupted by criminal activity and misconduct.
- Students and staff respect each other, personal and school property, and the mission of the school.

The key to this conception of a safe school is the notion of "every reasonable effort." No school can guarantee that every student and staff member will be free from harm. Schools, after all, are no different from families or other institutions in this regard. Even prisons, with all of their specially trained personnel and provisions for security, cannot guarantee that inmates or guards will be totally safe. The law recognizes that there are limits to the efforts that can be made to protect people. *Negligence* is the legal term reserved for those situations in which every reasonable effort has not been made. This book describes a variety of reasonable efforts that educators, students, and other citizens can, and should, be expected to make in order to provide their communities with safe schools.

Safety Standards

Much is heard these days about the importance of standards. The term typically is applied to student achievement. Politicians, pundits, and policy makers demand higher standards of student performance and call for huge investments in curriculum development and high-stakes testing to ensure that standards are met.

There is nothing wrong, of course, with expecting students to meet certain clearly defined and sensible standards. What *is* wrong, however, is *only* to hold students to high standards. It is this book's position that before students meet high academic standards, schools and communities should meet high standards of school support and school safety. Standards of school safety concern the conditions that should be in place to demonstrate that every reasonable effort has been made to provide a safe learning environment for students and staff. Current knowledge of best practice in the area of school safety supports seven basic standards of school safety.

Seven School Safety Standards
A reasonable effort to provide a safe school for all students has been made when

1. Students know how they are supposed to behave at school and understand the reasons why.
2. Rules are enforced and consequences are administered humanely, fairly, and consistently.
3. Students feel valued and cared for.
4. A balance exists between efforts to promote appropriate conduct, discourage misconduct, and effectively handle misconduct when and if it does occur.
5. School authorities anticipate and prepare for situations that could be disruptive or dangerous.
6. The physical environment of the school has been designed to promote the safety and well-being of students.
7. Parents and community members are involved in and committed to efforts to create and maintain safe schools.

Standard Number 1 recognizes that schools are complex organizations involving hundreds, if not thousands, of people. To function effectively and protect those they serve, schools depend on the observance of various norms and expectations. Many of these are codified in formal sets of rules or codes of conduct, but certain expectations are often not recorded or shared with students in a systematic way. If schools are to be as safe as they possibly can be, it is essential that students know how they are supposed to behave. Awareness of rules and other expectations, however, is only part of the first standard. Perhaps of greater importance is the fact that students understand *why* they are expected to behave in certain ways. When rules appear arbitrary, punitive, or intended primarily for a small number of "problem" students, they invite criticism and rejection.

The existence of rules and other forms of behavioral expectations presumes a system for ensuring their observance. The credibility of schools as rule-governed organizations depends on enforcement that is humane, fair, and consistent. These qualities also should characterize the administration of consequences for failure to obey rules. School discipline should not "teach" young people that justice is arbitrary or that consequences may vary depending on *who* you are.

Clear expectations and their conscientious enforcement are necessary, but they are insufficient alone to foster a safe learning environment. Students must feel valued and cared for. If they do not, rules will seem to exist primarily for the convenience and protection of teachers and school administrators. Arbitrary and unfair disciplinary treatment can be counterproductive, resulting in hostility, resentment, and acts of defiance. Feeling good about school is always the first line of defense against misconduct and dangerous activities. When school is perceived to diminish young people and cause them to feel inadequate and anonymous, school itself can be said to contribute to the erosion of safety and security.

Schooling is one of those fields of human endeavor in which there is always more to do than time available to do it. Educators therefore must give careful consideration to how they allocate their time and energy. In the area of school safety, such considerations mean maintaining a balance of effort among three primary tasks: promoting appropriate behavior, discouraging inappropriate behavior, and effectively handling inappropriate behavior when it does occur. The doctrine of pragmatic idealism dictates that educators refrain from placing all of their safety-promoting "eggs" in one basket.

Recent years have witnessed a small, but disturbing number of school-centered tragedies. Serious crime and acts of terrorism, once limited to the world beyond the schoolyard, now intrude in every type of school. Although it may be impossible to prevent all criminal or terrorist acts from occurring, steps can be taken to minimize the impact of these acts. By anticipating possible threats to school safety and developing crisis plans, educators and communities can reduce, and often prevent, the injuries, trauma, and loss of life that result from panic and disorder.

When threats to safety arise, they arise in a physical context. Researchers, architects, and educators have begun to understand many of the spatial characteristics of schools and school grounds that contribute to, and adversely affect, the safety and well-being of students. Aspects of a school's physical environment such as the overall size of the facility, the width of its corridors, and the location of lockers can affect student behavior. Careful consideration of the relationship between school design and student behavior can lower the likelihood of unsafe activity and reduce the victimization of students and staff.

The last standard acknowledges that schools do not exist in a vacuum. Many of the acts of violence that occur in school actually originate in the community. School safety, therefore, requires more than the attention and commitment of educators. Parents, other citizens, and community groups all have important roles to play in promoting safe schools. If safety is a high priority in the community, it is much easier to promote safety in the schools. Without the resources, concern, and involvement of the community, educators can do little to ensure that students have a productive and safe school experience.

References

Claiborne, William. "A 'Life in Chaos' Shaped Young Shooter," *Washington Post,* (March 2, 2000), pp. A1, A12.

Kaufman, Philip; Chen, Xianglei; Choy, Susan P.; Chandler, Kathryn A.; Chapman, Christopher D.; Rand, Michael R.; and Ringel, Cheryl. *Indicators of School Crime and Safety, 1998.* Washington, DC: U.S. Departments of Education and Justice, 1998.

SECTION I

Understanding the Challenge of School Safety

School safety is not a new issue. For decades people have worried over the well-being of children at school. Many efforts have been made to shed light on the origins of unsafe conditions and how best to eliminate or, at least, reduce them. Before taking action to improve school safety or confront unsafe conditions, it is crucial that educators, policy makers, and citizens in general understand how school safety has evolved as a public concern. They also need to realize that there are a variety of perspectives on—or ways to make sense of—school safety. Chapter 1 provides an overview of the recent history of school safety and identifies several important themes that characterize this period. Chapter 2 reviews various approaches to thinking about school safety.

1 The Rise of School Safety As a National Priority

MAJOR IDEAS IN CHAPTER 1

- All schools are not equally safe.
- Research has tried to determine why some schools are safer than others.
- Particular school safety problems vary in perceived seriousness over time.
- School safety no longer is exclusively a local concern.
- State and federal governments and the courts have come to play key roles in school safety.
- The variety and complexity of responses to school violence and disorder have increased considerably.
- Public concern over school safety does not necessarily reflect the actual levels of violence and disorder in schools.

It was a phone call that will stay with Denver Police Officer John Lietz for the rest of his life. Shortly after 11 last Tuesday morning [April 20, 1999], he picked up the line to hear the voice of Matthew Depew, the son of a fellow cop: Depew and 17 other Columbine High School students were trapped in a storage room off the school cafeteria, hiding from kids with guns. Lietz himself had a daughter in the school, and he could hear bursts of gunfire in the background. Lietz told the kids to barricade the door with chairs and sacks of food, and to be ready to attack the gunmen if they got in. Several times Lietz heard the shooters trying to break into the room; they were so close that he could hear them reloading cartridges. At one point, as they pounded on the door, Depew calmly told Lietz that he was sure he was going to die. "Please tell my father I love him," he said. ("Anatomy of a Massacre," *Newsweek,* May 3, 1999, p. 25)

When Dylan Klebold and Eric Harris, two clean-cut high school students from the Denver suburb of Littleton, murdered 12 of their classmates and a teacher before taking their own lives, the tragedy did not signal the beginning of public concern over school safety. Many Americans have worried about the well-being of their children at school for more than a century (Doyle, 1978). The Columbine High School massacre confirmed, however, what many had feared—that no school, however privileged, was immune from violence.

The shootings at Columbine also compelled politicians, pundits, parents, policy makers, and professional educators to confront a number of disturbing questions. How could such acts of naked aggression be committed by young men from seemingly normal families? What factors contributed to their hatred of their high school and many of their classmates? Had Klebold and Harris been influenced by violence on television, in films and music, and over the Internet? Had the strict caste system at Columbine, a system that divided students according to narrow notions of popularity, played a part in the alienation of the two killers? And what of the scope of the violence? Columbine High School had carefully-prepared crisis management plans; so did local law enforcement officials. Why hadn't these plans worked to minimize the carnage?

Some of these questions have a timeless quality to them, whereas others would not have been raised a century ago. This chapter looks at the evolution of school safety as a public concern since the fifties. It opens with an historical overview and follows with the identification of key themes characterizing the period.

The Road to Columbine and Beyond

Nostalgia can cloud recollections of the past. The present, no matter when it is, frequently seems more stressful, less safe, and less virtuous than the past. The decline of morality and civilization has been a consistent theme in Western history for centuries (Herman, 1997). It comes as no surprise that older adults, when confronted with shocking news about violence in schools, recall that life was more tranquil when they were young. In contemporary American society, for example, it is not unusual for people older than fifty to remember the fifties as a "golden age" when the economy was strong, schools ran smoothly, and children respected authority.

Early Warnings

In 1956, the National Education Association, the largest teachers' organization in the United States, published the results of a national study of teacher opinions regarding student behavior. The study was prompted by newspaper accounts of "juvenile gangsterism, stealing, armed assault, and even murder" (National Education Association, 1956, p. 52). Teachers, for their part, registered relatively little concern, however. Most teachers believed that their school neighborhoods and communities were not as troubled as the newspapers suggested. An impressive 95% of the teachers described their students as either "exceptionally well-behaved" or "reasonably well-behaved."

The behavior of young people, despite the positive feelings of the teachers, continued to surface as an issue in the fifties. The rebelliousness of teenagers became a theme in films, music, and plays like "West Side Story." For the most part, though, adolescent "acting out" was confined to the streets, not the schools. Fears, however, began to grow that schools soon would be forced to deal with these problems.

The December 1959 issue of *Phi Delta Kappan*, a respected education journal, was devoted almost entirely to articles related to increasing behavior problems among young people. One author noted that schools not only were victims of these problems, but also contributors (Morse, 1959, p. 109). Another author argued that schools were obliged to address the delinquent population, heavily represented by children of poor families, and prepare them for "a law-abiding lower-class way of life" (Widen, 1959, p. 106). Compulsory school attendance laws, according to a third writer, accounted for many behavior problems by compelling "unwilling" students to remain in school (Manning, 1959, p. 95).

In a pathbreaking book on American teenagers at the end of the fifties, James Coleman tried to place the growing concern over young people in sociological perspective. The book's title, *The Adolescent Society*, said it all: young people had formed their own society. Much of this society's identity derived from challenging adult norms and values, including the value of academic achievement and respect for the authority of elders. Although it was unclear whether teenagers had voluntarily pulled away from their parents or their increasingly busy parents had abandoned their children, the disturbing fact remained:

> The adolescent lives more and more in a society of his own, he finds the family a less and less satisfying psychological home. As a consequence, the home has less and less ability to mold him. (Coleman, 1961, p. 312)

Delinquency, Disruption, and Dissent

The sixties forever will be associated with generational conflict. There is no doubt that young people were more likely than in previous decades to question adult authority. Of course, much of this questioning was legitimate, given the nation's struggle to achieve racial equality and its involvement in an unpopular war in Southeast Asia. Young people played a major role in the civil rights movement and the anti-war movement, in the process exercising their First Amendment rights and sustaining a long tradition of public protest in the United States.

Not all of the challenges to authority during the sixties, however, were inspired by civic mindedness. The participation of some young people in school protests and demonstrations seemed to many to constitute sheer opportunism, an occasion to disrupt learning and misbehave. Juvenile delinquency and crime rose to alarming heights as well. In 1965, juvenile courts in the United States handled 697,000 delinquency cases (excluding traffic offenses), an all-time high up to that point (Schafer & Polk, 1967, p. 222). So concerned about crime in general was President Lyndon Johnson that he created the Presidential Commission on Law Enforcement and the Administration of Justice. The commission, in turn, formed the Task Force on Juvenile Delinquency.

In 1967 the task force published its report, titled *Juvenile Delinquency and Youth Crime*. The fact that the word "crime" was joined with the more moderate term "delinquency" suggested that youth problems were perceived to be growing more serious. The second chapter of the report focused on understanding the origins of juvenile delinquency and crime. Blame was distributed broadly and included conditions in America's urban slums, the erosion of the family, negative peer in-fluence, and problems with public education (Task Force on Juvenile Delinquency, 1967, pp. 41–56). The report noted that schools contribute to delinquency by using methods that "create the conditions of failure for certain students" (p. 49).

The recommendations of the task force reflected the idealism of the sixties, particularly the conviction that a combination of federal and state pressure, large infu-sions of money, and local initiative could overcome the effects of poverty and disad-vantagement. Among the report's suggestions were the following:

- Improve the quality and quantity of teachers and facilities in the slum school
- Combat racial and economic school segregation
- Relate instructional material to conditions of life in the slums
- Deal better with behavior problems [in school]
- Raise the aspirations and expectations of students capable of higher education

Educators faced the proverbial "chicken and egg" dilemma. Should they begin by concentrating on the establishment of order and control, or should they improve the quality of teaching and curriculum content in the hopes that better behavior would result? Risks and uncertainties, of course, were associated with either course of action. Complicating matters in many schools was the advent of desegregation. For the first time in the sixties, many previously White schools enrolled large numbers of African American students. Although desegregation proceeded relatively smoothly in some schools, others experienced considerable tension and occasional outbreaks of violence.

In his sweeping history of Hamilton High, Gerald Grant (1988) chronicled the integration and subsequent disruption of an eastern high school in the sixties. He noted that many students were fearful of associating with classmates of another race and that the mostly White teaching staff felt unable to deal directly with racial fric-tion. When the U.S. Civil Rights Commission conducted a field study at Hamilton High, it found that

> ...few teachers were prepared for desegregation. Most had no experience in interracial classrooms nor in teaching black students typically two years behind their white class-mates. Standards of discipline differed markedly from the predominantly black schools in the inner city to the mostly middle-class schools who received the black pupils. (Grant, 1988, pp. 25–26)

Prior to the sixties, threats to school safety tended to come in the form of indi-vidual acts or incidents involving a few students. With the sixties came the prospect of large-scale disruption—demonstrations, boycotts, riots, and racial confrontations. When a deeply concerned U.S. House of Representatives commissioned the "Survey of Student Unrest in the Nation's High Schools" in 1969, it learned that 18% of the more than 15,000 surveyed schools experienced disruptions (Pucinski, 1970, pp. E1178–E1180). The nature of the disruptions, however, had less to do with political or ideological matters than school policies. More than twice as many schools reported student disruptions related to repressive school rules and dress codes than to political reasons.

Student pressure for fair and reasonable treatment at school found favor in the courts during the sixties. In 1967 a nonschool case, *Gault v. Arizona*, set the tone for the coming decade when the U.S. Supreme Court declared that juveniles were covered by the same rights as adults. The right in question was due process, and the court stated that minors must be accorded due process, including timely notification of charges, access to legal counsel, and privilege against self-incrimination. Eight years later the Supreme Court reviewed a school discipline case, *Goss v. Lopez*, in which a number of students had been suspended from school in Columbus, Ohio. Although some students had committed documented acts of violence, Dwight Lopez claimed that he had been an innocent bystander. Given no opportunity to hear the charges or defend himself, Lopez also was suspended.

In a 5–4 opinion, the U.S. Supreme Court ruled that Lopez and other students were entitled to due process but they had been denied this right. School authorities, in effect, had denied the suspended students a property right—the right to an education—that was protected by the Constitution. The Court referenced an earlier case, *Tinker v. Des Moines Independent School District* (1969), which stated in unambiguous terms that young people do not "shed their constitutional rights" when they enter school.

By the end of the sixties, many educators felt, with ample justification, that their authority, traditionally protected by the principle of in loco parentis, had eroded to a point that they could no longer ensure the effective operation of their schools. Indicative of the assault on professional authority was a document titled *Academic Freedom in the Secondary Schools* that was published by the American Civil Liberties Union in 1968 (Grant, 1988, p. 51). The influential statement argued that students sometimes should be "permitted to act in ways which are predictably unwise so long as the consequences of their acts are not dangerous to life and property, and do not seriously disrupt the academic process." More than a few educators doubtless wondered about the dividing line between serious and nonserious disruption.

Some Encouraging Signs

Although public concern over delinquency and youth crime continued at high levels during the seventies, there also was reason to be encouraged. The federal government, for instance, began to play an active role in studying the problems of young people and supporting interventions intended to reduce crime in schools and communities. The decade commenced with a concerted federal effort to address one of the country's greatest safety concerns—the spread of drug use among the young. In 1970, Congress passed the Drug Abuse Education Act, Public Law 91-527, which called for the development of drug awareness curriculums, teacher training, and community education programs. This legislation was followed in 1972 by the Drug Abuse Office and Treatment Act, Public Law 92-255, which created an agency to coordinate federal drug abuse prevention efforts as well as the National Institute of Drug Abuse.

In 1974, Congress passed the Juvenile Justice and Delinquency Prevention Act (P.L. 93-415), thereby providing technical assistance, staff training, and other resources to develop programs aimed at keeping students in school and reducing suspensions and expulsions. The bill acknowledged that when young people remained in school, they were much less likely to commit crimes in the community. Retaining potential dropouts, however, posed a challenge to educators, who were expected to control young people who frequently were unmotivated to learn or obey rules.

As part of the Education Amendments of 1974 (P.L. 93-380), the Ninety-third Congress also mandated that the Secretary of Health, Education, and Welfare conduct a comprehensive study "to determine the incidence and seriousness of school crime; the number and location of schools affected; the costs; the means of prevention in use, and the effectiveness of those means" (U.S. Department of Health, Education, and Welfare, 1978, p. 1). Four years later a massive study, *Violent Schools–Safe Schools*, was published, providing educators and the public with the most systematic investigation of school safety ever conducted in the United States.

Drawing on surveys of school administrators, teachers, and students, as well as in-depth case studies of particular schools, researchers concluded that acts of violence and property destruction in schools had leveled off after the early seventies (U.S. Department of Health, Education, and Welfare, 1978, p. 2). Neill (1978, p. 303) supported this finding in a separate analysis of media coverage of education issues. Although school violence and vandalism in 1975 had been the most publicized issues, by 1978 concern had shifted to declining academic achievement.

To say that violence and vandalism had leveled off, of course, was not to say that they had ceased to be problems. *Violent Schools–Safe Schools* pointed out, for example, that the risk of violence to teenagers was greater *in school* than anywhere else, when the amount of time spent in school was taken into account. Though young people ages 12 to 19 spent no more than 25% of their waking hours in school, 40% of the robberies and 36% of the assaults on teenagers occurred in school (U.S. Department of Health, Education, and Welfare, 1978, p. 2). When the principals of 6,700 schools, both elementary and secondary, were surveyed, 8% reported that school crime was a serious problem (p. 2). The study confirmed what many people believed, that some schools were much safer than other schools. It also found evidence that junior high and middle schools were more dangerous in many ways than high schools.

Support for the principals' perceptions came from teachers and students. Researchers reported the following (U.S. Department of Health, Education, and Welfare, 1978, p. 5):

- 22% of all secondary students reported avoiding some restrooms at school because of fear.
- 20% of the students said they were afraid of being hurt or bothered at school at least sometimes.
- 3% of the students (approximately 600,000) reported that they were afraid most of the time at school.

- 12% of the secondary school teachers (approximately 120,000) said they were threatened with injury by students at school.
- 12% of the teachers said they hesitated to confront misbehaving students because of fear.

Despite these troubling statistics, *Violent Schools–Safe Schools* offered encouragement to advocates of greater school safety by identifying a number of characteristics of relatively safe schools. Schools where students and teachers were free of fear dealt with issues of order, discipline, and safety in a systematic way. Administrators were perceived to be firm, but fair, when it came to enforcing disciplinary policies. Policies were enforced consistently by teachers and administrators. Safe schools also tended to engage students and community members in efforts to reduce the likelihood of violence.

Years before the publication of *Violent Schools–Safe Schools*, a number of local schools and school systems, especially those in urban areas, had begun to develop systematic approaches to school safety. Offices of school security emerged in the early seventies, as larger school districts started to employ their own security personnel. Links between local police and schools were established. Changes were made in the physical environment of schools, including security locks on outside doors, intrusion alarms on windows, electronic surveillance systems, and hot lines between schools and local law enforcement offices. These initiatives likely contributed to some of the leveling off of safety problems that was noted in the government-sponsored study.

The courts began to shift their position somewhat on matters related to school discipline toward the end of the seventies. The singular focus on student rights was balanced against greater deference to the authority of school administrators. This move was initiated by the case of *Ingraham v. Wright* in 1977. Two junior high school students in Florida had been paddled for disciplinary reasons. They filed suit against school administrators, claiming that their corporal punishment violated the constitutional injunction against cruel and unusual punishment. The case eventually reached the U.S. Supreme Court, where the justices determined that the paddling, although excessive, did not violate the Eighth Amendment.

In 1985 the U.S. Supreme Court ruled, in *New Jersey v. T.L.O.*, that school officials did not have to observe the Fourth Amendment requirement of a search warrant when *reasonable suspicion* of a threat to school order existed (James, 1994, p. 193). The case involved a 14-year-old high school student who was caught smoking in a school restroom. The student denied smoking when questioned by a school administrator, so the administrator searched her purse. The search revealed not only cigarettes, but marijuana, rolling papers, a pipe, and other incriminating evidence. When the girl was suspended for possessing marijuana as well as smoking, she sued on the grounds that her Fourth Amendment rights had been violated. The Supreme Court ruling in *T.L.O.* recognized that educators face special challenges in preserving safe learning environments and should be partially exempted from the need to obtain search warrants.

Several developments during the seventies signaled a broadening of the scope of school safety, and with it, increased complexity for school authorities responsible for protecting students from harm. Title IX of the Education Amendments of 1972 addressed the issue of sex discrimination in schools, particularly in the area of athletics. Eventually, however, in the 1992 U.S. Supreme Court case of *Franklin v. Gwinnett County Public Schools*, Title IX became the basis for addressing sexual harassment in school.

Congress also acted to protect students with handicaps during the seventies. The Rehabilitation Act of 1973, Public Law 93-380, declared that no program receiving federal funds could discriminate against persons based solely on their handicaps. Two years later, the passage of the Education for All Handicapped Children Act, Public Law 94-142, established the right of children with handicaps to free and appropriate public education. As a consequence, school authorities were compelled to reconsider the exclusion of disabled students, including those who posed a threat to the safety of their peers and the orderly operation of school.

Schools at Risk

On August 26, 1981, Secretary of Education Terrel H. Bell created the National Commission on Excellence in Education and directed it to investigate the quality of schooling in the United States. Two years later the blue ribbon panel chaired by David Gardner issued a report, titled *A Nation at Risk*, that set the course for educational policy through the end of the century. Linking education to the prosperity, security, and civility of the nation, the report offered a comprehensive set of recommendations to address public concerns about the "rising tide of mediocrity" in the schools and to promote educational excellence. *A Nation at Risk* also reminded educators and the general public that schools were charged with a moral as well as an intellectual mission.

The relationship between learning and order became clear when the commission tendered recommendations for increasing the effective use of time in schools. The burden on teachers for maintaining discipline should be reduced, the group declared, through the development of firm and fair codes of student conduct that are enforced consistently, and by considering alternative classrooms, programs, and schools to meet the needs of continually disruptive students (National Commission on Excellence in Education, 1984, pp. 75–76).

Here was a clear cue for a shift in educational policy. After a decade of efforts to promote greater inclusion of problem students in mainstream school activities, the commission acknowledged that educational excellence might demand that certain uncooperative young people be assigned to alternative learning environments. All children, of course, must be accorded an opportunity to learn, but those who were unable or unwilling to abide by school rules should not be allowed to interfere with their classmates' opportunities to learn. Was such a tough position on school discipline warranted?

When the National Center for Education Statistics compiled data from the 1982 component of the High School and Beyond Study, it found that 29% of the students who were questioned believed that their school had a problem with student fighting (Plisko & Stern, 1985, p. 64). Other problems included class cutting (65%), poor attendance (54%), and threats or attacks on teachers (5%). Seven percent of the respondents indicated that they did not feel safe at school. The data also indicated that perceived safety problems in Catholic and other private schools were substantially less than in public schools. Such findings bolstered the Reagan administration's support for greater school choice for parents.

Students were not the only ones who registered concern over school safety in the eighties. When the U.S. Department of Education (Stern, 1987, p. 70) surveyed a sample of junior and senior high school principals during the 1983–84 school year, it found that:

- Students had been caught selling illegal drugs in 35% of the schools.
- Thefts of personal items valued over ten dollars had occurred in 82% of the schools.
- Police had been contacted for law violations in 72% of the schools.

The percentages of problems were substantially higher for schools of 1,000 or more students and schools in suburban and urban areas. Small schools and schools in rural areas reported lower percentages of safety-related concerns.

Another source of perceptions of problems in public schools was the annual Gallup Poll of the Public's Attitudes Toward the Public Schools. Throughout the seventies and early eighties, "lack of discipline" consistently appeared as the number one concern among citizens in general. Then, in 1986, an interesting change occurred. Lack of discipline dropped to the second position, supplanted by "use of drugs." By 1989, 34% of the people polled by Gallup believed that drug use was a big problem in schools (Elam & Gallup, 1989, p. 42). Lack of discipline was mentioned by only 19%. In an effort to address the growing concern over youthful drug use, First Lady Nancy Reagan launched her "Just Say No to Drugs" campaign in August 1986.

School violence resurfaced as a major source of public anxiety at the end of the decade. On January 17, 1989, a 26-year-old man armed with an AK-47 semiautomatic rifle entered the schoolyard at Cleveland Elementary School in Stockton, California, and began firing on children at recess. Five youngsters were killed. A shocked nation renewed pressure for gun control and greater protection for children at school. The coming decade, unfortunately, would prove that the Stockton massacre was not an isolated event.

A National School Safety Goal

In the fall of 1989, President George Bush convened an unprecedented meeting of the nation's governors at the University of Virginia. The purpose of the so-called Education Summit was to develop a truly national education initiative that would place American students in the front rows of the global classroom. The ultimate result of the Charlottesville meeting was a set of eight national goals and a commitment on the part of the states and the federal government to cooperate in achieving them. Goal 7 dealt directly with the issue of school safety:

> By the year 2000, every school in the United States will be free of drugs, violence, and the unauthorized presence of firearms and alcohol and will offer a disciplined environment conducive to learning.

To accomplish Goal 7, seven specific objectives were identified by the National Education Goals Panel (1995, p. 13):

1. Every school will implement a firm and fair policy on use, possession, and distribution of drugs and alcohol.
2. Parents, businesses, governmental and community organizations will work together to ensure the rights of students to study in a safe and secure environment that is free of drugs and crime, and that schools provide a healthy environment and are a safe haven for all children.
3. Every local education agency will develop and implement a policy to ensure that all schools are free of violence and the unauthorized presence of weapons.
4. Every local educational agency will develop a sequential, comprehensive kindergarten through twelfth grade drug and alcohol prevention education program.
5. Drug and alcohol curriculum should be taught as an integral part of sequential, comprehensive health education.
6. Community-based teams should be organized to provide students and teachers with needed support.
7. Every school should work to eliminate sexual harassment.

In the wake of the Goals 2000 program, as the initiative came to be known, school systems across the United States reviewed and revised student codes of conduct, introduced new curriculums to promote conflict management and civility, and developed alternative programs and schools for students who posed a threat to their teachers and peers. "Zero tolerance" became the watchwords of the nineties. Students caught with drugs, alcohol, or weapons on campus, as well as those who assaulted students or staff members, were subject to immediate suspension or expulsion. Schools employed school resource officers, electronic surveillance equipment, and metal detectors in an effort to reduce the likelihood of violence.

The federal government offered assistance to local school systems in various forms. In 1994, for example, Congress passed the Safe and Drug-Free Schools and Communities Act, which reauthorized funding and technical assistance for the development and implementation of school safety plans. In the same year, the Gun-Free Schools Act required each state to have a law requiring school districts to expel, for at least one year, any student who brought a firearm to school. The National Center for Education Statistics and the Bureau of Justice Statistics began compiling comprehensive data bases on school safety information (Kaufman et al., 1998).

In 1995, the halfway point for achieving the Goals 2000 initiative, the National Education Goals Panel published a progress report. Few signs of improvement, however, were reported for the indicators for Goal 7 (National Education Goals Panel, 1995). Use of illicit drugs and sale of drugs at school had increased, as had classroom disruptions reported by secondary teachers and victimizations reported by teachers at all levels. Alcohol use and classroom disruptions reported by tenth graders remained basically unchanged. The only sign of progress was a slight decline in victimizations reported by 10th-grade students.

Not until the eve of the new millenium did data on school safety offer substantial reason for celebration. In 1999 the secretary of Health and Human Services, Donna Shalala, announced that drug use among teenagers fell 15% in the previous year, to roughly 1 in 10 adolescents (Walsh, 1999). Government statistics in 1999 also indicated that crime in general, youth crime, and youth victimization all had dropped during the mid-nineties (*American School Board Journal*, 1999, p. 8). The good news, however, had to be tempered by the realization that the last half of the decade witnessed a spate of tragic school shootings. From Pearl, Mississippi, to Springfield, Oregon, to Paducah, Kentucky, teenagers gunned down their peers. Each incident reminded the public that no school, however well run, was invulnerable to acts of violence.

In one of his last addresses as president, Bill Clinton acknowledged the lessons of Columbine and other school-based acts of violence (Associated Press, 2001):

> Over the past few years, terrible tragedies at Columbine and other schools have forced us to take a hard look at youth violence, and an even harder look at what each of us can do and must do to ensure that such tragedies do not happen again.

Clinton went on to note the efforts his administration made to reduce youth violence. Initiatives included the Brady law to curtail the acquisition of firearms by criminals, the COPS in Schools program, and the GEAR-UP program to provide young people with mentors. One of the final acts of the Clinton administration was to establish a national hotline and Web site for young people seeking help with conflicts and others desiring information on how to combat youth violence.

School Safety Themes

Reflecting on school safety since the late fifties, several themes can be identified. Concern over school safety, for example, has persisted at relatively high levels over much of the period, though the particular problems of greatest concern have tended to vary. Other themes include the following:

- Expansion of the range of concerns associated with school safety
- Expansion of the types of school-based responses to safety concerns
- Expansion of the role of government and the courts in matters related to school safety
- Growing politicization of school safety
- Growth in the knowledge base regarding school safety

This section explores each of these themes in an effort to appreciate how school safety has evolved as a public and professional issue.

School Safety: A Persistent Concern

As suggested in the brief historical overview that opened this chapter, school safety has been a continuing source of concern for members of the public, their political representatives, and educators. Concern is revealed in statistics on school victimization, violence, drug and alcohol use, suspensions, and expulsions. When the Survey Research Center at the University of Michigan compared the percentages of high school seniors who annually reported being victimized at school, for instance, it found considerable consistency over the 18-year period from 1976 to 1993 (U.S. Department of Education, August, 1995). As Table 1.1 shows, victimization rates changed little during this time, with the exception of a slight increase in the percentage of students who reported being threatened both with and without a weapon. In the case of being threatened or injured with a weapon, Black high school seniors were more likely to report being victimized than White high school seniors.

Statistics are important for monitoring actual levels of reported victimization, but they may not reveal the entire story of school safety. Safety is, to a large extent, a matter of perception. Individuals sometimes believe that their safety is at considerable risk when statistics suggest something different. This situation, in fact, occurred in the late nineties. An unnerving series of school shootings in seemingly peaceful rural and suburban schools upset Americans, but the data on school violence actually indicated a decline in homicides and other violent acts. Data, of course, provided little comfort to young people and parents who watched the news coverage of Columbine High School. The message of Columbine was stark in its clarity—no student in any school is completely safe. Although violence in schools is relatively rare, each incident has a half-life that sustains its impact. When a school experiences a homicide or other tragedy, feelings of anxiety may continue for years.

Many people consider sending their children to private school because they perceive public schools to be more dangerous. When the Bureau of Justice Statistics compared student reports of criminal victimization at school in 1989 and 1995, it found, however, that public and private schools were not far apart in terms of personal and property victimization (see Figure 1.1). It is also interesting to note that the percentages of students reporting victimizations remained relatively stable over time.

School safety data do not necessarily reveal the ebb and flow of concern about particular school safety problems. Citizens responding to a national poll may list lack of discipline as the number one concern regarding public education, but the meaning of "lack of discipline" may range from disrespect for authority to disobeying rules to fighting. Since the late fifties, educators and the public in general have expressed alarm over the behavior of young people, but the particular behavior in question has varied over time. In the late sixties, for example, student demonstrations, disrespect for authority, and racial tensions resulting from school desegregation received considerable publicity. The early seventies brought fears of drug use, assaults, and

TABLE 1.1 Percentage of High School Seniors Who Reported Being Victimized at School, 1976–1993 (by type of victimization and race/ethnicity)

Year	Had something stolen		Property deliberately damaged		Injured with a weapon		Threatened with a weapon		Injured without a weapon		Threatened without a weapon	
	White	*Black*	*White*	*Black*	*White*	*Black*	*White*	*Black*	*White*	*Black*	*White*	*Black*
1976	39.9	35.9	25.1	30.1	5.0	7.8	11.4	16.3	13.2	14.3	21.2	24.2
1977	40.4	32.8	24.3	21.0	4.0	8.1	11.0	19.7	10.6	11.4	20.2	24.2
1978	38.8	32.4	25.7	21.2	3.9	7.2	11.2	13.3	11.5	14.4	20.4	17.5
1979	34.6	27.2	24.5	20.8	4.0	8.1	11.1	16.5	11.7	9.8	20.3	17.9
1980	34.3	33.1	25.3	21.9	3.5	9.9	9.5	17.8	10.3	14.9	19.0	20.0
1981	40.1	39.2	30.4	29.8	5.1	13.4	13.4	23.7	13.8	19.1	23.6	25.0
1982	37.9	42.0	25.6	25.4	4.2	4.5	11.1	15.9	11.8	11.7	21.3	19.5
1983	39.4	39.2	25.0	23.1	4.3	5.6	11.9	14.8	13.4	13.2	23.9	24.5
1984	38.4	35.3	24.3	21.8	3.2	6.0	10.9	16.7	12.1	13.3	23.0	24.4
1985	39.3	35.2	26.6	28.0	5.4	8.9	11.6	22.6	13.6	18.2	24.5	25.2
1986	41.1	36.3	25.7	24.5	4.9	6.9	12.6	15.7	14.5	12.8	25.7	22.7
1987	42.1	39.4	27.0	25.0	4.4	5.6	11.2	17.5	15.4	15.4	25.4	20.2
1988	41.4	46.6	27.4	25.8	3.9	9.0	11.3	22.2	13.5	16.6	24.3	27.7
1989	39.4	46.4	26.0	28.9	4.9	11.3	12.0	24.1	13.7	17.8	24.5	21.0
1990	41.6	42.2	28.9	26.1	4.6	10.0	12.0	16.0	13.6	10.0	26.1	21.7
1991	41.4	44.3	28.4	24.6	5.3	9.6	15.7	20.2	15.4	17.1	26.5	27.5
1992	36.2	44.2	25.7	28.3	4.5	5.2	12.3	19.4	12.7	13.6	25.5	20.5
1993	41.6	46.0	25.8	26.3	4.3	6.4	13.8	23.5	11.0	11.5	23.8	22.3

Source: University of Michigan, Survey Research Center, Institute for Social Research, *Monitoring the Future Study.* Distributed by the National Center for Education Statistics, Indicator of the Month No. NCES, 1995, 95–788.

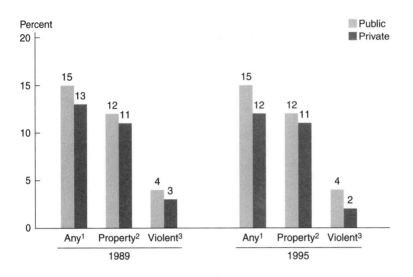

[1] "Any victimization" is a combination of reported violent and property victimization. If the student reported an incident of either, he or she is counted as having experienced any victimization. If the respondent reported having experienced both, he or she is only counted once under "Any victimization."

[2] Property victimization includes theft of property from a student's desk, locker, or other locations.

[3] Violent victimization includes physical attacks or taking property from the student directly by force, weapons, or threats.

Note: "At school" means in the school building, on the school grounds, or on a school bus.

Source: U.S. Department of Justice, Bureau of Justice Statistics, School Crime Supplement to the national Crime Victimization Survey, 1989 and 1995.

FIGURE 1.1   Percentage of students ages 12 through 19 who reported criminal victimization at school during the previous six months, by type of victimization and school control: 1989 and 1995

Source: Phillip Kaufman, Xianglei Chen, Susan P. Choy, Kathryn A. Chandler, Christopher D. Chapman, Michael R. Rand, and Cheryl Ringel, *Indicators of School Crime and Safety,* 1998 (Washington, DC: U.S. Department of Education and U.S. Department of Justice, 1998), p. 7.

vandalism. It is interesting to note that drug use in the seventies often was referred to as a "victimless offense" (U.S. Department of Health, Education, and Welfare, 1978, p. 3). This language later would be dropped as the harmful effects of the drug culture on non-drug users began to receive more attention.

When worries about violence and vandalism subsided a bit later in the decade, educators shifted their attention to truancy and chronic absenteeism. Drugs again surfaced as a leading issue in the eighties, eventually displacing lack of discipline as the public's number one school-related concern on the annual Gallup Poll of the Public's Attitudes Toward the Public Schools. The following decade witnessed an epidemic of school shootings and, with them, a national obsession with weapons on campus.

Whether these shifts in the focus of school safety concern reflect actual changes in the incidence of particular problems, selective attention by the mass media, evolving political and educational priorities, or other factors is unclear. It may be, for example, that educators do their best to address a school safety concern for several years and then decide that the root cause of the problem requires them to concentrate their efforts elsewhere. In other cases, the media appear to tire of coverage of a particular school safety issue, thereby creating the impression that the problem has diminished.

The Widening Scope of School Safety

Another theme characterizing recent educational history has been the widening scope of issues associated with school safety. Years ago school safety efforts focused mostly on fights, pranks, and disruptive acts in class. The perpetrators tended to be male students. Today school safety concerns have expanded to include an array of behaviors committed by male and female students as well as school employees. In some cases, such as the abuse of inhalants and computer-based crime, the acts are relatively new. In other cases, the problems have a long, but largely unrecorded history. Problems typically do not receive attention until they are named. Sexual harassment and child abuse doubtless occurred in the past, but until these acts were named, their victims tended to suffer in silence.

Current thinking recognizes a variety of direct and indirect threats to school safety. Direct threats include such acts as the following:

Abusive language	Homicide
Arson	Insubordination
Assault	Possession of communication devices
Battery	Rape
Child abuse	Robbery
Disruption	Sexual harassment
Distribution of controlled substances	Substance abuse
	Theft
Extortion	Threats of violence
False fire alarm	Vandalism
Gang-related acts	Weapons possession
Hate crimes	

Most of these problems constitute criminal acts, but some exist primarily within the domain of school discipline, an area in which local authorities generally exercise considerable discretion. In some schools, for example, student possession of a cellular phone is considered a direct threat to safety because it could be used to signal a drug deal or other illegal act. When two students went on a killing spree at Columbine High School, however, a student used his cellular phone to call the police for help. Weapons typically are banned from campuses, but in some rural areas students who go hunting before or after school are permitted to keep rifles locked in their vehicles.

Although what constitutes a direct threat to school safety has expanded somewhat over the years, perhaps the greatest increase has occurred in the area of indirect threats. Academic failure and retention long have been acknowledged to play a role in frustrating individual students and destabilizing schools. Today, however, what students wear to school and where they hang out can lead to violence. Students have been seriously injured and even killed because they wore a gang's colors or an article of clothing or jewelry that was coveted by others. Gangs and cliques often lay claim to certain areas of schools and campuses. Trespassers are subjected to taunts and possibly injury for wandering into the wrong territory.

The social structure of schools, particularly secondary schools, has been implicated as an indirect threat to school safety. Social structure differentiates between high-status and low-status groups. Members of low-status groups are likely to feel alienated from their peers and school in general. In some cases these feelings boil over into acts of defiance and aggression.

A particularly disturbing dimension of contemporary concerns about school safety involves acts by school employees. Although staff members doubtless took advantage of students in the past, these incidents rarely hit the newspapers. Today, however, it is not unusual to read about school employees charged with sexual harassment or molestation, assault, rape, and substance abuse. School systems have responded with police background checks of prospective employees and drug testing. The need to monitor the conduct of employees as well as students has added substantially to the complexity of school safety efforts.

A Growing Range of Responses

There was a time when most matters related to discipline and safety were resolved between teachers and students. Punishment was immediate. Over the years, as the variety of threats to school safety have increased, teachers have found it necessary to obtain help in dealing with the most serious cases. Schools now possess an array of means for dealing with threats to school safety.

So complicated, in fact, is the area of school discipline and safety that it is useful to classify the different types of responses. Elsewhere the author has subdivided these responses into three general categories of response: problem intervention, problem prevention, and problem management (Duke, 1980, pp. 16–31). Although the categories sometimes overlap, each has a relatively distinct purpose.

Problem intervention responses are intended to deal effectively with discipline problems and other threats to school safety that actually have occurred. The goal is to minimize the negative impact of these acts and ensure that they do not recur. As the next list suggests, educators may choose from a variety of problem intervention responses, ranging from direct communication with students to parental involvement. Preferences for particular responses tend to shift over time. In-school suspension, for example, was popular in the eighties, but educators increasingly have come to regard it as ineffective. Preferred interventions for the most serious threats to school safety, such as weapons possession and assault, are expulsion and assignment to an alternative education program.

Problem Intervention

Types of Response	*Examples*
Direct communication	Warning, direct order
Counseling	Active listening, contracts, assessment
Behavior modification	Plan for systematic reinforcement of appropriate behavior
Punishment	Loss of privileges, detention, extra assignment, work detail, in-school suspension, expulsion
Reassignment	Alternative education program, homebound instruction
Parental involvement	Parent–teacher conference, parent–student contract

Problem prevention responses derive from an understanding of the causes of dangerous and inappropriate behavior. The goal is to identify individuals and groups that are likely to engage in conduct that threatens their own safety or the safety of others and to respond in ways that prevent them from acting thus. School rules and punishments are obvious examples of problem prevention responses. Traditionally, educators have confronted student misconduct by promulgating more rules and harsher punishments. Because this approach has not always produced the desired effect, other problem prevention responses have been introduced. They include special training for students and staff members, parent education, and efforts to boost student self-esteem. One of the more controversial responses involves rewarding students for good behavior. As will be discussed later, critics argue that good behavior should be manifested because it is the right thing to do, not because it results in a reward.

Problem Prevention

Types of Response	*Examples*
Rules	Clear statements of how students should/should not behave
Punishment	Loss of privileges, detention, extra assignment, work detail, in-school suspension, expulsion

Instructional adjustment	Assistance for students experiencing academic difficulties; relevant and engaging assignments
Special skills training for students and staff members	Anger management, conflict resolution
Affective education	Self-esteem enhancement
Values education	Character education
Parent education	Parenting skills classes, parent focus groups
Rewards	Incentives and privileges for appropriate behavior and good citizenship

The third category of school-based responses is premised on the belief that threats to safety cannot be completely eliminated. The key to problem management responses, therefore, is to establish mechanisms for managing problems so that they do not adversely affect teaching and learning. A central task in problem management is to identify and reduce conditions that give rise to threats to school safety. For example, developing a crisis management plan for dealing with an armed stranger may not prevent such a person from entering school, but it can minimize the likelihood of widespread panic and injury. The area of problem management probably has seen the greatest growth during the past four decades. Contemporary schools boast a variety of specialized personnel, action teams, and sophisticated equipment for dealing with school safety.

Problem Management

Types of Response	*Examples*
Specialized personnel	Deans of students, school resource officers, hall monitors, crisis teachers, drug counselors
Team troubleshooting	Rumor management, data analysis, early detection of problems
Surveillance	Video cameras on buses and in poorly supervised areas of school
Conflict-resolution opportunities	Ombudsman, problem hotline, peer mediation
Downsizing	Smaller schools and subdivision of large schools into self-contained units
Environmental design	Elimination of hard-to-supervise areas, improved lighting, controlled access to school
Contingency planning	Development of crisis management plans, practice drills

The combined effect of the widening scope of problems associated with school safety and the expanded range of school responses has been to greatly increase the *complexity* of school organization and management. Staff members must devote a considerable portion of their time and energy to problem intervention, prevention, and management. In schools in which concerns over safety are particularly great, this time and energy may be allocated at the expense of teaching and learning. Students in safer schools, therefore, earn a double benefit. Not only can they attend school with relatively little fear of victimization, but they have more time to focus on learning and their teachers have more time to teach.

A Greater Role for Government and the Courts

Adding to the complexity of efforts to create and maintain safe schools has been the expanded educational role of state and federal governments and the courts. For much of the history of public education in the United States, discipline and school safety were largely local matters. Principals and teachers, working with the parents of misbehaving students, were expected to handle all but the most serious cases. In these instances, the superintendent and school board, and possibly local law enforcement officials, became involved.

Principals and teachers, along with parents, still are the first line of defense against threats to safety, but their actions increasingly are guided and constrained by laws, regulations, policies, and court decisions. In the sixties and early seventies, a number of the limitations on the discretion of local educators involved efforts to protect the Constitutional rights of students. Students, for example, were assured the freedom to assemble and to communicate their beliefs verbally, in writing, and symbolically. When students faced suspension or expulsion from school, they had to be accorded due process. Later the rights of students with disabilities were specified in law, creating new complexities concerning appropriate disciplinary measures for students whose offenses were related to their disabling condition.

Beginning in the mid-seventies, the emphasis on student rights began to be balanced by laws and court decisions designed to protect the safety of students and school employees. Bills were passed at the state and national levels in an effort to control drugs, alcohol, and weapons on campus. Zero tolerance policies were adopted that required the expulsion of students who posed a threat to school safety. Regulations called for the systematic collection and reporting of data on violations of school rules and actions taken by school systems. Legislation provided funds for special programs to address various school safety matters, from staff development on how to handle aggressive students to alternative education for expelled students.

To grasp the range of school safety and related issues that have attracted the attention of legislators, it is instructive to review the bills introduced during the Virginia General Assembly's 1999 session. The bills dealt with the following issues:

- Guidelines for school strip searches (HB 1489)
- Addition of school bus stops to territory included in designated drug-free school zones (HB 2426)
- Mandatory incarceration for battery of a teacher, principal, or guidance counselor (HB 2445)

- Pilot programs for disruptive elementary and middle school students who do not qualify for alternative education (HB 1248)
- Grants to fund school resource officers (HB 1445)
- Guidelines for mandatory school safety audits (HB 1521)
- Guidelines for dealing with truancy and violations of compulsory school attendance law (HB 1817)
- Guidelines for expulsion of students for drug offenses (HB 2144)
- Guidelines for placing students in alternative education (HB 2405)
- Guidelines for law enforcement officers involved in picking up and delivering truants (HB 2698)
- Required character education for all elementary schools (SB 817)
- Mandatory crisis and emergency management plans for all schools (SB 827)
- Modifications to zero tolerance guidelines for student expulsions (SB 1136)
- Reporting of student offenses to school authorities by law enforcement officials (SB 1244)
- Suicide prevention in schools (SB 1250)

All but one of these bills passed. The net impact of such legislation has been to increase the paperwork of school authorities and the complexity of handling school safety. Just keeping up with changes in the law is a major challenge! At the same time that educators' responsibilities have increased, their authority and discretion has been subject to limitations. Laws circumscribe educators' choices of punishments and specify procedures to be used in disciplinary cases. With laws also come fears of litigation. Once protected by the principle of in loco parentis, today's educators realize that practically everything they do, or do not do, in the name of school safety can be challenged in court.

The Politicization of School Safety

Although one might imagine that school safety would be a nonpartisan issue, the fact is that considerable controversy, contention, and conflict swirl around efforts to legislate safe schools. Educators have been compelled to become politically active in an effort to press for initiatives they feel will make a difference. Special interest groups have taken sides on various aspects of school safety. Politicians have chosen safe schools as a central plank in their platforms.

One indication of the politicization of school safety can be seen in the aftermath of school shootings. Invariably a cry for gun control is raised. Proponents argue that it is too easy for young people to get their hands on weapons. Opponents of gun control counter that those who intend to use guns for illegal purposes will always find ways to obtain them. The people who are adversely affected by gun control measures, they contend, are law-abiding citizens who use weapons for protection or sport. Gun control advocates respond by noting that semiautomatic weapons and "Saturday night specials" typically are not intended for either recreation or self-defense. They demand legislation that will limit the sales of firearms, require background checks, and compel gun manufacturers to add safety features to their products.

Another source of contention in recent years has been the exclusion from school of students who are deemed dangerous. Special interest groups representing parents of special needs students, for instance, resist efforts to exclude these young people from regular school settings when their dangerous behavior is linked to their disabling condition. Civil rights advocates point out that a disproportionate number of excluded students are members of minority groups. They claim that teachers and administrators treat minority students more harshly than majority students.

A third area of school safety in which politicization is evident concerns the abuse and harassment of students by teachers. Student advocates want swifter action and stiffer penalties for school employees who mistreat students. Teachers unions, although not condoning such behavior, point out that due process and teacher rights must be recognized. It is possible, they contend, for students to falsely accuse teachers of harassment or abuse and thereby ruin their careers.

It should come as no surprise that school safety has become an intensely political issue. Education is big business in the United States. Initiatives designed to make schools safer, whether they involve hiring more school resource officers, building smaller schools, or installing electronic surveillance equipment, carry hefty pricetags. Contention typically arises when decisions must be made concerning the allocation of public funds. In addition, some of the efforts to reduce the likelihood of violence and substance abuse among young people threaten wealthy and powerful industries. Unsafe behavior, for example, may be linked to violence and the glorification of drugs on television and in the movies, but lobbyists for the media exercise considerable political clout in Washington, D.C., and state capitals.

The Expanding Knowledge Base on School Safety

The rise of school safety problems has not gone unstudied. For decades, scholars from many disciplines have trained their talents on understanding the causes of and cures for youth violence, disruption, school failure, substance abuse, school absenteeism, and related concerns. Within the field of education have developed a variety of specialized areas of study, including behavior disorders, classroom management, and school discipline. Training programs for teachers, counselors, school psychologists, and school administrators have been expanded to accommodate new knowledge concerning the prevention and management of school safety problems. Special research centers concentrating on issues ranging from behavior modification to corporal punishment have been created at institutions of higher education.

Much of the growth in knowledge involves a deeper awareness of the conditions that give rise to or influence dangerous and dysfunctional behavior in children and adolescents. It has been noted that one implication of this research has been a shift of responsibility for misconduct from the individual to a host of forces external to the individual—a shift referred to by the author as the "depersonalization of blame" (Duke, 1978; Task Force on Juvenile Delinquency, 1967). Parents and family circumstances were among the first influences to be blamed for the misconduct of young people in school. Later the adolescent peer group was acknowledged by sociologists to constitute a powerful shaper of negative behavior. Other sociologists recognized that a link existed between student behavior and how schools were organized and operated. In other words, schools and their employees actually created conditions that increased the likelihood that young people would act out. Some of the alleged culprits included tracking and institutional insensitivity to student concerns. Eventually, the entire society came under fire from some scholars for fostering a culture of winners and losers and tolerating great disparities in access to resources and opportunities. Presumably such a culture compelled certain young people to engage in actions that were harmful to themselves and others.

Each explanation for the dangerous and dysfunctional behavior of young people has led to a set of prescriptions. Programs have been developed to train parents to deal effectively with discipline at home and to assist children who live in unstable homes. Other programs have concentrated on converting negative peer influence to positive. Staff development for teachers and administrators has focused on ways that educators contribute to and alleviate behavior problems. School and community-based programs have been designed to counteract the effects of inequities, racial tension, media violence, and other destructive social and cultural forces.

Although schools continue to face threats to their safety, it is clear that much more is known today than a half century ago about the causes of these threats and how to deal with them. The major challenge, to some extent, involves finding effective ways to share this knowledge with those who are in the best position to put it to constructive use.

Conclusion

In this chapter we have seen that school safety is not a new concern. Educators and the public in general share a longstanding fear that bringing large numbers of young people together in schools creates the potential for disorder, disruption, and danger. Protecting young people from harm, not surprisingly, has been a continuing focus of attention.

It would be a mistake, though, to assume that nothing has changed over the years with regard to school safety. The incidence of serious crime in schools is much higher than it was a half century ago. Criminal acts that used to take place in the streets now occur in classrooms and corridors. Students who once were dropouts or pushouts are now required to attend school, forcing educators to contend with individuals who are unmotivated to learn and resentful of having to sit in class.

Another change concerns the locus of decision making regarding school safety. Once the principal's office was the primary arena for dealing with threats to school safety, but now the courthouse, statehouse, and even the White House have become involved. With school shootings, drug busts, and gang activities front-page news, the public expects politicians and policy makers to take action.

One consequence of these changes is that teachers, school administrators, and other school employees operate under much greater scrutiny than they once did. Handling school safety and discipline has become a very complex matter requiring considerable teamwork and paperwork, an understanding of law and policy, and advanced training. There is no indication that these complexities are going to vanish in the future. Protecting the physical and psychological well-being of students likely will continue to be a primary goal of those who work in schools.

REFERENCES

American School Board Journal. "Despite Perception, Youth Violence is Down." vol. 189, no. 9 (1999) p. 8.

"Anatomy of a Massacre." *Newsweek* (May 3, 1999), pp. 25–31.

Associated Press. "Clinton Announces Hot Line and Web Site on Teen Disputes." *Washington Post* (January 14, 2001), p. A11.

Coleman, James S. *The Adolescent Society*. New York: Free Press, 1961.

Doyle, Walter. "Are Students Behaving Worse Than They Used To?" *Journal of Research and Development in Education*, vol. 11, no. 4 (Summer 1978), pp. 3–16.

Duke, Daniel L. "The Etiology of Student Misbehavior and the Depersonalization of Blame," *Review of Educational Research*, vol. 48, no. 3 (Summer 1978), pp. 415–437.

Duke, Daniel L. *Managing Student Behavior Problems*. New York: Teachers College Press, 1980.

Elam, Stanley M., and Gallup, Alec M. "The 21st Annual Gallup Poll of the Public's Attitudes Toward the Public Schools," *Phi Delta Kappan*, vol. 71, no. 1 (September 1989), pp. 41–53.

Grant, Gerald. *The World We Created at Hamilton High*. Cambridge, MA: Harvard University Press, 1988.

Herman, Arthur. *The Idea of Decline in Western History*. New York: Free Press, 1997.

James, Bernard. "School Violence and the Law: The Search for Suitable Tools," *School Psychology Review*, vol. 23, no. 2 (1994), pp. 190–203.

Kaufman, Phillip; Chen, Xianglei; Choy, Susan P.; Chandler, Kathryn A.; Chapman, Christopher D.; Rand, Michael R.; and Ringel, Cheryl. *Indicators of School Crime and Safety, 1998*. Washington, DC: U.S. Departments of Education and Justice, 1998.

Manning, John. "Discipline in the Good Old Days," *Phi Delta Kappan*, vol. 41, no. 3 (December 1959), pp. 94–99.

Morse, William C. "The School's Responsibility for Discipline," *Phi Delta Kappan*, vol. 41, no. 3 (December 1959), pp. 109–113.

National Commission on Excellence in Education. *A Nation at Risk*. Cambridge, MA: USA Research, 1984.

National Education Association. "Teacher Opinion on Pupil Behavior, 1955–1956," Research Bulletin of the National Education Association, vol. 34, no. 2 (April 1956).

National Education Goals Panel. *Building a Nation of Learners 1995*. Washington, DC: U.S. Government Printing Office, 1995.

Neill, S. B. "Violence and Vandalism: Dimensions and Correctives," *Phi Delta Kappan*, vol. 59, no. 5 (January 1978), pp. 302–307.

Plisko, Valena White, and Stern, Joyce D. (eds.). *The Condition of Education*, 1985 edition. Washington, DC: U.S. Department of Education, 1985.

Pucinski, Roman C. "Results of a Survey of Student Unrest in the Nation's High Schools," *Congressional Record* (February 23, 1970), pp. E1178–E1180.

Schafer, Walter E., and Polk, Kenneth. "Delinquency and the Schools." In *Task Force Report: Juvenile Delinquency and Youth Crime*. Washington, DC: U.S. Department of Education, 1967.

Stern, Joyce (ed.). *The Condition of Education*, 1987 edition. Washington, DC: U.S. Department of Education, 1987.

Task Force on Juvenile Delinquency. *Task Force Report: Juvenile Delinquency and Youth Crime*. Washington, DC: U.S. Government Printing Office, 1967.

U.S. Department of Education. *The Condition of Education*, 1995 edition. Washington, DC: U.S. Department of Education, 1995.

U.S. Department of Education. "Indicator of the Month No. NCES 95–788." Washington, DC: National Center for Education Statistics, U.S. Department of Education, August, 1995.

U.S. Department of Health, Education, and Welfare. *Violent Schools–Safe Schools: The Safe School Study Report to the Congress*, vol. I. Washington, DC: U.S. Department of Health, Education, and Welfare, 1978.

Walsh, Edward. "Teenagers' Use of Drugs Dipped in '98," *Washington Post* (August 19, 1999) pp. A1, A12.

Widen, Irwin. "Helpful Words on Theory and Practice," *Phi Delta Kappan*, vol. 41, no. 3 (December 1959), pp. 105–108.

Legal

Franklin v. Gwinnett County Public Schools. 503 U.S. 60, 112 S.Ct. 1028 (1992).

Gault v. Arizona. 387 U.S. 1. 87 S. Ct. 1428 (1967).

Goss v. Lopez. 419 U.S. 565 (1975).

Ingraham v. Wright. 430 U.S. 651 (1977).

New Jersey v. T.L.O. 469 U.S. 325 (1985).

Tinker v. Des Moines Independent School District. 393 U.S. 503 (1969).

2 Perspectives on School Safety

MAJOR IDEAS IN CHAPTER 2

- There is not only one way to think about school safety.
- School safety can be regarded as a function of learning to be safe.
- School safety requires an understanding of the causes of individual behavior.
- School safety is influenced by how schools are organized and structured.
- School safety is a "socially constructed" issue subject to the dynamics of the political process.
- Concerns about school safety reflect cultural norms and values.
- By taking into account various perspectives, schools can be designed to be safe and caring places.

Karen Ortiz, Millwood High School's prize-winning drama teacher, was distraught when she rushed into the principal's office. "Dr. Grogan, I just heard the news! I can't believe that you expelled Rick Palmer. He's supposed to graduate in three months."

Faye Grogan started to respond, then paused and motioned to Karen to sit down. "I'm upset, too, Karen. Everybody knows that Rick is a good kid. But my hands are tied. A policy is a policy, and the policy at Millwood is very clear. No weapons and no look-alikes."

"It was a water pistol," Karen blurted out. "You're ruining a student's future because he had a water pistol on the back seat of his car? I can't believe it. This is my fault, not Rick's. The water pistol was a prop for a one-act play we were working on."

"Karen, I understand how you're feeling, but Rick knew about our zero tolerance policy and so did you. Where do you draw the line? If we allow look-alike weapons on campus, how can we tell if someone sneaks a real weapon into school?"

Karen looked defeated. She rose to leave, then turned slightly. "I thought we were running a school, not a prison. I didn't become a teacher so I could watch responsible young people get thrown out of school because of paranoid policies."

Although the opening story is fictitious, it is based on an actual case from a Virginia high school. Such cases are becoming more common as school districts across the country adopt zero tolerance policies for possession of weapons, drugs, and alcohol and other serious offenses. Should Rick Palmer be expelled for having a water gun that was intended as a prop for a play? Should a student be expelled for giving an over-the-counter medication to a friend suffering from cramps? Should a student be banished from school for defending himself when assaulted by another student? The answers to such perplexing queries depend on an individual's perspective.

In the case of Rick Palmer, the principal operated from an organizational perspective. The school board adopted a zero tolerance policy regarding weapons and look-alikes. Rick Palmer violated the policy that Dr. Grogan was employed to enforce. Her obligation, as painful as it was to carry out, was clear. Karen Ortiz, however, saw the situation from a different perspective. As an educator, she believed her obligation was to teach and help students. Rick Palmer was not a troubled or dangerous young man. He posed no threat to his peers. In her mind, expelling him for bringing a prop to school contradicted everything that being an educator stood for.

This chapter considers a variety of perspectives on school safety. The intent is not to discredit some perspectives while championing others, but to convey a sense of the complexity involved in trying to determine how best to create and maintain schools in which young people are safe and cared for.

What Is a Perspective?

Various terms have been suggested for capturing the way people look at and make sense of the world around them. Paradigms, frames, and mental models are some of the terms that have become popular in recent years. Perspective is not necessarily different from these terms, but it will be used because its meaning may be more readily understood by a wider audience than the other terms.

A perspective represents a particular "angle of vision" or way of thinking about things. Perspectives may be distinguished by their implicit assumptions about such matters as why people behave as they do, the purpose of public institutions, and the nature of the good life. Different perspectives are characterized by different explanations for social problems and different means for resolving them.

Different perspectives frequently are associated with different role groups. An argument could be made, for example, that students, parents, teachers, school administrators, and police officers are likely to have distinct perspectives on school safety. For present purposes, however, distinct perspectives on school safety will not be limited to particular role groups. The six perspectives that are discussed in this chapter include the following:

1. Educational perspective
2. Psychological perspective
3. Organizational perspective
4. Political perspective
5. Cultural perspective
6. Design perspective

There are, of course, other perspectives on school safety besides these six. One could look at school safety, for instance, from public health, moral, sociological, biological, and legal perspectives. The six perspectives addressed in this chapter should provide, though, a good idea of how different purposes and assumptions can lead to distinctive ways of addressing school safety.

An educational perspective, for example, is concerned chiefly with learning and teaching. When looking at school safety through an educational "lens," then, it becomes important to determine how students learn to behave in ways that threaten their own safety and the safety of others. A question arising from this perspective is, Can such learned behavior be reversed through instruction? An organizational perspective, alternatively, focuses primarily on the goals of the organization—in this case, a school—and any obstacles to their achievement. If certain students behave in ways that undermine a school's ability to achieve its academic mission, this behavior, from an organizational perspective, must be eliminated, either through the application of various forms of organizational control or removal of the offending students.

Each perspective is analyzed in terms of its unique focus and assumptions. Questions that might be asked by individuals operating from the perspective are identified and used as a way to review representative approaches to dealing with the challenge of school safety. The discussion of each perspective concludes with a review of its implications and limitations. It should be noted that perspectives may overlap in various ways. Although distinct, they should not be regarded as necessarily incompatible.

An Educational Perspective

Key Aspects of an Educational Perspective on School Safety

Focus: Learning and teaching

Assumptions: Effective learning depends on order and security.
Safe and unsafe behavior is learned.
Safe behavior can be taught.

(continued)

| Questions: | What do young people need to learn in order to keep from harming themselves and others? |
| | How can young people be taught to care about their own well-being and the well-being of others? |

Focus.   An educational perspective on school safety begins with a concern for learning and teaching. Learning, of course, goes on all the time, whether or not teaching occurs. By focusing on teaching as well as learning, an educational perspective addresses the issue of intentional learning. We teach what we intend others to learn. The ultimate goal where school safety is concerned is to teach what will prevent threats to safety from occurring in the first place.

A case can be made that young people need to learn three things with regard to school safety. First, they must learn how to keep from harming themselves. Sometimes young people act in ways that are designed to harm themselves. Federal studies, for instance, have indicated that 1 in 5 high school students have considered suicide, and 1 in 10 actually have attempted it (Goldberg, 1999). At other times, the harm young people bring on themselves is inadvertent, the result of poor judgment or ignorance. Examples of such behavior include experimentation with drugs and risky activities such as driving at high speeds.

A second focus for learning concerns how to avoid victimization. Students need to understand their physical and social environment well enough to steer clear of locations and situations in which they could be harmed. They also can benefit from learning certain social competencies that reduce the likelihood of confrontations and negative interactions. These include listening carefully to instructions, accepting not getting one's own way all the time, receiving criticism without getting defensive, and ignoring teasing and name-calling (Embry & Flannery, 1999, p. 65).

Helping to keep others safe is a third focus of learning. Schools are complex social systems. The well-being of one individual is linked in many ways to the well-being of others. Many tragic school shootings can be traced to feelings of isolation and resentment toward peers. By learning how to appreciate others and how to discourage aggressive behavior and "put-downs," students can assume a measure of responsibility for the safety of their schools.

Assumptions.   Schools exist for the purpose of learning. Although learning can occur under a variety of adverse conditions, it is generally assumed that learning is most effectively achieved in an orderly and secure environment. How students behave toward their teachers and each other goes a long way to determining the orderliness and security of schools.

Behavior is learned. This goes for unsafe as well as safe behavior. It is just as much a consequence of learning when a student punches another student for making fun of him as it is when a student refrains from belittling a classmate. Often it is easier to determine how young people learn to behave appropriately than how they learn to behave inappropriately. Observing how adults behave is clearly one way that behavior is learned. When parents, teachers, and television and movie characters ridicule and take advantage of others and endorse aggressive acts, instruction is taking place.

If behavior is learned, young people can be taught how to behave safely and responsibly. This assumption is central to an educational perspective. In *Waging Peace in Our Schools* (Lantieri & Patti, 1996), the authors prescribe a curriculum designed to inspire caring and safe behavior. Their model for the "peaceable classroom" teaches young people "skills in cooperation, communication, expression of feelings, bias awareness, and decision making and conflict resolution, with the result...that young people become empowered to manage their own emotions and handle their own conflicts as they arise" (Lantieri & Patti, 1996, p. 47).

Questions. Different perspectives can be characterized by the kinds of questions that adherents are likely to ask. Individuals who look at school safety from an educational perspective might ask, for example, "What do young people need to learn in order to keep them from harming themselves and others?" The authors of *Waging Peace in Our Schools,* as indicated in the preceding passage, answered this question with one list of skills. Daniel Goleman (1995) focused on other skills, including self-awareness, handling emotions, self-motivation, and empathy. As noted earlier, Embry and Flannery (1999, p. 65) preferred to emphasize certain social competencies. Advocates of multicultural education believe that knowledge of the cultures and backgrounds of different students can reduce misunderstandings that lead to interpersonal friction.

Another question is "How can young people be taught to care about their own well-being and the well-being of others?" Although the first question dealt with the "what" of learning, the second involves the "how." There are many ways to teach, and some may be more effective than others. Those who operate from an educational perspective are concerned about finding instructional methods that reach all students. This concern may require the adoption of multiple methods or "differentiated instruction." For example, modeling may work best for some students, whereas direct instruction is better for others. Problem-based or hands-on learning and cooperative learning are other approaches that may be effective for certain students.

Implications and Limitations. Educators complain that the curriculum is always being added to, but the time available for teaching remains constant. If school safety is going to be addressed by teaching young people how to care for and protect themselves and others, time must be found to do so. Finding time to cover new and important issues is not just a matter of more efficient teaching or curriculum reorganization. It requires policy decisions concerning what instructional objectives can be eliminated to make room for instruction related to school and personal safety.

Getting agreement from parents and other community members regarding what to teach students is likely to generate heated debate. Consider reactions to efforts by educators to offer sex education and values education. Although few people may object to instructing students in what to do if an armed stranger enters school, support can erode when schools try to address such issues as self-esteem and emotional health, issues that may be related indirectly to individual conduct and school safety, but that are considered by critics to be too personal for the classroom.

One limitation of an educational perspective is that schools are not the only sources of learning for young people. They learn from their parents, peers, employers, and the media. If what is taught concerning safety in school is not reinforced elsewhere, the effectiveness of school-based instruction can be undermined. For this reason, any comprehensive effort to make schools safe for all students must involve the entire community.

A Psychological Perspective

Key Aspects of a Psychological Perspective on School Safety

Focus: Causes of behavior

Assumptions: Human beings do not necessarily behave the same.
                    Behavior is influenced by a variety of factors, including traits, needs, and environmental conditions.

Questions: Why are some young people more likely to harm themselves and others?
                    What causes of unsafe behavior can be effectively addressed by educators?

Focus.   There obviously are many points of similarity between an educational and a psychological perspective on school safety. Both, for example, address how behavior is learned. But differences also exist. An educational perspective is less concerned with the root causes of behavior than with instructing groups of young people in how they should behave in order to function effectively in society. A psychological perspective is primarily concerned with explaining why individuals behave as they do. Although they acknowledge that people are similar in many respects, proponents of a psychological perspective appreciate and attend to individual differences.

In trying to account for individual differences, psychologists have developed a variety of theories. These theories cover such matters as aggression, altruism, moral development, resilience, and social learning. To identify a perspective on school safety as psychological is not to suggest that all such theories are compatible or that all psychologists agree on the best ways to reduce unsafe and enhance safe behavior.

When proponents of a psychological perspective make practical use of their theories, they tend to follow a medical-style diagnostic-prescriptive process. In other words, they draw on their understanding of the root causes of behavior to diagnose the nature of an individual's problems and prescribe an appropriate treatment. A behaviorist, for instance, might determine that a student's disruptive acts in class derive from a need for attention, a need that is not being satisfied elsewhere in his life. One treatment could be to ignore the disruptive acts, thereby denying the student the reinforcing attention that he seeks through acting out. A parallel treatment might involve giving the student positive attention whenever he behaves properly.

Assumptions. Although social science has sought to identify the ways in which all human beings are similar, the fact remains that we behave in very different ways. This belief in individual differences serves as the fundamental assumption supporting a psychological perspective. It leads to the search for factors that cause individuals, when faced with similar situations or challenges, to respond differently. These factors are assumed to involve a combination of inherited attributes and environmental influences.

Traits are associated with individuals' ancestors and their genetic and biochemical makeup. Some individuals, for example, are more impulsive than others or more inclined to respond to frustration with aggressive acts (Feshback, 1964). Researchers have tried to demonstrate that certain patterns of behavior run in families or are linked to the presence or absence of a particular gene. Hoffman (1988) suggests that there may be a genetic basis for altruistic behavior that is rooted in an inherited capacity to empathize—to become aroused by another's distress.

Individuals also behave differently because they have different unmet needs. The fulfillment of needs is the basis for much of the work on human motivation. Psychologists such as Alderfer (1972) and Maslow (1970) have argued that individuals behave in ways that increase the likelihood of satisfying particular needs. These needs are sometimes seen as constituting a hierarchy. Until more "basic" needs have been adequately addressed, "higher" needs are unlikely to command attention. Maslow, for example, indicated that human beings first are motivated to satisfy physiological needs, including food and shelter. Once these needs have been met, individuals strive for safety and security. If students do not feel safe in school, Maslow would contend, they are unlikely to focus on higher needs, such as the need to achieve recognition for their academic efforts.

Another source of variation in behavior is the environment in which individuals are raised and schooled. Young people from poor families are more likely to exhibit higher levels of aggressive and delinquent behavior (Shaffer, 1994, p. 347). Peer influence begins to grow with the commencement of formal schooling. A study of aggression and victimization in elementary schools found that classmates single out certain individuals to pick on and, more disturbingly, that the status of "victim," once conferred, is difficult to overcome (Perry, Williard, & Perry, 1990). Parents generally are acknowledged to be the primary influence on the behavior of young children; although some have begun to question whether their impact has been overestimated (Harris, 1998). The fact that children who are abused by a parent frequently grow up to be abusers serves, however, as a tragic reminder of the power of environmental influence on behavior (Ney, 1988).

Questions.   As the preceding discussion suggested, proponents of a psychological perspective ask why some young people are more likely than others to harm themselves and others. A variety of explanations derive from behavioral, cognitive, developmental, personality, psychoanalytic, and social learning theories. There is more to a psychological perspective, though, than accounting for the origins of behavioral differences. It is also important to explore and identify ways that appropriate behavior can be encouraged and inappropriate behavior prevented. In this regard, it is critical that we ask about what can be done to eliminate or reduce the causes of unsafe behavior in schools.

Besides teaching and modeling appropriate behavior, which were addressed in the discussion of an educational perspective, educators and support staff, including counselors, school nurses, and school psychologists, can work with individual students who are likely to engage in unsafe behaviors or who already have done so. The type of help that characterizes a psychological perspective tends to be more clinical and therapeutic than that associated with an educational perspective. Through counseling, conferences with parents and teachers, individual instruction, and continuing case management, students receive the guidance and support necessary to avoid or overcome problems. Under certain circumstances, case managers may adopt special incentives, reinforcement schedules, punishments, or "logical consequences." They recognize that what is rewarding or punishing for one student may not be so for another. Effective treatment depends on an in-depth understanding of each individual, including their traits, physical characteristics, needs, and life circumstances.

Another way that educators and support staff can promote safe schools for all students is by studying individuals who manage to overcome the odds and turn their lives around. These young people are said to be "resilient," and the study of resilience has begun to attract considerable attention. Resilience refers "to the personal qualities and situational factors that allow individuals to adapt to difficult life circumstances" (Jaffe, 1998, p. 498). Young people who succeed despite adversity often manifest persistence and a high tolerance for frustration. They are able to derive support from at least one positive role model, which may be an individual at school or elsewhere.

Implications and Limitations.   To address school safety from a psychological perspective requires attending to individual differences among students, including those students who pose a threat to others and those who are victims. Trying to understand how best to meet the needs and deal with the problems of individuals demands a clinical orientation. Such an orientation is frequently associated with the norms of the caregiving profession, or what is referred to in the sociological literature as particularism. Particularism calls for every "client" to be treated as a unique individual with a unique history and characteristics.

Particularism is often contrasted with universalism, which characterizes the norms of a bureaucratic organization. Universalism represents the expectation that all clients will be treated the same, that none will receive favoritism or special treatment. Bureaucratic organizations, as will be seen in the next perspective, are expected to avoid differential treatment.

The problem for schools is that they are both professional organizations and bureaucratic organizations. Although treating every student as an individual makes sense from a psychological perspective, it is more problematic from an organizational (bureaucratic) perspective. For example, when a student gets into a fight and has no history of aggressive behavior, a case can be made from a psychological perspective that a severe punishment should not be imposed. If the school has a zero tolerance policy regarding fighting, however, the principal may have no choice, from an organizational perspective, but to suspend or expel the student.

In order to treat all students as individuals, educators and support staff must get to know each student. They must develop personalized plans to help both victimizers and victims. Frequent counseling, continuing case management, and close supervision are called for. Operating from a psychological perspective, in other words, can be very time-consuming and costly. When counselors must oversee the programs of 300 or more students, it is unlikely that most students will receive much individual attention. The challenge of school safety is that it must be achieved in schools, and schools are, for the most part, large, bureaucratic organizations.

An Organizational Perspective

Key Aspects of an Organizational Perspective on School Safety

Focus: School goals and organizational structure

Assumptions: Schools exist to achieve certain goals.
Schools have formal structures to enable them to achieve their goals.
The structure of a school influences the behavior of those who work and study in it.

Questions: To what extent is the physical and psychological safety of students and school employees a goal of schools?
What aspects of school structure are intended to promote the safety of students and staff members?
To what extent can problems related to school safety be attributed to school structure?

Focus.   Organizations exist to achieve goals that cannot be achieved by individuals alone or in informal groups. Organizations are characterized by structures that determine how work is allocated and coordinated (Bolman & Deal, 1997, p. 40). These structures consist of roles, formal relationships, and rules. Provisions exist for dealing with individuals who do not follow the rules. The overall purpose of organizational structure, at least from a rational perspective (Scott, 1992), is to enable organizations to achieve their goals.

Schools are considered to be formal organizations. Their roles range from the traditional—teachers, administrators, and students—to a variety of new roles, including school resource officers, crisis teachers, and transition specialists. Each role represents a set of expectations related to the mission of the school. Relationships typically are based on such factors as role, grade level, and academic department. The larger the school, the more complex are the relationships because larger schools tend to be subdivided into more units. Relationships are frequently portrayed by the lines on an organization chart. These lines designate the flow of authority between and among various role groups. Schools are rule-governed organizations, with regulations constraining the conduct of students and employees. Rules and regulations must be developed in accordance with local, state, and federal laws.

Assumptions.   Schools are assumed to exist for the purpose of achieving goals deemed important by society. Identifying these goals, however, is not always easy. Ambiguity often surrounds the meanings of certain goals—literacy, for example. People may disagree about what it means to be literate or how literacy can best be achieved. In some cases, it is difficult to distinguish between ends and means. Is school safety, for instance, a means to an end or an end in itself? Proponents of an organizational perspective are interested in determining what people believe to be the goals of schools and whether general agreement exists. School effectiveness can be adversely affected by confusion and disagreement regarding the mission of the school.

A second assumption concerns structure. The structure of a school is supposed to enable it to achieve its goals. When goals are not achieved, the first place to look, from an organizational perspective, is school structure. There are those who believe, for example, that one reason why some schools have lower student achievement than others is because teachers do not have a role in making school decisions. Others urge the downsizing of schools so students will receive more individual attention. Decision making and size are both structural concerns.

Structure is important because it is assumed to influence how people behave. If no such link were believed to exist, it is unlikely that organizational structure would attract much attention. Agreement about the exact nature of the relationship between structure and behavior has proven elusive, however. Some believe that the way to ensure greater productivity is to increase rules, a process known as formalization. Others argue just the opposite position—that people will be more productive if they are subject to fewer constraints. For many years, a predictable organizational response to school safety concerns has been to add more rules and stiffen punishments. Critics have observed, though, that this approach actually can be counterproductive (Duke, 1990).

Questions.   The first question regarding school safety that a proponent of an organizational perspective might ask is whether the physical and psychological safety of students and staff members is a stated goal of the school or school system. When safety is an "official" goal, it is probable that time, energy, and resources will be focused on protecting the well-being of members of the school community. Safety, of course, may not be a goal because leaders do not believe that there is any reason to be concerned about safety. Schools, like other organizations, must constantly guard against complacency.

Another question that can be asked concerns which aspects of school structure are specifically intended to promote the safety of students and staff members. Have new roles been added to the school roster in order to address safety issues? Have new rules and expectations been developed for the same purpose? How are decisions regarding possible violations of school rules made and by whom? Do safety mechanisms tend to focus more on reducing physical, rather than psychological, threats? Are staff members evaluated on, and held accountable for, school safety? Answers to such questions can produce a profile of organizational features that many believe impact school safety. Whether these features actually do so is a third focus for inquiry.

A key to assessing school safety involves making sure that aspects of organizational structure that are intended to promote safety actually *do* promote safety. Adding a variety of specialists, including crisis teachers and deans of students, to school staffs may do less to reduce threats to school safety than to facilitate "passing the buck" from one staff member to another. Increasing the number of school rules actually may contribute to more violations because the job of enforcing a large number of rules becomes more difficult. Certain punishments, such as suspension, may not be particularly effective for students who dislike school already. The benefit of an organizational perspective is that it compels people to be on constant alert for elements of school structure that fail to accomplish what they are expected to accomplish.

Implications and Limitations. An organizational perspective on school safety requires educational leaders to think about how schools are structured. Concern for structure is important because structure helps determine the climate and quality of life in schools. It is possible, for example, for school authorities to place so much emphasis on controlling students that attending school ceases to be an enjoyable experience. The purpose of organizational control is to safeguard students and staff members in order for productive teaching and learning to occur. When safety becomes an end in itself, rather than a means to an end, the risk of creating a prison-like atmosphere increases and valuable energy may be diverted from the school's instructional mission.

An organization consists of various control mechanisms that are intended to keep people focused on its mission. It is assumed that individuals, in the absence of organizational control, will tend to pursue their own self-interest rather than the goals of the organization. Schools typically employ a number of control mechanisms to keep students focused on academic achievement. They include grades, the threat of retention or loss of credit, direct supervision, punishments, and rewards. Questions have been raised about all of these forms of control. Recently, for instance, Kohn (1993) has raised serious doubts about the wisdom of using rewards as a means of getting students to cooperate and try hard in school.

A major limitation of an organizational perspective is that it tends to minimize the importance of individual differences. Unlike a psychological perspective, it concentrates on handling large numbers of "clients" at the same time. Unless they are careful, proponents of an organizational perspective can allow concern for efficiency and economy of scale to supplant a commitment to effectiveness. Most people have experienced what it is like to be treated "like a number" in a large organization. Such experiences should have no place in schools. Young people need to feel that they are valued and that their unique qualities are understood by those who teach and serve them.

A Political Perspective

Key Aspects of a Political Perspective on School Safety

Focus:	How to resolve differences of opinion regarding school safety
Assumptions:	Social problems, like unsafe schools, are socially constructed. People do not necessarily agree on what constitutes a social problem, why social problems exist, or how to resolve them. Costs and benefits are associated with different concepts of social problems.
Questions:	Who benefits from and who is harmed by defining school safety as a social problem? Who benefits from and who is harmed by particular causal stories that account for unsafe schools? Who benefits from and who is harmed by particular strategies for dealing with unsafe schools?

Focus.   If the essence of politics is compromise, then its impetus is disagreement. Disagreement is found throughout society, including organizations. Bolman and Deal (1997, p. 198), in fact, consider organizations to be arenas in which disputes are continually negotiated.

> As arenas, organizations house contests. Arenas help determine what game will be played, who will be on the field, and what interests will be pursued. From this perspective, every organizational process is political.

People, of course, disagree about many issues related to the education of the young. Different opinions are voiced about what schools should teach and how it should be taught and evaluated. Even school safety provokes its share of contention and debate. When school safety is looked at from a political perspective, the focus becomes how different ideas about the nature of school safety and how best to achieve it are raised and resolved.

Assumptions. Individuals invariably have problems with which they must deal. If enough individuals share the same problem, it may become a social problem. A social problem is defined as "a condition affecting a significant number of people in ways considered undesirable, about which it is felt something can be done through collective action" (Horton & Leslie, 1965, p. 4). Social problems are socially constructed, and this process is, to a great extent, political in nature. In other words, people do not necessarily agree on what constitutes a particular social problem, why the problem exists, or how it should be resolved.

One source of disagreement can be assumed to relate to the costs and benefits associated with particular conceptions of a social problem. To argue that unsafe schools constitute a social problem is not a value-neutral position. First of all, there are always more potential social problems than there are resources available to deal with them. Resources that are invested in making schools safer may be resources unavailable for addressing other issues, such as health care for the elderly or road improvements. In a world of limited resources, debate over which problems merit the investment of public funds is to be expected.

It is also reasonable to anticipate that people will disagree about why a social problem exists. In *Policy Paradox and Political Reason,* Stone (1988, p. 106) notes, "Problem definition is strategic because groups, individuals, and government agencies deliberately and consciously design portrayals so as to promote their favored course of action." For example, a teacher organization may explain school safety problems in terms of overcrowded classes, a situation that makes supervision and the building of positive teacher–student relationships very difficult. This *causal story,* as Stone refers to it, naturally leads to the recommendation that more teachers be hired and class sizes reduced. A taxpayer organization, concerned about the expense of hiring more teachers, may counter with the argument that teachers might control their students better if they were trained better. In other words, teacher competence, not class size, is the key to school safety.

When George W. Bush was campaigning for President in New Hampshire in the fall of 1999, he attributed student behavior problems to a state of "moral chaos" in public schools (Neal, 1999, p. A1). Instead of advocating more federal dollars for safe and drug-free schools, he urged that schools needed more moral education. Students did not require smaller classes; they needed to be taught the difference between right and wrong. It was no coincidence that Bush staked out his position at the same time that President Bill Clinton was trying to persuade Congress to appropriate funds to hire more teachers and reduce class sizes.

Questions. To understand school safety from a political perspective, it is important to learn about which groups are positively and negatively affected by decisions related to the subject. Benefits, of course, come in various forms and may include material benefits, support for a particular platform or ideology, and enhanced status.

The decision to define school safety as a social problem, for example, is likely to benefit certain people more than others. If public schools are declared unsafe, nonpublic schools may see increased interest among parents searching for less troubled learning environments for their children. School administrators, on the other hand, may try to minimize the seriousness of school safety problems because unsafe schools could be regarded as evidence of ineffective leadership on their part.

Questions also can be raised about who does and does not benefit from particular explanations, or causal stories, of why schools are unsafe. Critics of the separation of church and state may contend that the absence of moral instruction has contributed to youthful irresponsibility and recklessness. Gun control advocates may try to pin the blame for weapons-related school violence on the availability of firearms. Educators may claim that safety problems derive from inadequate resources for schools.

Different causal stories typically are linked to different approaches to achieving safer schools. If unsafe behavior on the part of young people is considered a consequence of poor parenting, interventions likely will be directed at parents. Family therapists and social workers stand to benefit because they are in the best position to provide services to parents. If unsafe behavior is understood to be a function of inadequate teaching, teacher educators and staff development specialists with skill in classroom management and disciplinary techniques are likely to benefit. If unsafe schools are linked to poorly designed school facilities, architects, designers, and companies selling electronic surveillance equipment may profit.

Implications and Limitations.   A major implication of a political perspective is that educators need to regard school safety initiatives as political activities requiring convincing arguments and the mobilization of support. It is not enough to assume that community members will endorse anything done in the name of school safety. Resources are always limited, and competition for them usually is keen. When funds are sought to hire school resource officers or install electronic surveillance equipment, policy makers and ultimately the public must be convinced that these additions are really necessary.

Educators, however, are not always prepared to act "politically." Sometimes they react defensively when members of the public question their requests and recommendations. It is important for educators and others committed to safe schools for all students to realize that costs and benefits are associated with particular explanations of why schools are not as safe as they could be and with particular approaches to improving school safety.

Resistance to some school safety initiatives, for example, may be anticipated from advocates for minority students. They do not believe that school safety measures always serve the interests of minority students. A disproportionate number of suspensions and expulsions, they note, involve minority students. Suspicion exists that White teachers and administrators may single out minority students for harsher treatment than White students. Confronted by this belief, educators must convince minority advocates that school safety initiatives actually serve students of all races and ethnic origins equally well.

Politics today is characterized by a variety of special interest groups. Well organized and often generously funded, these groups lobby elected officials in order to promote their agendas. The education arena is filled with such groups, each contending that it knows what is best for young people. Educators charged with the responsibility of protecting the students in their care can neither ignore nor automatically endorse special interest groups. Operating from a political perspective demands that educators understand what these groups stand for and who they represent. It also suggests that educators must develop expertise in forging coalitions among various community groups in order to initiate and sustain their efforts to promote safe and caring schools.

A Cultural Perspective

Key Aspects of a Cultural Perspective on School Safety

Focus:	Norms and values
Assumptions:	Between-school differences in safety may be a function of cultural differences.
	Unsafe behavior may be perceived as normal under certain circumstances.
Questions:	Do members of the school community value safety?
	What norms govern student behavior?

Focus. People shape culture, and culture shapes people. Among the cultural mechanisms that influence behavior are norms and values. A cultural perspective on school safety seeks to understand the normative structure of schools and the cultural contexts in which they exist. Normative structure is a primary source of information regarding how members of an organization are supposed to behave. Values represent the criteria by which individuals and groups select the goals of behavior, and norms constitute the acceptable means for achieving these goals (Scott, 1992, p. 16). The normative structure of a particular school may place high value on dressing in the latest and most expensive clothes. School safety is compromised, though, if students believe it is acceptable to obtain these clothes by stealing from each other.

The norms and values that characterize school culture are likely to reflect aspects of the greater culture. The greater culture helps determine, for example, the level of personal safety that people expect in schools and, indeed, the very conception of safety itself. The meaning of safety varies across cultures. One culture may define safety strictly in terms of protection from serious physical harm, whereas another culture may broaden the notion of safety to encompass protection from psychological abuse as well.

Studies over the years have found that certain cultures and subcultures are more aggressive and violent than others (Shaffer, 1994, pp. 347–349). Culture is closely linked to socioeconomic status and class. Because schools frequently enroll students from different backgrounds and classes, these cultural differences can lead to misunderstandings, rivalries, and open conflict. One critical function of schooling is to promote understanding among young people representing diverse cultures and reduce the likelihood of hostilities.

Assumptions.   A cultural perspective on school safety assumes that differences in the levels of safety among various schools may be a function of cultural differences. Schools in poor neighborhoods, for instance, often are characterized by higher levels of disruption, crime, and violence. Poverty, in fact, gives rise to its own culture, a culture that frequently is marked by "apathy, cynicism, helplessness, and mistrust of such institutions as police, courts, schools, and government" (Siegel & Senna, 1988, p. 124). Such conditions lead some young people to expect little in the way of benefits from their educational experiences. Behavior that may be judged dangerous in affluent settings is regarded as normal in some poor neighborhoods.

One of the prevailing theories in the study of juvenile delinquency is cultural deviance theory. It holds that "youth crime is a result of an individual's desire to conform to the cultural values of his or her immediate environment which are in conflict with those of the greater society" (Siegel & Senna, 1988, p. 125). Middle-class norms and values may be challenged for no reason other than the fact that they are associated with those in authority. They also may be challenged because those in authority are viewed as obstacles to the achievement of success by legitimate means (Cohen, 1955). Young people from poor backgrounds who struggle in school often convince themselves that their problems derive from unsympathetic teachers and administrators. Perceiving themselves to be unfairly blocked from progress, these frustrated students feel justified in defying school personnel.

Questions.   In applying a cultural perspective to school safety, it is important to determine whether the normative structure of a school places a high value on safety, and, if so, what meaning is attached to safety. The task of protecting young people obviously becomes more challenging when risk is valued over safety or when different groups define safety in different ways. Students may not be the only source of confusion. When teachers tacitly condone fighting among male students because "boys will be boys," they unwittingly undermine the development of a culture of caring in school.

It is also important to inquire about the norms governing student behavior in a particular locality. In parts of the United States, for example, students are expected to defend themselves when attacked by another student. School codes of conduct reflect this expectation by not punishing students who fight in self-defense. In other places, students are instructed to report any physical attack to school authorities. When students fight, all parties are punished. No attempt is made to differentiate between aggressors and defenders.

Local norms also govern appropriate responses to name-calling and derisive comments. In some places a physical reaction to a racial slur or derogatory comment about one's parents is condoned. In other places, victims of verbal abuse are expected to exercise self-restraint. As a consequence of varying norms, it is unwise to offer sweeping generalizations about the nature of school safety expectations in different settings.

Implications and Limitations.   Schools today enroll students from various cultural backgrounds. The challenge, from a cultural perspective, is to acknowledge diversity without undermining the importance of shared norms and values. No organization, including schools, can function very effectively when certain groups are allowed to disregard rules and expectations on the basis of cultural differences. These differences have become highly politicized in recent years. As a result, educators may face resistance when they condemn conduct in school that is condoned at home.

A cultural perspective can be valuable when educators want to understand the origins of divergent views concerning school safety. This perspective also can be frustrating, though, because there is little that educators alone can do to change cultural and subcultural influences that threaten to subvert school norms and values. A critical component of any comprehensive school safety plan, therefore, is student, parent, and community involvement. Only broad-based participation can produce sufficient consensus about what behavior is and is not appropriate in school.

A Design Perspective

Key Aspects of a Design Perspective on School Safety

Focus:	Creating schools in which safety and caring are valued
Assumptions:	No one perspective on an issue as complex as school safety is sufficient alone.
	Safe schools for all students are most likely to result from examining various perspectives and involving various stakeholders.
Questions:	Under what conditions are members of a school community most likely to value safety?
	How can these conditions be combined to create a good learning environment?

Focus.   It is understandable why many people consider unsafe schools to be a social problem of surpassing importance. Once a problem has been identified and validated, the logical next step is to explore ways to eliminate the problem and prevent it from recurring. What is unique about a design perspective is that the focus is not on problem elimination and prevention. Instead, energy is concentrated on the act of creating something desirable. Proponents recognize that it is possible to become so absorbed in eliminating problems that people lose sight of what they really want.

In *The Path of Least Resistance* (1989, p. 34), Robert Fritz explains the limitations of problem solving.

> The structure is this: The problem leads to actions designed to reduce the problem. The problem is reduced. This leads to less need for other actions. This leads to fewer future actions. This leads to the problem remaining or intensifying anew.

If we apply Fritz's reasoning to an unsafe school, we find educators confronting threats to safety as they arise. Once the threats have been reduced or eliminated, the temptation grows to shift energy elsewhere. Such shifts are easy to understand because there is always more to do in schools than time available to do it. Once attention is diverted to other problems, threats to safety may reemerge.

A design perspective on school safety, however, calls for an act of creation, not prevention or elimination. The goal is to create a school in which safety is valued. To accomplish this design challenge, it is also important to create a school in which caring is valued. As indicated earlier in the book, safety without caring can beget repression and alienation. Schools do not exist for safety alone. Their primary purpose is learning. As will become clearer in subsequent chapters, a key to creating safe schools for all students is promoting a culture of caring. This kind of thinking illustrates a key element of a design perspective—systemic thinking. Good designers attend to the connections between desired goals and the conditions most likely to support their achievement (Senge, 1990, p. 68). McDonald (1996, pp. 17–18) observes that schools cannot be designed without "dealing in depth with issues of belief; issues involving the distribution of power, energy, and information within the school; and issues involving the schools' links to outside values and ideas."

Assumptions. The fundamental assumption supporting a design perspective is that no single approach is sufficient to provide an answer to a concern as complex as school safety. Systemic thinking requires an examination of various perspectives. Assumptions must be challenged, key questions explored, and potential limitations identified. This book reflects contributions from all six perspectives. Each one contains important considerations regarding the creation of safe schools for all students. The combining and coordinating of these contributions to create a good learning environment is the central challenge for the educational designer.

Who is an educational designer? Anyone with an interest in designing a learning environment and a commitment to exploring a variety of perspectives and possibilities. Obviously some individuals possess more experience and expertise in design than others, but everyone has something to offer. Teachers and school administrators have just as much to contribute to designing safe and caring schools as politicians and policy makers. Parents and students also can play important roles in the design process. Design that is detached from context is little more than an academic or aesthetic exercise. Safe and caring schools do not exist in a vacuum. They are part of communities with their own cultures, concerns, and constituents. The greater the number of participants in the design process, the more likely it is that the final products will be compatible with their contexts.

A school consists of various "design elements." These include time, space, curriculum content, materials, activities, groupings of students, and staffing arrangements. A design perspective assumes that one key to achieving a desired environment involves attending to the relationships between and among these elements. An educational designer, for instance, would not consider a new school schedule without anticipating its impact on physical space. Given an overcrowded facility, a staggered bell schedule might be necessary to reduce the likelihood of pushing and shoving during transitions between classes.

Questions.   A fundamental design question is this: Under what conditions are members of a school community most likely to value safety? The question implies that it is preferable to focus on a positive goal instead of concentrating on preventing or eliminating a negative situation. By adopting a design perspective and incorporating contributions from other perspectives, it is possible to identify conditions that support the valuing of safety.

From an educational perspective on school safety, for example, we discover the benefits of actually teaching people about the value of personal safety and treating others with care. A psychological perspective informs us that people are characterized by differences as well as similarities and that differences may be reflected in many ways, including adjustment to school expectations and capacity for working effectively with others. That the way we organize and structure schools influences how students and staff behave is the central message of an organizational perspective. A political perspective teaches us that members of a school community may not necessarily agree on the nature of a safe learning environment or how best to achieve it. Agreements must be worked out through discussion and negotiation. A cultural perspective reminds us that many of our beliefs about how to behave in school are derived from our cultural background. A shared set of beliefs about school safety must begin with an understanding of our differences.

By studying these perspectives, designers may come to understand that members of a school community are more likely to value safety if they are taught about the benefits of safety, if they feel cared for and about as individuals with distinct needs and interests, and if their cultural backgrounds are appreciated and taken into account. Furthermore, designers must recognize the relationship between organization structure and individual behavior and the fact that there are costs and benefits associated with particular conceptions of school safety. How to integrate this knowledge into a viable school organization is the art of design.

Implications and Limitations.   Adopting a design perspective on school safety implies that school leaders balance their orientation to solving problems with a commitment to creating something positive—an environment in which safety and caring are valued by students, parents, and staff members. The likelihood of achieving this goal is a function of the range of viewpoints considered during the design process and the imagination of the designers. Safe and caring schools cannot be created by mandate. Ultimately, they must emerge from the sharing of aspirations and beliefs by stakeholders. Good designers are skilled at eliciting desires and understandings from all members of a school community.

Good designers also realize that design is a process, not an event. It is ongoing because conditions change and stakeholders come and go. A safe school in the sixties does not resemble a safe school in 2000. Developing a capacity for continuous design distinguishes outstanding designers from the rank and file.

A limitation of a design perspective is that the design process is very time-consuming. It takes time to involve stakeholders. It takes time to understand various cultures and resolve differences of opinion regarding how best to create safe and caring schools. It takes time to continually assess the effectiveness of programs, practices, and policies intended to promote safety and caring. Given all of the responsibilities of contemporary school leaders, it is understandable why many might prefer to dictate the conditions of school safety rather than design them. Ease and convenience, in the long run, of course, are no substitute for ownership and effectiveness.

Conclusion

This chapter has reviewed a number of perspectives on school safety. Although they are certainly not the only perspectives, they do illustrate the variety of foci, assumptions, and questions that need to be addressed in order to promote the safety and well-being of young people. Educators are advised to consider various perspectives in the process of creating and maintaining safe schools for all students.

This book draws on all six perspectives in order to identify the conditions necessary to foster safe and caring learning environments. The seven school safety standards that serve as the framework for this book derive from them.

Standard 1, which concerns student awareness of appropriate behavior in school, is based on an educational and organizational perspective on school safety. The humane, fair, and consistent enforcement of rules, the focus for Standard 2, is associated with a psychological, organizational, and political perspective. Standard 3, which states that students should feel valued and cared for, reflects a psychological perspective with its recognition of the human need for support and appreciation, and a design perspective, with its focus on creating desirable learning environments. Standard 4's call for a balance of approaches to school discipline can be traced to a number of perspectives, including educational, psychological, organizational, cultural, and design. Standards 5 and 6, which involve contingency planning and thoughtful approaches to the physical environment, are influenced by an organizational and design perspective. The last standard, which focuses on the involvement of parents and other community members in school-based efforts to promote safety, exemplifies a political and cultural perspective.

The next section of *Creating Safe Schools for All Students* explores each standard in depth. It is the obligation of educators and other citizens to take these standards, representing an understanding of "best practice" in school safety, and weave them together into a set of conditions that support the mission of the school.

REFERENCES

Alderfer, Clayton P. *Existence, Relatedness, and Growth.* New York: Free Press, 1972.

Bolman, Lee G., and Deal, Terrence E. *Reframing Organizations,* second edition. San Francisco: Jossey-Bass, 1997.

Cohen, Albert K. *Delinquent Boys.* New York: Free Press, 1955.

Duke, Daniel L. "School Organization, Leadership, and Student Behavior." In Oliver C. Moles (ed.), *Student Discipline Practices.* Albany, New York: State University of New York Press, 1990, pp. 19–46.

Embry, Dennis D., and Flannery, Daniel J. "Two Sides of the Coin: Multilevel Prevention and Intervention to Reduce Youth Violent Behavior." In Daniel J. Flannery and C. Ronald Huff (eds.), *Youth Violence.* Washington, DC: American Psychiatric Press, Inc., 1999, pp. 47–72.

Feshback, S. "The Function of Aggression and the Regulation of Aggressive Drive," *Psychological Review,* vol. 71 (1964), p. 257–272.

Fritz, Robert. *The Path of Least Resistance.* New York: Fawcett Columbine, 1989.

Goldberg, Carey. "Poll Finds Decline in Teen-age Fear and Violence," *New York Times* (October 20, 1999), pp. A1, A22.

Goleman, Daniel. *Emotional Intelligence.* New York: Bantam Books, 1995.

Harris, Judith Rich. *The Nurture Assumption.* New York: Free Press, 1998.

Hoffman, M. L. "Moral Development." In M. H. Bornstein and M. E. Lamb (eds.), *Developmental Psychology: An Advanced Textbook.* Hillsdale, NJ: Erlbaum, 1988.

Horton, Paul B., and Leslie, Gerald R. *The Sociology of Social Problems.* New York: Appleton-Century-Crofts, 1965.

Jaffe, Michael L. *Adolescence.* New York: John Wiley & Sons, 1998.

Kohn, Alfie. *Punished by Rewards.* Boston: Houghton Mifflin, 1993.

Lantieri, Linda, and Patti, Janet. *Waging Peace in Our Schools.* Boston: Beacon Press, 1996.

Maslow, Abraham H. *Motivation and Personality,* revised edition. New York: Harper & Row, 1970.

McDonald, Joseph P. *Redesigning School.* San Francisco: Jossey-Bass, 1996.

Neal, Terry M. "Bush Cites 'Moral Chaos,' Urges Religion in Schools," *Washington Post* (November 3, 1999), p. A1, A9.

Ney, P. G. "Transgenerational Child Abuse," *Child Psychiatry and Human Development,* vol. 18 (1988), pp. 151–168.

Perry, D. G.; Williard, J. D.; and Perry, L. C. "Peers' Perceptions of the Consequences that Victimized Children Provide Aggressors," *Child Development,* vol. 61 (1990), pp. 1310–1325.

Scott, W. Richard, *Organizations.* Englewood Cliffs, NJ: Prentice-Hall, 1992.

Senge, Peter M. *The Fifth Discipline.* New York: Doubleday Currency, 1990.

Shaffer, David R. *Social and Personality Development,* third edition. Pacific Grove, CA: Brooks/Cole Publishing Company, 1994.

Siegel, Larry J., and Senna, Joseph J. *Juvenile Delinquency,* third edition. St. Paul: West Publishing Company, 1988.

Stone, Deborah A. *Policy Paradox and Political Reason.* Glenview, IL: Scott, Foresman, 1988.

SECTION II

The Elements of a Safe School

Although the challenge of school safety is considerable, so too is the knowledge base from which educators can draw assistance. Research and professional judgment regarding the key elements of safe schools have been distilled in this book into seven school safety standards. Each of these standards is addressed in Section II. Chapters 3 and 4 deal with the development and enforcement of clear guidelines for student behavior. The importance of balancing rules and consequences with caring and compassion is the focus of Chapter 5. Balance is the theme of Chapter 6 as well. A key to safe schools is a combination of efforts to promote appropriate conduct, discourage misconduct, and intervene effectively when misconduct occurs. Chapter 7 concerns preparedness for emergencies and unanticipated situations. Facilities design and its role in school safety is the subject of Chapter 8. The final chapter in Section II examines the role of parents and communities in achieving safe schools.

3 Standard 1: Knowing What Is Expected

MAJOR IDEAS IN CHAPTER 3

- Guidelines for student conduct can be expressed in a variety of ways.
- Some guidelines are dictated by state and federal law.
- Students and parents may contribute to developing guidelines for conduct in school.
- Behavioral guidelines should be taught to and modeled for students.
- Guidelines need to be reexamined and updated periodically.
- Guidelines may vary depending on the age and maturity level of students and the size and nature of the school.

Driving in a foreign country for the first time can be a confusing and potentially dangerous experience. Why is this? We already know how to drive. But there is more to driving than a technical understanding of how an automobile operates. We must share the road with other drivers. The anxiety of driving abroad results partly from lack of knowledge of local laws and customs. In Cairo, for example, lane markings are painted on the streets, but few motorists observe them. A four-lane street suddenly expands to accommodate six cars abreast. Trying to obey the lane markings in this circumstance actually can contribute to an accident. In the United States, drivers generally are permitted to turn right on a red light, if they first come to a full stop and if no traffic is coming from the left. This option, however, is not available to drivers in some countries. A driver from one of these countries consequently may remain stopped at an intersection in the United States, causing those behind him to grow impatient and angry.

School can be like a foreign country to some students. Although all schools have rules, the nature of the rules and how they are interpreted can vary considerably from one school to another. In addition to formal rules, schools also are characterized by a host of unwritten norms and expectations. One school, for example, may permit upperclassmen to exercise certain privileges unavailable to other students. Another school may acknowledge no such distinctions between students. Add to such unofficial differences the fact that teachers may vary in the kinds of behavior that they deem acceptable and unacceptable, and the challenge of knowing how to behave in school can become truly daunting.

Educators are advised never to assume that students arrive at school already knowing how to behave appropriately. The first key to a safe school, therefore, is making certain that students know and understand how they are expected to conduct themselves.

Standard 1
Students know how they are supposed to behave at school and understand the reasons why.

This chapter examines various aspects of school rules and expectations. The first part of the chapter discusses some of the different forms that expectations may take and the range of behaviors that schools attempt to control. Subsequent parts investigate the conditions under which students are most likely to know and understand how to behave appropriately in school. Indicators of good practice are noted along with unresolved issues and controversies.

The Need for Clear Guidelines

Imagine a young person growing up in a poor neighborhood, one characterized by street gangs, criminal activity, and distrust of authority. To survive in such a setting, it may seem necessary for the individual to adopt the persona of an aggressor, someone who initiates acts of disruption and defiance. When the young person shows up at school, however, the behavior that served him well in his neighborhood is likely to get him into trouble or thrown out of school. The first lesson that this person must be taught is that appropriate behavior in school is different from behavior in other settings. In school, self-interest and the common good are not incompatible.

This point was recognized almost a century ago when William Chandler Bagley wrote his famous manual for teachers. *Classroom Management* (1908, p. 92) informed teachers thusly:

> The problem of discipline looks first to the welfare of the whole. The conditions that are most favorable for the concentration of attention by the entire class must be established and preserved...This requirement implies that each member of the class inhibit any impulse that may be inconsistent with these conditions; each member of the class must subordinate his own desires to the welfare of the class as a whole.

Schools and classrooms are intended, first and foremost, as learning environments—places where young people are expected to learn what is necessary to move successfully into adult roles. Because it is expensive, and possibly undesirable, to deliver this learning on an individual basis, young people are compelled, for the most part, to attend schools where they must learn in groups. The presence of large numbers of young people, along with dozens of adults, in one location necessitates a measure of order and control that would be unnecessary in a home or a private tutorial.

The need for order and control is often expressed in calls for schools to be "disciplined" environments. A Department of Education work group exploring ways to achieve the national goal of safe and drug-free schools indicated that disciplined school environments are characterized by a strong emphasis on academic goals, an ethic of caring reflected in interpersonal relationships, and clear behavioral standards that are firmly, fairly, and consistently enforced (Goal 6 Work Group, 1993, p. 9). The last characteristic is the focus of this and the following chapter. When students are unclear or confused about how they are expected to behave, the likelihood of inappropriate and unsafe behavior increases (Duke, 1990; Gottfredson & Daiger, 1979; Gottfredson & Gottfredson, 1985; Perry, 1980).

Clear guidelines concerning appropriate behavior help young people acquire a sense of right and wrong. Researchers have noted that unsafe and disruptive behavior can be traced, in part, to the reluctance of educators and parents to tell young people in direct ways what is right and what is wrong (Kilpatrick, 1993, pp. 13–29; Liedloff, 1977). It is unlikely that children and adolescents will spontaneously discover the nature of right and wrong behavior unless they are provided with clear guidelines and instruction.

The challenge for schools is to help young people recognize that only by respecting the rights of others and serving the common good can they safeguard their own welfare. In other words, they must understand the need to relinquish a measure of their independence in order to secure it.

To develop a set of clear guidelines governing behavior in school, educators have to address a number of difficult questions. The remainder of this chapter deals with these queries.

What Form Should Guidelines Take?

When many people think about guidelines for student behavior, they imagine a set of rules. The term "discipline" is often associated with rule enforcement. Wolfgang (1999, p. xi), for example, states that discipline is "the required action by a teacher or school official, toward a student (or group of students), after the student's behavior disrupts the ongoing educational activity or breaks a preestablished rule or law created by the teacher, the school administration, or the general society." Just as it is difficult to conceive of driving in a place where no "rules of the road" exist, it is hard to imagine a school without rules. Emmer, Evertson, Clements, and Worsham (1997, p. 16) conclude that it is "just not possible for a teacher to conduct instruction or for students to work productively if they have no guidelines for how to behave...."

Rules may be expressed in two basic forms. Fuller (1969, p. 5), in his text on the morality of law, observes that one type of morality—what he terms the "morality of duty"—"starts at the bottom" and "lays down the basic rules without which an ordered society is impossible." These rules take the form of "thou shalt nots." The "morality of aspiration," on the other hand, "starts at the top" and addresses "the morality of the Good Life, of excellence, of the fullest realization of human powers." These rules are expressed in positive terms, as "thou shalts."

Many states mandate that school districts and schools develop and implement a uniform code of student conduct. The form in which the rules are to be written, however, is usually not specified. Some rules follow a morality of duty—for example, "No student, while on school property, including school buses, shall behave in a disorderly manner or in any other way interrupt or disturb the orderly operation of school." Other rules reflect a morality of aspiration—"Students are expected to exhibit proper conduct in school, on school grounds, buses, and at all school-sponsored functions."

Whether expressed negatively or positively, rules constitute behavioral expectations. Typically, they cover two domains: classroom conduct and behavior outside of class. School rules are more inclusive and generally supercede classroom rules. Classroom rules often vary, depending on the nature of the activities in the class, the makeup and maturity of the students, and the style and instructional orientation of the teacher. Rules in a resource room for emotionally disturbed students, for example, are likely to differ in some ways from rules in an advanced-placement calculus class.

Some educators feel that a complete education should involve more than adherence to various organizational rules. They want young people to strive for behavioral ideals as well as meet basic behavioral expectations. Such ideals may encompass virtues, ethics, and character development. Schools increasingly are engaging in activities designed to teach young people about personal integrity, responsibility, and moral conduct. The Walker Upper Elementary School in Charlottesville, Virginia, for example, expressed a set of behavioral ideals in its credo, The Walker Way:

The Walker Way

As a Walker student, I agree…

To be an active listener;

To respect all people even if they are different from me;

To strive for my personal best and to take responsibility for the choices that I make;

To solve problems through cooperation, not with violence or put-downs;

To be truthful and earn the trust of others;

When I do this, I will help to make Walker a place where all people feel safe, respected, and challenged to learn.

The statements in The Walker Way represent guidelines for student conduct, but they do not constitute rules. Rules imply formal consequences for disobedience. It would be inappropriate, of course, to punish a Walker student who failed to be an active listener or strive for her personal best.

Behavioral guidelines may take other forms besides rules and ideals. Research on teaching effectiveness stresses the importance of clear routines and procedures. These guidelines "usually apply to a specific activity, and they are usually directed at accomplishing something rather than at prohibiting some behavior or defining a general standard" (Emmer, Evertson, Clements, & Worsham, 1997, p. 18). Effective teachers establish routines for many classroom tasks, including taking roll, being excused from class, checking out classroom texts, asking questions, correcting homework, and conducting seatwork. Clear routines actually reduce the need for disciplinary intervention by eliminating circumstances in which students are unsure of what to do. Rules are less necessary when such guidelines are built into the daily operations of each class. Students who resent rules may find routines and procedures more acceptable, a reasonable outgrowth of class activity.

CASE IN POINT

Consider situations when students come late to class. The teacher may have to stop teaching, ask the students why they are tardy, and inspect their passes. On their way to their desks, students may inadvertently or purposely bump a seated student or say something to a classmate that might result in a further interruption of instruction.

A savvy teacher, aware of the disruptive potential of late arrivals, establishes a routine for handling tardy students. An empty desk can be placed just inside the door to the class. Students who arrive late are informed that they must sit in this desk until there is a transition point in the lesson, at which time the teacher will come over and inspect their pass. Then they may proceed to their desk.

Guidelines also may take the form of responsibilities and obligations. This form is often used along with lists of student rights. The notion is that students enjoy certain rights when they are in school, but that these rights oblige them to assume certain responsibilities as well. Linking responsibilities to rights is considered by some educators to be a more acceptable way to convey behavioral expectations. Gathercoal (1993, p. 15) maintains that deriving behavioral guidelines from rights and responsibilities is compatible with the principles of a democratic society: "In democratic classrooms, responsibility flows from a principled level of thinking where students learn to balance individual freedoms with the welfare interests of the school community."

Norms are one other way that behavioral guidelines can be conveyed. Schools frequently foster distinctive organizational cultures, and these cultures encompass a variety of implicit as well as explicit expectations. Norms may or may not be conveyed in a direct way. Freshmen, for example, may not be told by older students that they are supposed to avoid the "senior corridor" to get to class. They may learn about this "tradition" the hard way by taking the "wrong" corridor and suffering taunts and threats. Part of the socialization process for new students involves learning the expectations that are not written down anywhere. Although they can be powerful shapers of behavior, norms do not always constitute a positive force. Many norms perpetuate traditional patterns of bias and unfair treatment. Reculturing a school so that prevailing norms reflect constructive guidelines can be one of the most daunting challenges facing a school leader.

Guidelines thus can take many forms: rules in the form of "thou shalts" and "thou shalt nots," ideals, procedures and routines, responsibilities and rights, and norms. Is one particular type of guideline preferable?

No evidence exists that school safety depends on adopting a particular type of guideline, but research is clear that students need guidelines of some kind in order to know how they are expected to behave. Common sense would seem to dictate that as many expectations as possible be expressed in positive, rather than negative terms, but in cases involving serious acts of misconduct and crimes, it is necessary, for legal purposes, to specify proscribed behavior. Ideals are important when educators strive to teach young people that rules and laws only cover minimum expectations, not the exemplary behavior on which a good society depends. Classroom rules are helpful to a point, but expressing expectations in the form of routines and procedures may be more acceptable to students. Helping students to recognize and examine norms can be a useful way to raise questions about behavioral expectations in school, but formalizing norms into lists of official guidelines may prove counterproductive.

> **Recommendation 1.1:** Consider the various forms that behavioral guidelines may take and which forms are most appropriate for particular types of behavior, instructional purposes, and settings.

What Are Characteristics of a Good Rule?

Because most schools have *rules,* the discussion will concentrate on this form of behavioral guideline. Not all rules are necessarily good rules, of course. Older readers may remember when drivers were not allowed to turn right at a red light, even if no traffic was coming from the left. When gasoline prices skyrocketed during the OPEC crisis in the seventies, transportation specialists pointed out that unnecessary gasoline was wasted at red lights when vehicles waited to turn right. The traffic law was changed, resulting in significant gasoline savings and a smoother flow of traffic.

Weinstein (1996, p. 53) offers four principles for developing classroom rules.

1. Rules should be reasonable and necessary.
2. Rules need to be clear and understandable.

3. Rules should be consistent with instructional goals and with what we know about how people learn.

4. Classroom rules need to be consistent with school rules.

One sure way to undermine the credibility of efforts to promote school safety is to include rules that make little sense to students. A good rule is one that most individuals understand is necessary for the welfare and safety of all. Arbitrary restrictions and rules that seem to exist for the convenience or benefit of certain individuals or groups invite disrespect for all rules, even those that are sound. Examples of unreasonable rules may include requirements for complete silence at times other than when tests are being taken and rules that permit adults to do things, such as smoke, when students are forbidden to do so.

In *School Policy*, Duke and Canady (1991, p. 7) contend that a "good school policy is one that increases the likelihood that school goals will be achieved without adversely affecting any particular group of students." This statement also applies to classroom and school rules. Students do not have to like every rule, but they need to understand that the rules are not intended to single out or discriminate against a particular group of students. A rule requiring all homework to be typed, for example, may be regarded as placing poor students—those without access to a typewriter or computer at home—at a disadvantage.

> **Recommendation 1.2:** Make certain that school and classroom rules are reasonable and that they do not discriminate against any particular group.

Weinstein's second principle holds that rules should be clear and understandable. Rules are of little benefit if students cannot figure out what they are expected to do or not to do. Unclear and ambiguous rules also invite uneven enforcement because teachers and administrators have trouble determining when a violation has occurred. Uneven enforcement undermines the credibility of school safety efforts.

An example of a rule that may be misinterpreted appears next. The rule pertains to "disruption of the educational process" and comes from the code of conduct of a high school.

Disruption of the Educational Process: This includes, but is not limited to food fights, verbal confrontations among students, fighting, assault and battery, "pranks" which disrupt and create unsafe conditions, and willful disobedience or open defiance of authority of any teacher or staff member.

This rule invites misinterpretation by trying to cover too much territory. It combines relatively minor problems, such as food fights, and criminal conduct—assault and battery. Certain concerns, like verbal confrontations, may mean vastly different things to different people. The fact that the rule is not limited to the examples that are given creates additional possibilities for misunderstanding.

> **Recommendation 1.3:** Develop rules that are stated clearly and that are unlikely to be interpreted differently by different people.

The last two principles that Weinstein recommends relate to the issue of consistency. She suggests that classroom rules should be consistent with the instructional mission of the teacher. It makes little sense, for example, to expect students to question ideas during lessons but forbid them to raise questions about the nature of authority or school discipline. Classroom rules also should be in line with school rules and, it may be added, the rules of other teachers. Students and parents compare notes on the expectations of different teachers. A student's disciplinary record should not be jeopardized because he happens to be assigned to a teacher who is far more strict than other teachers.

One further provision regarding rule consistency should be noted. Rules must be consistent with the rights enjoyed by all citizens under the Constitution. Dworkin (1985, p. 12) has observed that "compliance with the rule book is plainly not sufficient for justice; full compliance will achieve very great injustice if the rules are unjust." A principal personally may object to interracial dating, but that does not give her the right to prevent interracial couples from attending school dances. Schools must stand for more than rules and safety; they must stand for the principles upon which the nation and its legal system are founded.

> **Recommendation 1.4:** Develop rules that are consistent with the Constitution and the mission of the school.

One area of controversy concerning school rules concerns the extent to which rules should be developed in anticipation of possible problems. Should the behavior of all students be restricted because the potential exists for a few students to behave irresponsibly? Is it right, in other words, to curtail everyone's freedom because of the possible actions of some? Consider the case of cellular phones and pagers. Most students probably are capable of bringing these devices to school without disrupting instruction or using them for wrongful purposes. Should the prospect of misuse by some lead to a total ban?

> *Controversy*
> Should the behavior of all students be restricted because the potential exists for some students to behave irresponsibly?

The Supreme Court of the United States has declared that young people enjoy rights under the Constitution, regardless of whether they are in school. "Fear or apprehension of disturbance" is an insufficient basis for denying individuals their rights, according to Hudgins and Vacca (1985, pp. 319–363). Others counter that it sometimes is necessary to restrict rights for the sake of the general welfare. Just because there is a right to freedom of speech does not mean a student can yell "Fire!" in a crowded auditorium, thereby causing panic and possible injury.

Sometimes rights may conflict. Students have a right to an education. Toward this end, they are required to attend school. Can a case be made that it constitutes cruel and unusual punishment, a violation of the Eighth Amendment, to require students to attend schools where safe and orderly conditions cannot be ensured? An attorney general of California once threatened a lawsuit against the Los Angeles school system on these grounds!

How far should school authorities be allowed to go in order to assure students and their parents that schools are safe? The answer to this difficult question ultimately hinges on how much risk people are willing to accept in order to protect their rights. Efforts to control the sale and possession of firearms have been thwarted because the powerful gun lobby has been unwilling to restrict the right to bear arms.

Can a School Have Too Many Rules?

Besides being clear, reasonable, and consistent with the law, school rules should be enforceable. Unenforceable rules detract from school discipline and invite disregard for all rules. Sometimes the enforceability of a school rule is a function of the rule itself. An injunction against chewing gum is difficult to enforce because the act itself is relatively easy to conceal. In other cases, enforceability is a function of the sheer number of rules. Codes of conduct with dozens of rules may be unenforceable, given the size of school staffs, their various responsibilities, and the capacity of individuals to remember a large number of rules.

Controversy
Is it better to have a few rules or a lot of rules?

Advocates for school safety take several positions regarding the number of school rules. Some, for example, adopt a "comprehensive" position that calls for the promulgation of highly specific rules for every conceivable disruptive or unsafe act. These individuals try to anticipate problems before they develop and create rules to cover them. Others adopt a "minimalist" position. Assuming that most students understand how they should behave in school, minimalists prescribe short lists of general rules. Teachers and administrators are expected to exercise discretion in determining when a general rule, such as one regarding respect for the rights of others, has been violated. Minimalists contend that there is little value in having more rules than people can manage. Advocates of the comprehensive position respond that short lists of general rules invite different interpretations and the probability of inconsistent enforcement.

In *Judicious Discipline,* Gathercoal (1993, p. 13) makes a case for the minimalist position: "Trying to remember 'all the rules' is much more difficult than accepting and abiding by a moral and ethical code of relatively few principles from which all interactions would flow."

It is possible, of course, to imagine certain young people who, for whatever reason, take advantage of the absence of highly specific rules covering every possible behavior problem. Should educators design school codes of conduct with these individuals in mind? Or should they remember that most students do not misbehave or threaten the safety of others? Duke and Canady (1991, p. 96) warn that "lengthy lists of rules and proscribed behaviors may communicate distrust and invite rule avoidance by students." They go on to point out, "Overly restrictive learning environments are often perceived as oppressive by those subject to the rules, and those who must enforce the rules can lose sight of the fact that their first obligation is to help students learn, not act as disciplinarians."

There is no simple way to resolve the controversy over how many rules are enough. What is clear is this—determining the appropriate number of rules requires a careful consideration of context. Certain situations demand more rules than others. A small school, for example, may need fewer rules than a large school. Duke and Perry (1978) compared alternative schools and nearby high schools in a study of school discipline policies and practices. They found that alternative schools had relatively few rules and relatively few discipline problems when compared with the high schools. What made the finding more interesting was the fact that the alternative schools enrolled large percentages of students who had been removed from regular high schools because of behavior problems. Alternative-school educators did not feel a need for lots of rules covering every possible contingency because they knew and cared about all of the students. For their part, students understood what was expected of them despite the absence of lots of rules. As will become clearer in Chapter 5, rules are a poor substitute for relationships.

What Behaviors Do Rules Need to Address?

In one sense, educators have no choice when it comes to school and classroom rules. They are not free to condone behaviors that constitute violations of local, state, and federal laws. Consequently, students cannot assault each other or staff members, use or distribute illegal substances, possess weapons, or commit hate crimes. Besides the rules covering behavior proscribed by law, educators typically develop rules related to the safe and efficient operation of school.

> **Recommendation 1.5:** Develop rules related to illegal acts, classroom deportment, attendance, behavior outside of class, and academic work.

Illegal acts encompass a broad range of behaviors. In a comparative study of codes of conduct in 11 large school systems, Duke (1992) found that every code contained rules prohibiting assault and battery, possession and use of weapons, extortion and intimidation, theft, vandalism, and possession, use, and distribution of controlled substances. Other acts covered in at least some of the codes included arson, gambling, threats against staff members, trespassing, acts intended to incite, possession of drug paraphernalia, possession of stolen property, possession of "imitation" controlled substances, and pretending to be under the influence of a controlled substance. Because these are illegal acts, they apply to staff members as well as students.

Blauvelt (1999, pp. 22–23) offers a comprehensive listing of criminal offenses to assist educators in developing a standardized vocabulary. Ensuring that staff members share a common understanding of the nature and definition of particular offenses is a crucial component, he contends, of an effective school safety program. Blauvelt's classification system consists of 16 "primary offenses:"

Alcohol	Larceny/theft
Arson	Robbery
Assault	Sex offenses
Bomb incident	Trespassing
Disorderly conduct	Vandalism
Drug offenses	Vehicle complaints
Extortion	Weapons
Fire	Miscellaneous complaint

Rules also are needed to ensure that teaching and learning can occur in class. Emmer, Evertson, Clements, and Worsham (1997, pp. 20–21) offer a simple, yet comprehensive set of rules for classroom deportment at the secondary level.

Rule 1. Bring all needed materials to class.
Rule 2. Be in your seat and ready to work when the bell rings.
Rule 3. Respect and be polite to all people.
Rule 4. Listen and stay seated when someone is talking.
Rule 5. Respect other people's property.
Rule 6. Obey all school rules.

Although all rules are important, one rule should take precedence over all other classroom rules. Schools exist for the purpose of learning. If learning cannot take place, there is no reason to have schools. Consequently, students should be helped to realize that no individual can be allowed to deprive another person of the opportunity to learn.

Opportunity to learn is also a function of attendance. If students are not in class, they are unlikely to learn what they need to learn. Furthermore, if they are not in school, they are more likely to get into trouble in the community. Schools, therefore, have rules related specifically to attendance. Typically, four categories of attendance rules can be found in codes of conduct. They relate to the following behaviors:

- Absence from school without permission (truancy)
- Absence from class without permission (cutting, skipping)
- Late arrival to school or class (tardy)
- Leaving school or class without permission

Truant officers once were familiar figures in communities. Their task was to pick up young people who were absent from school without permission. Although truancy persists and some school systems have revived the role of truant officer or enlisted the help of local police, it is now common to find young people coming to school, but not attending class. Detecting these individuals presents school authorities with a challenge, because data processing on class cutting can be slow. Many schools now employ attendance officers to expedite the process.

One of the challenges posed by attendance rules involves the determination of when an absence is "excused." Excused absences entail no punishment; although some school systems deny academic credit to students who miss more than a specified number of school days—excused or unexcused. Duke (1992, p. 58) found that school systems vary considerably in what they consider to be legitimate reasons for missing school. All school systems excuse students who are sick, experience a death in the immediate family, or observe a religious holiday. Variations exist for excuses such as college visitation, trips with parents, and isolated conditions making travel difficult or dangerous.

The fourth area in which rules are necessary concerns behavior outside of class. This domain includes conduct on school buses, in corridors and areas where instruction is not taking place, and at school-sponsored events. It also involves behavior on field trips. Examples of the acts that may be addressed by rules in this domain include smoking, public displays of affection, improper attire, loitering, littering, possession of "nuisance equipment" such as radios, and running in the halls. Enforcing these rules presents special problems because various staff members may be involved. Interpretation of the rules and consistency of enforcement can vary.

The last area in which rules should be developed concerns academic work. Among the problems that teachers must address are failure to do assignments, turning work in late, coming to class without appropriate materials, cheating on tests, copying classmates' work, and plagiarizing published material. In some cases, the consequences for violating these rules are limited to lowered grades. In other instances, additional consequences are involved.

Which Rules Can Cause Confusion?

Rules are intended to prevent problems, but some rules create problems as well. The cause of school safety is not advanced when those subject to rules and those who must enforce them are confused about what the rules mean or why they permit no exceptions. Poorly conceived rules distract from the primary mission of schools by prompting contention and protest. Although it may not be possible to develop a perfect set of rules, educators need to review rules periodically to make sure that sources of confusion are kept to a minimum.

> **Recommendation 1.6:** Periodically reassess rules to determine if revisions are necessary.

Zero tolerance policies concerning weapons, alcohol, and drugs have spawned considerable debate regarding school rules. Contention is based on the fact that the students who violate these policies pay a heavy price—expulsion or long-term suspension from school. Consider a zero tolerance policy regarding weapons. What constitutes a weapon? Almost any object can be used to harm another person. A pencil can puncture the skin. A book bag can be used to strike someone. Then there is the matter of possession. Should rules focus on the possession of a weapon or the use of a weapon? If a student takes a weapon away from another student and is caught with it before she can turn it over to a school official, has she broken the rule concerning possession of weapons?

What about look-alikes? Although it is understandable that rule enforcement becomes more difficult when school staff must try to distinguish between real weapons and pretend weapons or real drugs and ersatz substances, should students receive the same punishment for having a water pistol as a semiautomatic rifle? In some ways, schools are less understanding than the courts when it comes to the nuances of rule violations.

CASE IN POINT

A fourth grader was asked by her teacher to bring something to class for "Show and Tell." The girl brought an unopened can of "Billy Beer" the next day, indicating that her father kept it as a collector's item. The beer had been bottled as a spoof on President Jimmy Carter's brother.

 Alarmed that the girl had violated the school's zero tolerance policy regarding alcohol, the teacher reported her to the principal. The principal called the girl's parents and reluctantly notified them that their daughter had to be suspended from school. She could not be reinstated for 10 school days. During this time, she and her parents were required to participate in an alcohol awareness program.

Another school rule that can create problems involves the ban on fighting. First, there is the matter of whether the participants were "serious." Presumably some physical interactions are not intended to injure. Should a distinction be drawn between relatively harmless wrestling and more serious fighting? Who should decide—the combatants or school authorities? A further issue concerns the distinction between aggressor and defender. Should both parties be subject to the injunction against fighting, or only the person who initiated contact? Should a student be permitted to defend himself without fear of punishment? What if the aggressor was provoked by a racial slur or crude remark? Do provocative words justify physical retaliation? Trying to resolve such thorny problems has prompted some school systems to declare that anyone involved in a fight will be considered to have broken the rule against fighting. Such blanket interpretations, of course, do not eliminate disputes and appeals.

The issue of self-defense presents school authorities with other challenges. Should students, for example, be permitted to carry pepper spray, mace, or other means of personal protection? One Kansas school system allowed students to possess pepper spray in school until one student used it for offensive purposes. Does occasional abuse of a privilege justify denial of the privilege to every student? Are precautions taken for the sake of self-protection a privilege or a right?

Controversy
To what extent should students be permitted to defend themselves against hostile acts in school?

One fear about permitting students to defend themselves is that they may be more likely to be seriously injured. Refusing to strike back and opting to report an attack to a school official can be the more prudent course of action in some cases. If the attacker intends from the outset to do serious harm, however, "turning the other cheek" may be of little benefit.

Pranks pose another challenge for educators. When the author was a school administrator in New York, "senior prank day" was an unofficial tradition, a much anticipated cultural ritual. Most of the pranks were clever and harmless, but occasionally students stepped over the line and committed an act that was tasteless or harmful. Should a rule exist forbidding all pranks because of the potential for such excessive acts? Is it better to try and contain pranks by not forbidding them, but urging students to exercise good judgment and holding them accountable for "crossing the line"?

Rules that apply to students, but not to staff, also have the potential to provoke confusion and controversy. The ability to smoke on campus used to be one area in which a double standard frequently applied, but most school systems now forbid all individuals from smoking on campus. School rules typically prevent students from verbally abusing teachers, but nothing may be written in school policy manuals about teachers or other staff members verbally abusing students. Many teachers expect students to complete assignments on time, but they may not always return corrected and graded assignments in a timely manner. School rules are more likely to be accepted by students when they believe that the rules exist as much for their benefit as the benefit of adults in the school.

Who Should Make the Rules?

The development of school and classroom rules offers an opportunity to learn about what guidelines students and parents think are important. Although some rules are based on laws and school board policies and, therefore, are not subject to debate, a number of rules are discretionary. Involving students and parents in developing rules is not without its problems, however.

> *Controversy*
> To what extent should students and parents be involved in making school and classroom rules?

A case can be made that the challenge of enforcing rules is reduced when those subject to the rules play a part in their development. Telling people what they must do is less likely to produce a sense of ownership in school and classroom discipline than asking them for their opinion regarding what guidelines make sense. Parents, for their part, may be more likely to support school discipline if their feelings on the subject have been heard. From a philosophical perspective, it can be argued that broad-based involvement in rule development is consistent with the spirit of a democratic society. What better way for students to learn about democracy than practicing it in school?

The few studies of student involvement in rule development, however, have yielded mixed results (Duke, 1990). In addition, classroom-management specialists point out practical problems related to student involvement. Secondary teachers who teach five or six classes, for example, find it taxing to develop and enforce five or six different sets of classroom rules (Emmer, Evertson, Clements, & Worsham, 1997, p. 22). Handling student-proposed rules that are frivolous or not carefully thought out may present teachers with a dilemma. Should students be allowed to discover the hard way that certain rules are inappropriate, or should teachers exercise their authority, veto such proposals, and run the risk of being perceived as authoritarian? Emmer, Evertson, Clements, and Worsham (1997, p. 22) conclude thusly: "...a teacher who is authoritative, who establishes reasonable rules and procedures, who provides an understandable rationale for them, and who enforces them consistently will find the great majority of students willing to abide by them."

Although it may not always be prudent to involve students in deciding on school and classroom rules, teachers certainly should discuss with students the importance of having rules in organizations and periodically solicit their input regarding how well the rules are working. The same goes for parents. Teachers need to know how parents feel about school and classroom rules. If a school creates a committee to review the code of conduct or develop a new set of behavioral expectations, students and parent representatives certainly should be appointed.

How Should Rules Be Shared with Students?

Anyone who has spent time in a school recently has probably seen a list of school or classroom rules posted on a wall. Parents may have received a copy of the student code of conduct in the mail or been handed copies of classroom rules by teachers at Back to School Night. Displaying rules and giving copies of them to parents are important, of course, but the real value of rules derives from their internalization, from making rule-governed behavior part of one's life. Because individuals may interpret written rules in different ways, the best way to ensure that students understand what the rules mean, and equally importantly, why the rules are necessary, is to teach them the rules and the reasons for them.

Recommendation 1.7: Instruct students about the meaning of school and classroom rules and help them understand why the rules are necessary.

Instruction related to rules can be delivered in various ways, including orientation sessions, curriculum infusion, special classes, and disciplinary intervention.

Orientation sessions scheduled for the summer or the beginning of the school year provide one occasion for teaching students about rules and how they are expected to behave. Although some may contend that focusing on rules is the wrong way to commence a new school year because it can "send the wrong message" to students, such a beginning activity has the benefit of giving all students a clear idea of the guidelines before they actually start their classes. Misunderstandings about expectations can be cleared up, and incoming students can be instructed on what to do if other students threaten or mistreat them.

Because many schools are characterized by high student mobility during the school year, it is not sufficient to offer orientation sessions only at the beginning of the year. With new students arriving throughout the year, school officials also need to develop a program to orient each new arrival to school rules and expectations. One possibility is to produce a videotape covering the subject. Another is to ask counselors to meet with each newcomer and review the code of conduct.

A second instruction option involves infusing lessons about school and classroom rules into the content of every subject. It is important that young people learn that rule-governed behavior is not unique to schools. All organizations, from hospitals to professional sports teams, rely on rules to ensure that people are treated fairly and the goals of the organization are undertaken with seriousness of purpose. It is easy to imagine a discussion in language arts regarding how rules are written and how people can interpret words to mean different things. Social studies provides a basis for investigating the evolution of laws and the process by which they are established in a democratic society. Students taking drama may act out various rules and the consequences of disobeying them.

Many schools delegate instruction related to rules to one particular course, such as health, or they create special classes that meet periodically. These classes may be taught by counselors or school resource officers. In Danville, Virginia, for example, school resource officers teach middle school students a special curriculum covering state laws and the consequences for violating them. Some of these laws pertain to behavior in school. Developed by the Virginia Department of Education, "Class Action" apprises students of their rights and responsibilities as citizens. An explanation of the juvenile justice system also is provided.

Sometimes schools use advisory periods or homerooms as the locus for instruction about rules. Students are encouraged to raise questions about actual instances of rule violation and make suggestions concerning how to improve school discipline. As with any effort to promote learning, the quality of the experience is dependent on the talent and commitment of the instructor. Teachers who do not feel it is their responsibility to teach students how to behave are unlikely to make effective instructors.

One way that discussions of school rules can be generated, either in special classes or across the curriculum, is in conjunction with character education and social skills programs. Character education lessons typically focus on particular values or virtues, such as tolerance, respect, and honesty. Social skills instruction deals with anger management, conflict resolution, cooperation in groups, and impulse control. Students not only read and hear about strategies for avoiding harm and unsafe situations, but they also have opportunities to role-play and practice them. These subjects are closely related to school rules and safety. More will be said about character education and social skills instruction in Chapter 5, in which the topic is the development of schools in which all students are valued and cared for.

The last context in which instruction related to rules may be provided involves the administration of school discipline. Students, and sometimes their parents, can be required as a consequence of breaking a school rule to take classes dealing with the violation. Many school systems run special classes for students caught possessing or using drugs and alcohol. Although not as common, classes for students who exhibit aggressive or violent behavior also are offered. In these classes, students may be exposed to individuals who have gone to prison or had their lives ruined by uncontrolled aggression.

Learning about school and classroom rules, why they exist, and the consequences for breaking them is consistent with the educational mission of schools and reflective of an educational perspective on school safety. Structured lessons, of course, are not the only way that learning about rules takes place. An argument can be made that the most powerful source of learning about rules is adult modeling. Young people today are bombarded with negative role models: famous athletes who cannot control their aggressive tendencies, evangelists who take advantage of the faithful, and dishonest politicians and business leaders. As Curwin and Mendler (1997, p. 31) observe, being a positive role model is hardly easy: "How we resolve conflicts with students illustrates what we believe far better than what we say about acceptable behavior. It is easy to tell children to walk away from a personal put-down on the playground. It is difficult for us to walk away when a student puts us down in the classroom."

Students tend to believe that the information that should be taken most seriously is that on which they will be tested. Rightly or wrongly, what is not tested typically is disregarded. Before getting a driver's license, young people must pass a test concerning the rules of the road. Although education is a right, not a privilege like driving, it may still make sense to test students on their knowledge of school rules, consequences for disobeying them, and how to handle situations when they are threatened by other students or when they see another student breaking a rule.

One approach is to extend certain privileges to students who demonstrate a thorough understanding of school and classroom rules. A benefit of testing students on school rules is that those who pass the test cannot claim later that they were unaware of the rule they are accused of breaking.

CASE IN POINT

A high school in New York gives all students a test on school rules during the second week of school. Because all students take English, the test is given by English teachers. Students who pass the test are allowed to choose from a variety of options during the periods when they are not in class. Options range from going to the media center or computer lab to working out in the weight room and assisting a staff member. Students who do not pass the test must attend a restricted study hall that is supervised by a teacher. If these students eventually pass the test, they, too, are permitted to choose how to use their time outside of class. Students caught breaking a school rule must return to the restricted study hall for a specified period of time.

Conclusion

The first standard of a school that is safe for all students requires that students know how they are supposed to behave at school and understand the reasons why. Teachers cannot assume that young people come to school knowing how to behave appropriately. Part of every school's educational mission must be to teach and model rules and expectations concerning how students should act in class, in school when not in class, coming to and leaving school, and at school-sponsored events.

Standard 1 is met when clear and reasonable guidelines for student behavior are developed and communicated to students in a systematic way.

REFERENCES

Bagley, William Chandler. *Classroom Management.* New York: Macmillan, 1908.
Blauvelt, Peter D. *Making Schools Safe for Students.* Thousand Oaks, CA: Corwin, 1999.

Curwin, Richard L., and Mendler, Allen N. *As Tough As Necessary.* Alexandria, VA: Association for Supervision and Curriculum Development, 1997.

Duke, Daniel L. "School Organization, Leadership, and Student Behavior." In Oliver C. Moles (ed.), *Student Discipline Practices.* Albany, NY: State University of New York Press, 1990, pp. 19–46.

Duke, Daniel L. "Variations in School District Discipline Policies," *Record in Educational Administration and Supervision,* vol. 13, no. 1 (Fall/Winter 1992), pp. 54–61.

Duke, Daniel L., and Canady, R. Lynn. *School Policy.* New York: McGraw Hill, 1991.

Duke, Daniel L., and Perry, Cheryl L. "Can Alternative Schools Succeed Where Benjamin Spock, Spiro Agnew, and B. F. Skinner Have Failed?" *Adolescence,* vol. 13 (Fall 1978), pp. 375–392.

Dworkin, Ronald. *A Matter of Principle.* Cambridge, MA: Harvard University Press, 1985.

Emmer, Edmund T.; Evertson, Carolyn M.; Clements, Barbara S.; and Worsham, Murray E. *Classroom Management for Secondary Teachers.* Boston: Allyn & Bacon, 1997.

Fuller, Lon L. *The Morality of Law,* revised edition. New Haven: Yale, 1969.

Gathercoal, Forrest. *Judicious Discipline,* third edition. San Francisco: Caddo Gap Press, 1993.

Goal 6 Work Group. *Reaching the Goals: Goal 6.* Washington, DC: Goal 6 Work Group, Office of Educational Research and Improvement, U.S. Department of Education, 1993.

Gottfredson, Gary D., and Daiger, Denise C. *Disruption in Six Hundred Schools.* Report No. 289. Baltimore: Center for Social Organization of Schools, 1979.

Gottfredson, Gary D., and Gottfredson, Denise C. *Victimization in Schools.* New York: Plenum, 1985.

Hudgins, H. C., and Vacca, Richard S. *Law and Education,* second edition. Charlottesville, VA: Michie, 1985.

Kilpatrick, William. *Why Johnny Can't Tell Right from Wrong.* New York: Touchstone, 1993.

Liedloff, Jean. *The Continuum Concept,* revised edition. Reading, MA: Addison-Wesley, 1977.

Perry, Cheryl L. *Adolescent Behavior and Criminogenic Conditions in and around the High School.* Ph.D. dissertation, Stanford University, 1980.

Weinstein, Carol Simon. *Secondary Classroom Management.* New York: McGraw-Hill, 1996.

Wolfgang, Charles H. *Solving Discipline Problems.* Boston: Allyn & Bacon, 1999.

4

Standard 2: Humane, Fair, and Consistent Enforcement

MAJOR IDEAS IN CHAPTER 4

- Educators should not assume that all students are prepared to obey school and classroom rules.
- Various members of the school community have a role to play in rule enforcement.
- To ensure that school discipline is fair, it is important to monitor closely which students receive particular consequences.
- A good consequence entails more than reducing the likelihood that rule-breaking will recur.
- Not all consequences are equally effective with all students.
- Those who enforce school rules must realize that students have a right to due process.

Maintaining safe schools depends on students knowing how they are expected to behave. This knowledge is sufficient to ensure appropriate conduct for many students. For others, though, consequences for inappropriate and unsafe behavior are needed in order to discourage such action. In the case of a relatively small percentage of students, even the presence of consequences may fail to serve as a sufficient deterrent. Educators must weigh the interests of these individuals against the welfare of the entire school community.

In Biblical times, enforcement of laws was based on the principle of *lex talionis* or "an eye for an eye." Punishment was supposed to correspond in degree and kind to the offense. If someone took the life of another, the killer's family might be expected to give up one of its own in order to compensate the victim's family. Western legal systems have moved away from consequences based solely on restitution and retribution. Injunctions exist against "cruel and unusual punishment." Concern for making transgressors pay their "dues" is balanced against the desire to rehabilitate. There are people, of course, who feel that today's approach to law enforcement favors victimizers over victims. They lobby for harsher punishments and "victims' rights." Rule enforcement has become a political as well as a legal and organizational matter.

Schools are expected to prepare young people to become productive members of adult society. Because adult society is characterized by consequences for disobeying the law, schools would be negligent if they permitted students to break rules without cost. The challenge for educators is to provide a system of rule enforcement that is effective, reasonable, and consistent with the educational mission of schools.

Standard 2: Rules are enforced and consequences are administered humanely, fairly, and consistently.

This chapter examines a number of complex issues related to the enforcement of school rules. After addressing the nature of rule enforcement, three criteria for judging its quality are presented. Subsequent parts of the chapter consider what constitutes an effective consequence and the range of consequences available to educators. Among the controversial topics covered in the chapter are corporal punishment, the use of rewards to achieve behavior improvement, the disciplining of special education students, and zero tolerance policies.

The Nature of Rule Enforcement

What does it mean to enforce a school or classroom rule? Three basic decisions are involved in rule enforcement. First, a determination must be made that a rule has been broken. This judgment requires familiarity with the rules, no small feat when many codes of conduct are crammed with dozens of rules. Problems also can arise when teachers and school administrators do not actually witness a violation. Relying on reports from others requires additional judgments regarding the accuracy of information and the validity of conflicting accounts.

A second decision entails determining who is guilty of breaking a rule. When only one individual is involved, the matter is fairly straightforward, but when several students may have played a part, the judgment process becomes more difficult. When pressed for time, educators may be tempted to make summary judgments about the guilt of all involved parties. Hasty decisions regarding guilt, or innocence, can undermine the credibility of school safety efforts and lead to accusations of unfair treatment. Investing time in careful preliminary factfinding can save considerable time and energy later if individuals who feel falsely accused seek redress.

When it has been decided that one or more students have violated a rule, the third decision concerns what consequence to impose. In some school systems, educators exercise considerable discretion regarding the choice of consequences, whereas in other school systems the consequences for particular violations are clearly spelled out in policy. The issue of discretionary authority and how much of it is desirable surfaces throughout this chapter.

Consequences may be thought of in various ways, including punishments, negative reinforcements, natural consequences, and logical consequences. Specific options range from the purely punitive to the instructive. Students may be expelled or suspended from school, placed in an alternative school or program, required to attend detention hall or in-school suspension, and assigned to service activities. Milder consequences include warnings, parent conferences, and behavioral contracts. Regardless of the consequence, the process of enforcing school and classroom rules should meet three criteria.

Humaneness

Humans are imperfect. Efforts to enforce rules that fail to recognize this fact may be regarded as inhumane. Many minor violations of school and classroom rules are understandable, given the conditions under which many students are schooled and their personal histories. Compelling young people to sit quietly for long periods of time or expecting them to walk slowly to their bus on the last day of school may not always be reasonable. A humane approach to rule enforcement takes account of the fact that some behavior problems are understandable and deserve no more than a gentle reminder or warning.

Even when students are caught committing serious offenses, they should be treated humanely. The focus of attention should be the violation, not the individual's personality or life circumstances. These latter factors are relevant for counseling and other therapeutic interventions, but not rule enforcement per se. Educators also must avoid reacting to rule-breaking in vindictive and irrational ways, lest they provide students with powerful negative lessons concerning how problems should be handled. If angered or upset by a student's behavior or attitude, an educator is better off postponing dealing with the student or delegating responsibility to someone else.

Humane rule enforcement also requires careful consideration of the consequences imposed on students. In the early nineteenth century, teachers hung wooden logs from the necks of overly talkative children and punished more serious offenders by suspending them from a basket attached to the school roof so all their classmates could see them (Oakes & Lipton, 1999, p. 242). Cruel and unusual punishment is proscribed by the Constitution and should not be found in schools. Public humiliation and ridicule have no place in educational institutions.

Fairness

The fairness criterion requires that rule enforcement efforts avoid discriminating against particular groups or individuals. When the courts have reviewed school discipline practices, they have rarely challenged the nature of school rules. They have examined, however, the consequences applied to students accused of violating rules and the process by which guilt was determined. Questions have been raised in recent years regarding suspension and expulsion practices. Minority advocates point to statistics that indicate a disproportionately large percentage of suspensions and expulsions involve minority students. They accuse educators of imposing harsher consequences on minority students than on nonminority students. Counteraccusations are made that teachers and administrators are actually afraid to discipline minority students because of threats of community action and lawsuits.

In the fall of 1999, the Reverend Jesse Jackson focused national attention on the fairness of school discipline practices when he rallied support for a group of students who were expelled from a Decatur, Illinois, high school for fighting in the stands at a football game. The students, all of whom were black, initially were expelled for two years with no option to attend alternative school. The school board later reduced the sanctions to one-year expulsions with the option to enroll in a county-run alternative school. A U.S. district judge did not find any evidence of racial discrimination on the part of the board, but the case occasioned a national review of expulsion and suspension statistics. In Phoenix, Arizona, for example, blacks were found to make up 4% of the high school population, but received 21% of the expulsions and suspensions (Claiborne, 1999).

The issue of fairness also has been raised with regard to the disciplining of special education students. Critics observe that it is less likely that a special education student will be disciplined than a regular education student. In the case of the most severe consequences, law prohibits suspending or expelling special education students for offenses that are related to their disability or handicapping condition. Such protection is not afforded other students.

Rule enforcement requires judgment, and when judgment must be exercised, there always exists the possibility of error. To ensure fairness, it is therefore important that students accused of violating school rules be afforded an opportunity to present their side of the story. When several students are involved, school administrators should be careful to interview each student separately. Someone other than the administrator should be present to take notes. Students faced with suspension or expulsion must be accorded due process. The Goss decision required only that students be given an opportunity to tell their side of the story when they object to the accusation. Policies in many states, however, call for a formal hearing, witnesses, representation by legal counsel, and other protections (Zirkel & Gluckman, 1990).

Recommendation 2.1: Provide students accused of serious violations of school rules with a hearing and an opportunity to appeal a disciplinary decision.

Consistency

The third criterion of good rule enforcement is consistency. Consistency should characterize several aspects of school discipline. First, each individual charged with responsibility for enforcing rules should strive for consistency in interpreting and enforcing rules. This means that a teacher should not overlook a student loitering in the hall just because the teacher is in a rush. When educators allow their mood or level of activity to influence rule enforcement, they risk undermining the credibility of the entire discipline system.

The same can be said for inconsistencies across various individuals responsible for rule enforcement. When one teacher permits certain rules to be ignored while another teacher enforces them, students may begin to think of school discipline as a game. The object of the game is to break rules without getting caught, or at least without getting punished. Students learn to play one teacher or administrator against another, shrewdly reminding their accusers that some staff members allow behavior that others do not. It is a primary responsibility of school administrators to see that school rules are interpreted similarly by all staff members and enforced consistently.

Recommendation 2.2: Monitor rule enforcement efforts on a regular basis to ensure consistent interpretation of rules and application of consequences.

The credibility of rule enforcement also can be jeopardized when some teachers or administrators mete out harsher consequences than others. Students should not be at risk of receiving a severe punishment because they happen to be assigned to a particular teacher or they happen to be caught by a particular individual. One goal of school safety efforts is to convince students that the system applies to everyone equally, that it does not favor some and discriminate against others.

CASE IN POINT

One large school system handles the issue of student makeup work in an inconsistent manner. When a student is absent from school for an unexcused reason, he is not permitted to make up any work that was missed. The student receives a zero for every day he is absent.

If a student is suspended from school for 10 days, on the other hand, he has the right to make up any work that was missed during the suspension.

It hardly seems right that a student who misses school to attend a college interview (an unexcused absence) receives a zero for the day, when another student who is suspended for 10 days for fighting is allowed to make up all missed assignments.

Consistent, fair, and humane enforcement of school and classroom rules may be necessary for a good school safety program, but there is also another matter to be considered. What of the consequences themselves? Are all consequences equal? Of what value is humane, fair, and consistent rule enforcement if the consequences are morally objectionable or ineffective?

Understanding Consequences

The point already has been made that educators may draw on a variety of consequences to reduce the likelihood of rule violations and unsafe behavior. How does a teacher or administrator know, however, that one particular consequence is preferable to another? What is known about the nature of consequences and their relative effectiveness?

Consequences may be thought of in various ways. Probably the most common notion of a consequence is a *punishment.* Redl (1980, p. 251–252) defined punishment as a planned attempt to influence either behavior or development through exposure to an unpleasant experience. A key aspect of punishment concerns intentionality. The unpleasant experience has to be designed or intended to achieve a particular outcome.

In analyzing the concept of punishment, the author (Duke, 1985, p. 4150) found that thinking about the purposes of punishment varies. One possible purpose is to effect an immediate change in behavior, either by stopping an unwanted behavior or prompting a desired behavior. Deterrence is a second purpose of punishment. The idea is that the mere possibility of punishment will serve to discourage misconduct. In *Portrait of the Artist as a Young Man,* James Joyce provided a vivid account of how one of the priests beat a student in front of his classmates. By making an example of the boy, the priest believed he would deter future behavior problems.

In certain societies punishment is intended to achieve retribution, to ameliorate the effects of the wrongful act as well as expose the perpetrator to an unpleasant experience. Requiring a student to clean the walls she defaced is an example of such a punishment. Punishment need not be associated solely with unpleasantness, however. The so-called detergent theory of punishment holds that the ultimate purpose of punishment is to provide wrongdoers with opportunities to cleanse themselves of guilt through suffering, thereby freeing them to resume their regular activities.

Though widely used, punishment is by no means the only concept used to characterize the outcome of rule enforcement. Many educators and psychologists, in fact, feel that the concept of punishment is either too limiting or incompatible with the overall mission of educational institutions. Teachers trained in behavioral approaches to discipline, for example, supplement punishment with terms such as positive and negative reinforcement. The power of reinforcement derives from the belief that behavior is controlled by its consequences (Kerr & Nelson, 1989, p. 104). Although some specialists insist that behavior problems result from what occurs prior to their occurrence, experts in behavior analysis maintain that what occurs *after* a problem behavior is the real key. Depending on the consequences, the problem behavior may strengthen, weaken, or remain at the same level.

Reinforcement is the term used to describe consequences that strengthen or maintain behavior. Positive reinforcement pertains to situations in which the presentation of a consequence leads to the maintenance or increase of a behavior. Negative reinforcement achieves the same outcome by avoiding or eliminating aversive stimuli. Punishment is also used by behavior analysis experts, but its meaning is very specific. Punishment entails either presenting an aversive consequence (a verbal reprimand, for example) or removing a positive consequence (loss of free time, for example) immediately following inappropriate behavior. Unlike reinforcement, the expected result of punishment is weakened or diminished behavior. Besides clarifying the concept of consequences, behavior analysis stresses the fact that consequences need not be only negative.

Another view of consequences was offered by Rudolf Dreikurs, a psychiatrist and follower of Alfred Adler. He differentiated between natural consequences and logical consequences. The former were defined as "the natural results of ill-advised acts" (Dreikurs & Grey, 1968, p. 63). Because educators cannot remain uninvolved while the children for whom they are responsible experience the natural consequences of their acts, Dreikurs advocated the development of logical consequences, consequences that were directly related to a violation or act of misconduct. He assumed that young people reject or rebel against punishment because they see no connection between their wrongdoing and the sanctions imposed by adults (Dreikurs, Grunwald, & Pepper, 1982, p. 117). If, therefore, a student deprived his classmates of the opportunity to learn about electrons because he was disruptive in science class, he should be required to teach the class about electrons. Detaining him after school for a week would be unrelated to the offense or, in Dreikurs' terms, illogical.

Consequences also can be divided into proactive and reactive consequences (Walker, Colvin, & Ramsey, 1995, p. 142). In general, most consequences in school are reactive. They involve some form of punishment based on the alleged offense, but there is no effort to understand the root causes of the offense or provide assistance in identifying positive alternatives. Proactive consequences are based on the assumption that the wrongdoer needs support, help, and direction. Examples include counseling, conferences, contracts, modeling, instruction, and behavior plans.

A final way to differentiate consequences is based on the object of the consequence. The object may be an individual or a group. Typical disciplinary practice in schools involves meting out consequences for individuals. Special education teachers and advocates of behavior modification, though, sometimes rely on group consequences (Kerr & Nelson, 1989, pp. 148–152). The latter derive from the assumption that students influence each other and constitute a potent source of reinforcement. Various types of group-oriented contingencies have been developed for use in schools. Dependent group-oriented contingencies, for example, tie consequences for all group members to the performance of certain group members. Interdependent group-oriented contingencies require every member to reach a specified level of performance in order for the group to receive a reward.

> **Controversy**
> How necessary and desirable are consequences for promoting good behavior?

Questions about the value of punishment and other forms of consequences have a long history. Critics have noted that harsh sanctions do not necessarily result in fewer violations. In *Beyond Discipline: From Compliance to Community,* Kohn (1996) presents a comprehensive indictment of all types of consequences as the key to good behavior in schools. One component of his argument is based on research findings that suggest punishment, at best, produces only temporary compliance. At worst, it results in alienation and avoidance. Reliance on punishment also teaches young people that power, rather than reason and cooperation, is the appropriate way to correct behavior (Kohn, 1996, p. 27). Educators, to be effective, must build relationships with their students, a goal that is hardly advanced by rule enforcement.

Kohn also questions the desirability of apparent alternatives to punishment. Whether it is called punishment or consequences, he contends, the impact is the same—young people are being acted on rather than worked with (Kohn, 1996, p. 38). He rejects Dreikurs' notion that young people automatically will accept consequences when they see a logical connection between them and acts of wrongdoing.

Instead of compelling students to comply with rules and expectations, educators should cultivate a feeling of community in which all students feel cared for. Kohn believes that rules and consequences alone do not foster an environment conducive to respect, cooperation, and learning. Much of what he advocates will be taken up in Chapter 5, when the issue of valuing and caring for students is addressed.

How Can Consequences Be Used Conscientiously and Effectively?

Although Kohn is correct to point out that consequences alone are unlikely to produce safe and caring schools, it is difficult to imagine a school—or any other institution—in which individuals experience no consequences for their actions. The appropriate question is not how can consequences be eliminated, but how can consequences be used most effectively and conscientiously to promote safe schools for all students.

Determining the effectiveness of a consequence requires clarity regarding its purpose. As the preceding discussion indicated, consequences may be intended to reduce the likelihood that a wrongful act is repeated, deter such acts from occurring in the first place, permit the wrongdoer to atone, or compensate those victimized by the offense. Effectiveness is the extent to which a consequence achieves its intended purpose. But is it enough for a consequence to produce desired results?

In a civilized society, concern for ethical conduct demands that effectiveness be achieved through conscientious means. Public flogging of students may ensure that rule violations do not recur, but resorting to such a consequence offends the sensibilities of many people and demeans the educational mission of schools. Educators should choose consequences for rule enforcement that are likely to achieve their purpose without breaching professional ethics, legal standards, local values, and common decency.

Recommendation 2.3: Clarify the purposes for which particular consequences are intended.

Recommendation 2.4: Ensure that consequences are legal, ethical, and consistent with the educational mission of the school.

Consequences, as the preceding discussion indicated, come in various forms. They may be punitive or nonpunitive, negative or positive. It might seem that positive consequences, such as rewarding students for appropriate behavior, would be preferable to punishing them for violating rules, but some experts object to the use of rewards and incentives.

Controversy
Should students be rewarded in order to promote good behavior?

Many parents occasionally resort to "bribes" in an effort to encourage good behavior by their children. The strategies used by advocates of behavior modification often depend on positive reinforcement to promote rule-governed conduct in school. Who could argue against the use of positive consequences?

Kohn (1996, pp. 32–36), for one, considers rewards to be almost as objectionable as punishments. Young people should not obey school and classroom rules simply because they expect to be rewarded. They should obey rules because they understand the importance of rules in a social context. Not only do rewards do little to promote such understanding, but they can lead to negative feelings when they are no longer forthcoming or perceived as worthwhile. Kohn cites research that suggests children who are frequently rewarded tend to be less generous and cooperative than those who are not rewarded. At best, rewards produce temporary compliance, not a long-term commitment to good behavior. Getting young people to realize that good behavior is its own reward, he asserts, should be the focus of educators' efforts.

Although Kohn's concerns merit thoughtful consideration, they represent a somewhat extreme position. Walker, Colvin, and Ramsey (1995, p. 142) offer a more prudent course of action when they urge educators to "develop a reasonable balance between proactive and reactive consequences." They recognize what every educator knows, that students and circumstances vary greatly and that one consequence is unlikely to be universally appropriate or effective.

> **Recommendation 2.5:** Develop a range of consequences, including positive as well as negative, nonpunitive as well as punitive.

In thinking about the effectiveness of consequences, it is useful to distinguish between intentions and perceptions (Duke & Canady, 1991, p. 99). Just because a consequence is intended to be punitive or rewarding does not mean it will be perceived as such. A school official may regard a 10-day suspension as a punishment, but to a chronic truant, it can seem more like a reward. For this reason, many school systems prefer to assign truants to in-school suspension.

The fact that particular consequences may not be perceived as they are intended leads to one of the thorniest problems in rule enforcement. If individual students respond to particular consequences differently, should educators "individualize" consequences? In other words, should two students who violate the same rule receive different consequences because one consequence is more likely to be effective for one student than the other? At issue are several concerns, including equitable disciplinary practices, recognition of individual differences among students, and the appropriate amount of discretion for educators engaged in rule enforcement.

What Is Known about School-Based Consequences?

The discussion of rule enforcement and consequences thus far has been somewhat generalized. What specific consequences actually are used in schools to maintain order, and what is known about their strengths and weaknesses?

When the author compared discipline policies across 11 school districts, he found a wide range of punitive and nonpunitive consequences (Duke, 1992). Table 4.1 presents a list of both types of consequences and the number of districts in which each was used. Although it is possible to identify additional possibilities, these consequences probably represent the primary ones used by public schools in the United States.

Expulsion and Suspension. The most severe consequence that a school system can exact is expulsion—denying a student access to school. Expulsion is reserved for the most serious offenses, those regarded as jeopardizing the safety and welfare of the school community. Contemporary zero tolerance policies require expulsion for acts such as bringing a weapon to school, attacking a school employee or student, and possessing or distributing drugs. In some cases, expelled students may apply for

TABLE 4.1   Punitive and Nonpunitive Consequences for Violating Rules in 11 School Districts

Punitive Consequences	# of Districts	Nonpunitive Consequences	# of Districts
Expulsion	11	Conference between student and:	
Suspension, short-term	11	administrator	8
Detention—after school	11	teacher	7
		school staff	7
Loss of privileges	11	Participation in an	
Suspension, long-term	10	awareness-building	
Suspension, in-school	7	or rehabilitation	
Corporal punishment	7	program	6
Detention—during school	6	Referral to an:	
		agency	4
Restoration/restitution	6	alternative school or program	4
Work detail	5	Warning	4
Probation	4	Referral to a district	
Time-out	3	student-services	
Suspension, from class	2	unit	3
Confiscation of illegal materials	1	Parent notification	2
		Behavior contract	2
Appearance before a district review panel	1	Parent intervention	1
Saturday school	1		

Source: From Daniel L. Duke, "Variations in School District Discipline Policies," *Record in Educational Administration and Supervision,* vol. 13, no. 1 (Fall/Winter 1992), p. 56.

readmission after a designated period of time—rarely less than the remainder of the school year or 365 days. In other cases, expelled students are not allowed to apply for readmission to the school from which they were expelled.

Depending on the school-leaving age permitted by state law, an expelled student still may have to be provided educational services at public expense. If the student is incarcerated as a result of the offense, these services may be provided by juvenile justice authorities, often in conjunction with a school system. Otherwise, the student may be assigned to homebound instruction, referred to an alternative school or self-contained program, or advised to apply to another school system. With expulsion, the primary goal is to remove a potentially dangerous student from a regular school setting in which she might harm others. Rehabilitation and reinstatement are secondary concerns.

Suspension, on the other hand, presumes that a student will return to school in a relatively short period of time, usually 10 days or less. As a result, school authorities must consider whether the act of suspension is likely to discourage the student from repeating the offense. Out-of-school suspension, as suggested previously, may not be very effective in reducing truancy. Although in-school suspension seems more logical, there is little evidence to indicate that it is a particularly effective alternative. In-school suspension typically requires the allocation of a room and a coordinator to supervise students. When more than 10 students are assigned to in-school suspension, an additional room and coordinator may be needed. It goes without saying that the effectiveness of in-school suspension is highly dependent on the quality of the coordinator.

One advantage of in-school suspension is that students are supervised as they complete assignments that they would have worked on in class. If they receive out-of-school suspension, adequate supervision cannot be assumed. School administrators also must develop a policy regarding makeup work if students are assigned to out-of-school suspension.

Suspension has become one of the most complicated areas of rule enforcement. Some school systems, for example, differentiate between long-term and short-term suspension. In certain states, teachers are permitted to suspend a disruptive student from class, but the student is free to attend other classes. To deal with students who repeatedly violate less serious school rules, some administrators regularly suspend them. A series of short-term suspensions, however, may be tantamount to expulsion, because the overall effect is to deny the student access to an education. As a result, many school systems have been compelled to provide students with due process and limit the number of days a student can be suspended (Zirkel & Gluckman, 1990).

Further complicating the process of suspension is the requirement of contingencies. Prior to being reinstated following a suspension, a student may have to attend a workshop related to the rule that was violated or have a parent meet with the principal. Before suspending a special education student, it is necessary to carefully review the student's Individual Education Program (IEP). More will be said about disciplining special education students in the next part of the chapter.

Corporal Punishment. One of the most controversial consequences involves inflicting physical punishment on students. Although the Supreme Court upheld the right of school personnel to administer corporal punishment in *Ingraham v. Wright,* just over half of the states have prohibited the practice (Harp & Miller, 1995, p. 24). Calls for corporal punishment often are politically motivated, a reaction by individuals and groups to concern over youthful disrespect for authority and irresponsible behavior.

Various reasons exist for not using corporal punishment to enforce school rules. The "message" that reliance on physical force as a means to control behavior sends to young people is hardly consistent with the values of a civil society. Hyman and Snook (1999, p. 157) have observed, with more than a touch of irony, that the Constitution prevents prisoners from being beaten, but not students. Surely a case can be made that corporal punishment of students constitutes cruel and unusual punishment.

Another reason for avoiding corporal punishment concerns the fact that those who administer such punishment are not accorded immunity from litigation in most states. Lawsuits against school administrators for excessive use of force have been increasing. Essex (1989, pp. 43–44) lists 10 ways that school administrators risk lawsuits or criminal charges when they employ corporal punishment:

1. When they administer corporal punishment for offenses that clearly do not warrant physical force
2. When they do not inform students in advance that certain specific infractions will result in corporal punishment
3. When they totally ignore the age, size, sex, or physical condition of the child
4. When they fail to use a reasonable instrument
5. When they do not provide minimal due process for the child prior to administering corporal punishment
6. When they fail to have a witness present during the administration of corporal punishment
7. When they administer corporal punishment with malice or anger
8. When they use excessive force or exercise poor judgment
9. When they insist that corporal punishment is the only option and administer punishment over a student's or parent's objection
10. When they fail to follow local or state policy

Besides legal and moral objections, there is no solid evidence that corporal punishment is an effective means of enforcing school rules.

Can a line be drawn between corporal punishment and the reasonable use of force to prevent a student from hurting himself or others? Several states have passed teacher immunity laws in order to protect teachers and administrators who intervene when students become physically dangerous. Clearly there is a difference between paddling a student who breaks a rule and restraining a student who is attempting to injure a classmate or harm herself. School policy needs to specify the circumstances under which staff members can make legitimate use of physical force and when such force is not in the best interests of students or the school.

Other Consequences.   Table 4.1 presents a variety of other consequences besides expulsion, suspension, and corporal punishment. Punitive consequences include loss of privileges, detention, Saturday school, restoration and restitution, and school service (work detail). Nonpunitive consequences include warnings, conferences, special rehabilitation programs, behavior contracts, and referral to an alternative school or program. Educators probably can think of occasions when particular consequences have and have not worked. Students, of course, vary in their reactions to different consequences and their desire to cooperate in general with school-based disciplinary efforts.

Particular consequences tend to be favored by advocates of comprehensive approaches to classroom management and school discipline. Those who endorse behavior modification, for example, rely on sending students—or having them choose to go—to time-out when they feel upset or unable to work effectively in class. Glasser (1978) believes that students who disobey rules should help to draft behavior "contracts" specifying what they will do to improve their conduct. Canter's Assertive Discipline program (1976) makes use of after-school detention as a consequence designed to encourage greater student respect for teacher authority. Although these and other consequences are likely to be effective with certain students under certain circumstances, research has failed to determine that any consequence constitutes a panacea to behavior problems (Emmer & Aussiker, 1990).

Experts, however, offer some useful guidelines for the application of consequences. Brophy (1983), for example, has noted that mild forms of punishment, such as loss of privileges, demerits, and detention, can effectively communicate the school's commitment to order and civility. Emmer (1987, pp. 247–250) provided the following research-based advice on the choice of punitive consequences:

1. Whenever possible, the punishment should relate logically to the misbehavior.
2. Severe punishment is frequently no more effective than moderate punishment and, at times, less so.
3. Punishment procedures should be focused on helping the student understand the problem and make a commitment to change to more acceptable behavior.
4. Punishment should not be overused with respect to either time or frequency.

Emmer's last point is worth underscoring. Applying certain consequences entails a substantial commitment of time on the part of teachers and administrators. Educators have better things to do than supervising consequences that do not achieve desired effects. For this reason, every school needs to review and evaluate, on a regular basis, the impact of particular consequences on student behavior.

> **Recommendation 2.6:** Evaluate the effectiveness of consequences on a regular basis and adjust or eliminate consequences that fail to produce desired effects.

When dealing with relatively minor behavior problems, Walker, Colvin, and Ramsey (1995, pp. 136–139) recommend that educators follow a graduated series of strategies. Their seven-step protocol ensures consistency and fairness. The steps include:

1. Remove adult and peer attention from the student who is displaying inappropriate behavior.
2. Redirect student to the expected behavior with a gesture or verbal prompt.
3. Provide immediate opportunities for practice and acknowledge compliance.
4. Deliver a warning by providing an opportunity for the student to choose between the expected behavior and a penalty or loss of privilege.
5. Deliver the penalty or loss of privilege.

6. Use additional resources, such as a staff meeting, to address the problem.
7. Document the problem and the interventions that were used.

The strength of this protocol is that it offers students several opportunities to adjust their conduct before a negative consequence is applied. Students are given clear indications of how they are expected to behave, rather than simply being told to stop whatever they are doing. Along with the expected behavior comes verbal reinforcement. Although these steps may not always lead to the elimination of behavior problems, the individual who employs them knows that a reasonable and systematic attempt has been made to address the matter.

Alternative Schools.   In a relatively small percentage of cases, teachers and administrators can do little to make a difference in a student's behavior. For whatever reasons, particular individuals are unable or unwilling to conform to expectations. The problem may rest with a particular mix of students. In other cases, a student may dislike his teacher, or vice versa. Additional factors, including the size of the school, the way instruction is delivered, the presence of too many temptations, and circumstances outside of school also can play a part. When such situations arise, the interests of the student and the school may best be served by referral to an alternative school or program.

Recommendation 2.7: Provide students who find it difficult to conform to expectations with access to alternative schools and programs.

Many school systems today offer a continuum of alternatives to address the needs of students who are not experiencing success in conventional settings (Duke, Griesdorn, & Kraft, 1998). Options may range from schools-within-schools to district alternative schools to special regional facilities serving several school districts. There are even single-sex schools, military-style boot camps, residential programs, and homebound, computer-based programs. The last three alternatives typically are for students with major behavior disorders and those who have committed serious offenses.

Alternatives offer a variety of benefits not available in most regular school settings. The ratio of staff to students is low, often around 1 staff member to 10 students. This provision ensures that every student receives lots of individual attention and no one gets "lost in the shuffle." Alternative schools operate less formally, in many cases, than regular schools and place more emphasis on teacher-student relationships than on rules in order to effect good behavior (Duke, 1990, pp. 30–32). Students assigned to alternatives also may be more motivated to cooperate because they know that their placement constitutes "the last resort."

Some alternative schools strive to return students as soon as possible to regular schools, whereas others are designed to enroll students until they complete their studies. The latter group include programs that prepare students to earn a high school diploma, to pass the General Education Diploma (GED) test, and to secure job training and placement. Although no alternative succeeds with every student, there is compelling evidence that they provide a substantial number of young people with the tools and support they need to finish school (Duke, 1990, pp. 30–32; Duke, Griesdorn, & Kraft, 1998).

Discipline and Special Education Students

Between 3% and 6% of the school-age population in the United States has been estimated to suffer from serious emotional and behavioral disorders (Kauffman, 2001, p. 49). Emotional and behavioral disorders refer to disabilities that are characterized by "affective responses and conduct...that are so deviant from acceptable age-appropriate norms that educational performance in one or more of the following areas is adversely affected: academics, classroom behavior, personal and work adjustment, self-care, and socialization" (Cangelosi, 2000, p. 215). Ensuring that individuals with these disabilities comply with school and classroom rules and avoid harming themselves and others is a major challenge for educators.

The educational interests of students with disabilities are protected by law. Disciplining special education students requires a thorough familiarity with the provisions of the Education for All Handicapped Children Act (P.L. 94-142) and the Individuals with Disabilities Education Act. Public Law 94-142 specified that special education students had "a right to placement in the least restrictive learning environment, insofar as possible, with nonhandicapped children and, whenever possible, at the same school they would attend if they were not handicapped" (O'Reilly & Green, 1992, p. 140). Each special education student must have an IEP, which has to be reviewed at least on an annual basis to ensure that the program is appropriate. Perhaps the provision that has stirred the most controversy for those charged with maintaining school safety concerns the right of students with emotional and behavioral disorders "to remain in present placement during any administrative or judicial proceedings" (O'Reilly & Green, 1992, p. 141).

At issue when special education students commit an offense that normally carries with it suspension from school is whether suspension constitutes a change in placement. This matter was taken up by the U.S. Court of Appeals, Ninth Circuit, in *Honig v. Doe*. The court ruled that a suspension in excess of 10 days did not constitute a change in placement. When the case went to the U.S. Supreme Court, however, the ruling was reversed (O'Reilly & Green, 1992, pp. 164–166). Suspending a special education student was found to represent a change in placement and, therefore, required due process, including a review of the student's IEP. What the Supreme Court did not clarify, however, was whether the 10 days of suspension were consecutive or cumulative.

Another issue related to the discipline of special education students concerns alternative placement. Under what circumstances is it appropriate to place students in private educational facilities as a consequence of their behavior? Do the school districts always have to pay the tuition in these cases?

CASE IN POINT

Rachel continually disrupted her class and intimidated other students. She was diagnosed with Tourette's Syndrome, a behavior disorder characterized by involuntary actions, hyperactivity, and rapid mood swings. Rachel was placed on an IEP that included medication.

When Rachel's behavior did not improve, she was moved to an adaptive behavior classroom for three subjects. Her parents grew concerned that Rachel was exposed to students in this classroom who could harm her. They decided to enroll her in a costly private program.

After several months, Rachel's parents no longer could afford to keep her in the private program. At this point they sought to have her tuition, including what they already had paid, covered by the school system. Rachel's lawyer argued that her original IEP had been inappropriate and that the district was obliged to pay for Rachel to be in an appropriate placement.

This example is based on an actual case that resulted in litigation (Zirkel, 1997). After reviewing the student's IEP, the court decided that the school district had provided an appropriate program. As a result, the student's parents had no basis for insisting that the school district cover the cost of tuition. A district is obliged to pay for private education only when it is unable to offer an appropriate program.

Suspending a special education student for more than 10 days requires a determination that the offense was unrelated to the individual's disabling condition. If a "group of persons knowledgeable about the student" decides that the student's misconduct was a manifestation of his or her disability, the options available to educators include the following (U.S. Department of Education, 1998, p. 1205):

- Suspension for up to 10 days
- Conflict management strategies
- Behavior management strategies
- Teacher training initiatives
- Student training initiatives
- Use of time-out, study carrels, or other restrictions in privileges

As a last resort, a change of placement may be considered in accordance with established procedural guidelines. In addition, a school district always has the option to seek a court order to remove a student from school in cases in which the individual is presumed to pose a threat to other students. Recent amendments also permit educators to make immediate interim changes of placement for up to 45 calendar days for students with disabilities who bring firearms to school (U.S. Department of Education, 1998, p. 1205).

The Complexities of Rule Enforcement

Once upon a time, rule enforcement in schools was relatively straightforward. Teachers and principals developed rules and determined when rules were broken. Consequences were meted out without challenge or appeal. No need existed for complicated faculty handbooks, codes of conduct, procedural guidelines, and attorneys' opinions. Educators enjoyed the discretionary powers of parents.

As the preceding discussion of special education students indicates, however, rule enforcement has become a highly complex undertaking. Complexity is a function of several developments, including role differentiation, role conflict, and role confusion. To ensure safe schools for all students, educators must understand the nature of these challenges and how to mitigate their negative impact on school safety efforts.

Role Differentiation

Rule enforcement once was the responsibility of classroom teachers and, if they were unable to handle the problem, school principals, but today a veritable legion of special personnel stand ready to play a role in school safety. Principals, particularly those in larger middle and high schools, may be assisted by assistant principals, deans of students, school resource officers, and security guards. Students experiencing behavior problems may be referred to guidance counselors, special counselors trained to deal with drug-related problems, crisis teachers, school nurses, in-school suspension coordinators, school psychologists, and school social workers. Additional supervision may be provided by hall and cafeteria monitors, playground attendants, parking lot supervisors, and teaching assistants. Students and community volunteers also may be enlisted in efforts to mediate disputes and promote safe schools and classrooms. On occasion, school administrators must deal with police officers, probation officers, and attorneys representing both students and the school district.

Role differentiation means more staff members with specialized training to help with rule enforcement and deal with particular kinds of problems. The downsides of role differentiation, though, are coordination problems and buck-passing. When one principal handles all rule enforcement, there is no possibility for miscommunication, but when more than one individual is involved, problems may result from different interpretations of rules, different preferences for consequences, and failure to share disciplinary decisions in a timely manner. Students who frequently break rules soon learn which administrators are less likely to impose harsh sanctions. They can take advantage of the heavy volume of disciplinary referrals in some schools to play one administrator off against another.

Buck-passing results when one staff member chooses to refer a troubled student to another staff member rather than handling the problem personally. In some cases, of course, the referral is justified because another individual possesses greater expertise to deal with the problem. In other cases, though, the student is referred because it is the path of least resistance, the easy way out. Students who are said to have "fallen through the cracks" are often those who keep being passed from one staff member to another. No one is willing to "own" the student and her problems.

To reduce the negative effects of role differentiation, schools can take several steps. First, clear sets of expectations must be developed for every staff member with a role to play in school safety. If school resource officers are expected to teach units on safety, patrol school grounds, and make court appearances, they should understand the nature of their job before they start. Clear expectations allow individuals to request supplementary training when necessary and help other staff members understand when these persons should be called on for assistance. Figure 4.1 contains a sample list of school safety responsibilities. Principals should make certain that all staff members are clear about who is expected to assume each of these safety-related responsibilities.

Another step in reducing coordination problems involves the development of a School Safety Team, a core group of individuals who assume responsibility for overseeing rule enforcement and other aspects of the school safety program. It makes sense to involve school administrators, counselors, regular education teachers, and special education teachers on the team. Where specialized individuals, such as school resource officers, are employed, they also should be represented. The School Safety Team needs to develop and periodically review and update the list of responsibilities associated with school safety and rule enforcement. It also should determine who is best suited to undertake various responsibilities.

Coordination problems are a function, in part, of gaps in communication. To minimize the likelihood of such gaps, the School Safety Team, or a subgroup, should meet daily. In hospitals and police stations, briefings are held with each change in shift. It makes sense for School Safety Team members to "touch base" before school begins in the morning and at the close of the school day. A 10-minute briefing and debriefing each day allows plans to be made, information to be shared, and rumors to be checked. Experienced educators know the price to be paid when people in key roles fail to inform each other of emerging concerns, potentially thorny disciplinary cases, and unilateral decisions made during the course of the school day.

Recommendation 2.8: Create a School Safety Team to develop and review responsibilities associated with school safety and rule enforcement.

FIGURE 4.1   Partial List of Responsibilities Associated with School Safety

What staff member(s) or role group(s) is responsible for the following:

1. Enforcing classroom rules
    Classroom teachers
    Teacher aides
    Volunteers
    Visiting administrators or teachers

2. Enforcing school rules
    Classroom teachers
    Teacher aides
    Volunteers
    Principals and assistant principals
    Counselors
    Hall and cafeteria monitors
    School resource officers or security guards
    School nurses

3. Breaking up fights and restraining aggressive students
    Principals and assistant principals
    School resource officers and security guards
    Hall and cafeteria monitors
    Teachers with special training

4. Searching school property for weapons, drugs, and contraband
    Principals and assistant principals
    School resource officers and security guards
    Police officers
    Teachers with special training

5. Searching individuals for weapons, drugs, or contraband
    Principals and assistant principals
    School resource officers and security guards
    Police officers
    Teachers with special training

6. Hearing appeals related to rule enforcement
    Principals and assistant principals
    Faculty committee
    Central office designee
    Student court

7. Supervising detention hall
    Teachers who assign students to detention hall
    Detention hall supervisors
    Various staff members (on a rotating basis)

(continued)

FIGURE 4.1   Continued

8. Counseling a student who is extremely upset or "in crisis"
    Guidance counselors
    Crisis teachers
    School psychologists
    School nurses
    Peer counselors

9. Checking out strangers in school
    Principals and assistant principals
    School resource officers
    Police officers

10. Questioning students accused of rule violations
    Principals and assistant principals
    School resource officers

Role Conflict

Educators are called on to play many roles in the course of carrying out their school responsibilities. A teacher, for example, serves as an instructor to groups of students, a tutor for individual students, a classroom manager, and a disciplinarian. In some cases, what teachers must do to carry out one role may undermine their ability to fulfill another role. This problem is referred to by sociologists as role conflict, and it can adversely affect school safety efforts (Duke, 1980).

A case can be made, for example, that fulfilling the role of tutor requires that students trust and feel comfortable with teachers. Developing these feelings is more difficult when students also regard teachers as disciplinarians who enforce rules and administer punishments. There are many teachers, of course, who are able to satisfy the expectations of both these roles quite effectively, but they only can do so because they are perceived by students to be fair and to care.

> *Controversy*
> Should a counselor disclose confidential information about a student if school safety is involved?

There is no clearer example of role conflict than that of the guidance counselor. Counselors are expected to listen to students who are experiencing problems. In order to do so, they must assure students that what they hear will not be shared with anyone, including parents and school administrators. Counselors, however, are also members of a school community and, as such, they share responsibility for the safety and welfare of everyone in the school. Should a counselor respect a student's confidentiality when it is learned that the student plans to harm someone? Is it better to avert a tragedy by disclosing to school officials the student's intentions and risk further alienating and isolating the student? Are there legal consequences for breaching confidentiality or failing to do so?

To ensure safe schools it is necessary for counselors to regard themselves as part of the "team." This means that they must share privileged information when the safety of others is at risk. Counselors naturally may try to do all they can to redirect the feelings of an angry student and help him understand that hurting others is not the answer to his problems, but if these efforts are believed to be unproductive, the counselor has an obligation to serve "the greater good."

Cottone and Tarvydas (1998, p. 96) offer a useful list of exceptions to the general requirement for counselors to hold student communications confidential. These include situations when

- The student is dangerous to self or others.
- The counselor receives a court order requiring the release of information.
- Counseling occurs with a third party present.
- The student discloses the information to advance a criminal or fraudulent activity.
- Child abuse is suspected by the counselor.

School administrators also experience role conflict. It is possible, for instance, that a principal may serve as arresting officer, jury, and judge for the same case. In other words, she may catch a student who seemingly has violated a school rule, determine that the student is guilty, and mete out a consequence. There is a reason, of course, why these three functions are separated in our legal system. Concern for fairness requires that judge and jury consider evidence impartially. It may be difficult for an arresting officer to see all sides of an expected violation.

To ensure that rule enforcement efforts are perceived as fair, it may be prudent to involve various members of the School Safety Team. A staff member who apprehends a student or students and believes that a rule has been violated may wish to refer the matter to another staff member to adjudicate. Although this process is time-consuming, it reduces the likelihood of errors in judgment resulting from heated emotions. In serious cases, prudence may dictate that a consequence be determined by a third party. The long-term interests of school safety are not well served by rule enforcement that is perceived to be hasty, arbitrary, or vindictive.

Role Confusion

When an individual is unclear about what he is expected to do in order to fulfill his role effectively, role confusion is said to exist. A combination of factors, including closer scrutiny of school disciplinary actions by parents and the courts and greater centralization of disciplinary policy making, have led to questions about the amount of discretion over rule enforcement that school administrators should exercise. Contemporary administrators are often confused about the limits of their authority.

In *School Policy,* Duke and Canady (1991, p. 100) examine the arguments for and against administrative discretion in rule enforcement. An argument in favor holds that no two disciplinary cases are exactly the same. Students may or may not be repeat offenders. One student may have been motivated by malicious reasons but another was goaded into breaking a rule by a bully. A particular consequence for rule-breaking may be perceived quite differently by different students. To deal effectively with these and other contingencies, school administrators need a healthy measure of discretionary authority.

An argument against discretion, on the other hand, is that it invites "sanctioned inconsistency," which in turn can produce real or perceived discriminatory treatment. Critics of discretion point to statistics, for example, that indicate minority students receive a disproportionately high percentage of suspensions and expulsions. Nowhere has the tension over administrative discretion been greater than so-called zero tolerance policies.

> ### Controversy
> Should school administrators be prevented from exercising discretion when it comes to the enforcement of certain rules?

Curwin and Mendler (1999, pp. 119–120) acknowledge that zero tolerance policies requiring administrators to impose specific consequences, typically suspension and expulsion, for serious offenses derive from legitimate concerns over school safety. They also note that such policies send "a powerful message to the school community that violent, aggressive behavior will not be tolerated" (pp. 119–120). They go on, though, to question the wisdom of any policy that can create new difficulties in the process of trying to resolve the original problem.

Examples of the abuse of zero tolerance policies are abundant. Curwin and Mendler offer several illustrations, including a student who was expelled for bringing a gun to school. On further investigation, it was learned that the student had taken the gun from his father, who had threatened to kill the boy and his younger brother. In other words, the student had the gun in his possession in order to save lives, not harm others. Other examples of zero tolerance policies gone awry include the expulsion of a student for bringing a gun with its barrel welded shut to school and the suspension of a primary school student for kissing another student and thereby violating the policy against sexual harassment.

Proponents of zero tolerance policies point to resulting declines in serious incidents in many schools (Johnston, 1999, p. 12). They add that students who are suspended or expelled typically have an opportunity to attend an alternative school. Many school administrators express relief over the fact that they no longer have to make difficult decisions regarding how to punish students who have broken major rules.

If there is an answer to the challenges of rule enforcement, it is not to eliminate the need for professional judgment. The world of schools and young people is complex. Creating the illusion of simplicity through zero tolerance policies does not alter this fact. The point was noted by a federal district judge in Tennessee when he ruled that a school board went too far in expelling a high school student for having a knife in his car (Walsh, 1999, p. 10). Evidence indicated that the student was not even aware of the weapon. The judge's message was clear—the need for discipline does not justify ignoring the Constitutional rights of students.

Educators engaged in rule enforcement should exercise the same discretion recognized in a court of law. Determining the disposition of a disciplinary infraction, in other words, should take account of the particular circumstances of the violation, the prior records of those involved, and the impact of the offense on others. Because a consideration of these matters requires skill in investigation, analysis, and judgment, educators responsible for rule enforcement need to receive special training.

Conclusion

The second standard for a school that is safe for all students requires that rules are enforced humanely, fairly, and consistently. A critical part of the process by which young people mature into responsible adults involves learning that there are consequences, both positive and negative, for their actions. Educators need to give careful consideration to these consequences and determine which ones are and are not effective in promoting good behavior and school safety. Rule enforcement presents educators with a variety of challenges, including how to handle special education students, the proliferation of new roles related to school safety, role conflict, and confusion over the proper amount of discretionary authority for school administrators.

Standard 2 is met when everyone in a school understands the process of rule enforcement, when the process is conducted conscientiously, and when clarity exists concerning the consequences for violating school and classroom rules.

REFERENCES

Brophy, Jere E. "Classroom Organization and Management," *Elementary School Journal,* vol. 83 (1983), pp. 265–286.

Cangelosi, James S. *Classroom Management Strategies,* fourth edition. New York: Wiley, 2000.

Canter, Lee. *Assertive Discipline.* Santa Monica, CA: Lee Canter, 1976.

Claiborne, William. "Disparity in School Discipline Found," *Washington Post* (December 17, 1999), p. A3.

Cottone, R. Rocco, and Tarvydas, Vilia M. *Ethical and Professional Issues in Counseling.* Columbus, OH: Merrill, 1998.

Curwin, Richard L., and Mendler, Allen N. "Zero Tolerance for Zero Tolerance," *Phi Delta Kappan,* vol. 81, no. 2 (October 1999), pp. 119–120.

Dreikurs, Rudolf, and Grey, Loren. *A New Approach to Discipline: Logical Consequences.* New York: Hawthorne Books, 1968.

Dreikurs, Rudolf; Grunwald, B. B.; and Pepper, F. C. *Maintaining Sanity in the Classroom: Classroom Management Techniques,* second edition. New York: Harper Collins, 1982.

Duke, Daniel L. "Disciplinary Roles in American Schools," *British Journal of Teacher Education,* vol. 6, no. 1 (January 1980), pp. 37–50.

Duke, Daniel L. "Punishment." In *International Encyclopedia of Education.* New York: Pergamon Press, 1985, pp. 4150–4153.

Duke, Daniel L. "School Organization, Leadership, and Student Behavior." In Oliver C. Moles (ed.), *Student Discipline Practices.* Albany, NY: State University of New York Press, 1990, pp. 19–46.

Duke, Daniel L. "Variations in School District Discipline Policies," *Record in Educational Administration and Supervision,* vol. 13, no. 1 (Fall/Winter 1992), pp. 54–61.

Duke, Daniel L., and Canady, R. Lynn. *School Policy.* New York: McGraw-Hill, 1991.

Duke, Daniel L.; Griesdorn, Jacqueline; and Kraft, Mike. "A School of Their Own: A Status Check of Virginia's Alternative High Schools for At-Risk Students." Charlottesville, VA: Thomas Jefferson Center for Educational Design, 1998.

Emmer, Edmund T. "Classroom Management and Discipline." In Virginia Richardson-Koehler (ed.), *Educator's Handbook.* New York: Longman, 1987, pp. 233–258.

Emmer, Edmund T., and Aussiker, Amy. "School and Classroom Discipline Programs: How Well Do They Work?" In Oliver C. Moles (ed.), *Student Discipline Strategies.* Albany, NY: State University of New York Press, 1990, pp. 126–166.

Essex, Nathan L. "Corporal Punishment," *Principal,* vol. 68, no. 5 (May 1989), pp. 42–44.

Glasser, William. "Disorder in Our Schools: Causes and Remedies," *Phi Delta Kappan,* vol. 59, no. 4 (December 1978), pp. 322–325.

Harp, Lonnie, and Miller, Laura. "States Turn Up Heat in Debate over Paddlings," *Education Week* (September 6, 1995), pp. 1, 24.

Hyman, Irwin A., and Snook, Pamela A. *Dangerous Schools.* San Francisco: Jossey-Bass, 1999.

Johnston, Robert. "Decatur Furor Sparks Wider Policy Debate," *Education Week* (November 24, 1999), pp. 1, 12–13.

Kauffman, James M. *Characteristics of Emotional and Behavioral Disorders of Children and Youths,* seventh edition. New York: Merrill/Prentice Hall, 2001.

Kerr, Mary Margaret, and Nelson, C. Michael. *Strategies for Managing Behavior Problems in the Classroom,* second edition, Columbus, OH: Merrill, 1989.

Kohn, Alfie. *Beyond Discipline: From Compliance to Community.* Alexandria, VA: Association for Supervision and Curriculum Development, 1996.

Oakes, Jeannie, and Lipton, Martin. *Teaching to Change the World.* Boston: McGraw-Hill, 1999.

O'Reilly, Robert C., and Green, Edward T. *School Law for the 1990s: A Handbook.* New York: Greenwood Press, 1992.

Redl, Fritz. "The Concept of Punishment." In N. J. Long, W. C. Morse, and R. G. Newman (eds.), *Conflict in the Classroom.* Belmont, CA: Wadsworth, 1980, pp. 251–257.

U.S. Department of Education. "Disciplining Students with Disabilities." In Michael I. Levin (ed.), *1998 United States School Laws and Rules.* New York: West Group, 1998.

Walker, Hill M.; Colvin, Geoff; and Ramsey, Elizabeth. *Antisocial Behavior in School: Strategies and Best Practices.* Pacific Grove, CA: Brooks/Cole, 1995.

Walsh, Mark. "Federal Judge Draws the Line on District's Zero-Tolerance Policy," *Education Week* (February 10, 1999), p. 10.

Zirkel, Perry A. "But When He Was Bad, Was He Horrid?" *Phi Delta Kappan,* vol. 79, no. 3 (November 1997), pp. 250–251.

Zirkel, Perry A., and Gluckman, Oran B. "Due Process for Student Suspensions," *Principal,* vol. 69, no. 3 (March 1990), pp. 62–63.

5 Standard 3: A Caring School Community

- A substantial number of school safety problems can be traced to students who feel mistreated or uncared for.
- Rules and consequences are no substitute for constructive relationships and a sense of belonging.
- Caring is a matter of perception as well as intention.
- Peers can be a positive as well as a negative influence on school culture.
- The curriculum should reflect community-oriented values such as caring, civility, and responsibility.
- Students benefit from being taught social skills such as anger management and conflict resolution.
- Schools must ensure the psychological as well as the physical safety of students.

Clear behavioral expectations and consequences for disobeying rules may reduce the likelihood of unsafe acts, but they do little to ensure that young people want to attend school. Young people are no different from adults in the sense that they are attracted to places where they feel valued and cared for. When people are "treated like a number," when their concerns are minimized or ignored altogether, and when there is little encouragement to build constructive relationships, they hardly can be blamed for feeling alienated and unappreciated.

Most schools manage to make some students feel valued and cared for, but often these "small victories" are achieved at the expense of other students' feelings. Educators are accused of devoting considerable energy to sorting and selecting young people into groups with a high likelihood of success and groups "at risk" of not experiencing success. The overarching goal of a safe school for *all* students requires that *all* students feel valued and cared for, regardless of their background, behavior, and academic performance.

> **Standard 3:** Students feel valued and cared for.

This chapter opens with an examination of school cultures that might best be termed "toxic." These cultures repel rather than welcome large numbers of students. When students feel no sense of positive connection to school, they are more likely to engage in conduct harmful to themselves and others.

How to create caring school communities in which all students feel "connected" is the focus of this chapter. A variety of "design principles" are presented and discussed. These principles underscore the fact, stressed throughout this book, that school safety requires more than preventing young people from "behaving badly." The ultimate key to school safety is for students to learn to be constructive, contributing members of a community. The closing part of the chapter addresses several sensitive issues related to the psychological safety of young people and what caring schools can do about them.

Toxic School Cultures

Not all school cultures are created equal. Some cultures are robust and welcoming, whereas others are fragmented and repelling, more a collection of subcultures than a definable culture. Some cultures promote school safety by embracing positive values such as caring and mutual respect, but others actually contribute to safety problems by alienating certain groups and reinforcing negative values. Cultures in this last category may be referred to as *toxic*. They are inimical to the psychological well-being of many students and staff members. Peterson and Deal (1998, p. 29) note that toxic school cultures are places where "negativity dominates conversations, interactions, and planning: where the only stories recounted are of failure, the only heroes are anti-heroes."

Imagine being asked, as part of some misguided planning exercise, to design a school culture that discouraged caring. How would you go about it?

One critical element of an uncaring culture probably would involve the allocation of rewards and incentives. Students and staff would have to be shown that the benefits of insensitivity and competition outweighed the benefits of caring and cooperation. Such a goal could be accomplished by ensuring that the culture produced winners and losers. Valuing levels of achievement that only some students could reach in the time allotted would be one means to reach this end. Another would be to take some people's problems more seriously than others. For example, a discipline problem involving a popular cheerleader could be handled with greater understanding than a teenage mother's late arrival at school because of child care responsibilities.

Expectations also would play a role. To design an uncaring culture, it would be important to avoid high expectations for caring and cooperation. Students would not be expected, for example, to make newcomers feel welcome. Areas in which high expectations were stressed would be limited to individual accomplishment. Furthermore, those who failed to reach those high standards would be told in direct and indirect ways that the fault was theirs, not their teachers' or school system's.

To ensure that staff members would not model care for students, class sizes and caseloads would be high. Care requires time—time to seek out, time to listen, time to help. If staff members had large numbers of students for whom they were responsible, caring for all students would seem next to impossible. Faced with such an insurmountable obstacle, many staff members would be likely to grow discouraged and abandon efforts to care for any students.

The "design" that has been outlined is not a very inviting one, but it is precisely the image of school that many students hold. It is an image characterized by failure, frustration, isolation, and detachment. That some young people see schools as impersonal and uncaring places but others regard them with enthusiasm and hopefulness is a reminder that the full benefits of schooling have yet to be extended to all young people.

In the wake of the Columbine High School tragedy, an editorial appeared in *Education Week* that noted how alone and psychologically imperiled many teenagers feel. The author attributed these feelings in large part to a contemporary culture supporting few alternative models for success and harsh consequences for lack of conventional achievement. She went on to point her finger at large high schools in general, stating,

> ...in a culture that prizes athletic prowess, access to bucks, and narrowly defined good looks above all else, large high schools...replicate and intensely magnify a grueling, cruel, social-caste system that makes George Orwell's *Animal Farm* look like a barnyard picnic. (Lanier, 1999, p. 34)

Concerned over the toxic cultures in many secondary schools, the Educational Excellence Alliance surveyed almost 33,000 students in 130 Northeastern schools (Educational Excellence Alliance, 1999). Nearly 1 in 10 students said they were "insulted, teased or made fun of" almost daily. Harassment was routine for approximately a third of the male juniors and more than a fifth of the female juniors. Substantial numbers of students believed that classmates ridiculed or made fun of them behind their backs. These findings led the Alliance to characterize secondary schools as "insult cultures."

When Patricia Hersch (1998) spent several years tracking the lives of eight suburban Virginia teenagers, she found considerable evidence to support the Alliance's findings. One of her students put it thusly:

> Parents don't have a clue to what school is like these days. If all I had to do was go to classes and learn it would be a huge relief...But every day, we have to deal with being knocked around the halls, having to look over our shoulders, having classes absolutely taken over by rude kids. School is basically chaotic and it is really hard to learn. (Hersch, 1998, p. 89)

Although the causes of toxic school cultures are complex, they clearly derive from the actions of adults as well as young people. Teachers, for example, sometimes tolerate or even encourage aggressive behavior in boys. One study found that elementary teachers believe that being tough is a key to the popularity of some boys (Rodkin, Farmer, Pearl, & Van Acker, 2000). Another study found that teachers contribute to student behavior problems by overlooking, making light of, or minimizing students' personal concerns (Duke, 1978). When students feel that their worries mean little to teachers and administrators, they are less likely to be cooperative and to feel good about being in school.

If it is possible to design school cultures that are toxic, it is also possible to create school cultures in which students and staff feel valued and cared for. To do so, however, requires an understanding of the nature of caring and community.

What Is a Caring School Community?

One need look no further than childrearing to appreciate the complexity of the concept of caring. Parents sometimes tell their children that it is because they care for them that they are not going to bail them out of a jam. They believe that the long-term interests of their children are best served by allowing them to experience the negative consequences of their actions. Sometimes this strategy works, and sometimes it does not. Caring, it turns out, is a matter of perception as well as intention. If the actions we intend as caring are not perceived as such, then a critical condition of caring has not been satisfied.

In examining conceptions of care, Grogan (1999, pp. 22–23) points out that care is both a practice and a sensibility. The practice of care requires action for the sake of others. The disposition of care entails an awareness of the needs and interests of others. The two are obviously linked. Sensibility without action is as likely to come across as "care-less" as action without sensibility. Sensibility regarding others' needs and interests, Grogan notes, depends on and derives from relationships. It is difficult to imagine a caring school community in which students have no constructive relationships with staff members. The old adage applies: I do not care what you know until I know that you care.

Wuthnow (1995, pp. 40–41) observes that it is one thing to care in informal or primary settings, such as the family, and quite another to do so in formal and institutionalized settings, such as schools. As he puts it, "Whereas one may allow people to develop deep bonds of trust based on extensive personal interaction, the other may depend more on strict adherence to rules that do not necessitate extensive knowledge of personal traits or situations" (p. 40). It is a challenge, in other words, to foster the caring that might be found at home in schools and classrooms. The challenge, of course, is even greater when the home is bereft of care.

The term "community" is used to capture the fact that care is a collective as well as an individual enterprise. Kohn (1996, pp. 101–102) conveys the sense in which schools and classrooms can be communities when he describes them as places

> ...in which students feel cared about and are encouraged to care about each other. They experience a sense of being valued and respected; the children matter to one another and to the teacher. They have come to think in the plural: they feel connected to each other; they are part of an "us." And, as a result of all this, they feel safe in their classes, not only physically but emotionally.

A commitment to creating caring school communities requires that educators ask not only what do students need to know in order to graduate, but how can they learn to get along with each other in the process of getting an education. Noddings (1992, p. 65) maintains that "a great moral purpose" of schools is "to care for children so that they, too, will be prepared to care." Designing environments characterized by pervasive cooperation and caring requires, according to Kohn (1996, pp. 109–110), attention to three matters: class schedules, class size, and relationships. Community is unlikely to develop in settings in which time for building relationships between teachers and students is scarce, teachers must work with large numbers of students, and teachers themselves do not feel part of a professional community.

Sometimes community is associated with shared values. Although it is likely that true communities do share some key values, Selznick (1992, p. 358) is correct to point out that the essence of community is a commitment to live and work together despite differences. Defining community in terms of shared values can lead to exclusion of those who do not "fit" or worse, as evidenced by Nazi Germany.

Designing caring school communities involves an understanding that caring is learned behavior and that certain knowledge and skills can be important in promoting and sustaining care. Caring school communities require constant awareness of how students are feeling and continuing efforts to "connect" students to the school. Finding ways to build relationships between teachers and students and use the student peer group as a positive force are also essential. These concerns are represented by six "design principles" for caring school communities. The next part of the chapter addresses each of these principles in detail.

Design Principles for a Caring School Community

---

1. Caring is learned.
2. Special skills are needed to deal with situations that threaten a caring school community.
3. Students and staff members must be alert to early signs of problems.
4. The student peer group has a constructive role to play in a caring school community.
5. Students benefit from feeling connected to school and community.
6. A caring school community embraces differences.

Learning to Care

People are not born with the competence and commitment to care. They learn to care. Sometimes they learn by the direct experience of care, which for many individuals begins at birth and continues through childhood and beyond. They also learn to care by observing others in the act of caregiving. Finally, they may benefit from instruction in care.

In a perfect world educators could assume that young people come to school already familiar with the importance of care and a rudimentary understanding of caregiving. Unfortunately, all too many children receive too little care in their early years. Even those whose homes include nurturing parents need to know that caring is important outside the family as well as at home. For these reasons, educators should incorporate lessons related to care and caregiving into their instruction.

Recommendation 3.1: Address issues of care and caregiving in the formal curriculum.

That which is included in the formal curriculum of a school is more likely to be regarded as worthy of learning than that which is excluded. If we consider care and caregiving to be important subjects for study, the question arises, What is the best way to address care and caregiving in the curriculum? The position taken in this book holds that these subjects are best handled in the context of values education.

Calls for schools to incorporate values education into the formal curriculum have increased in recent decades as the public has become alarmed over youthful incivility and disrespect for authority. How best to address the subject of values, however, has not been resolved. Some states, such as Virginia, have mandated that all schools develop programs for character education. Louisiana has legislated that students be taught and held accountable for civility. The American Civil Liberties Union believes, however, that requiring students to say "yes, ma'am" or "no, sir" to teachers, as Louisiana has done, is a violation of their freedom of speech (Pressley, 2000, p. A3).

Controversy
How should schools handle the subject of values?

In *Why Johnny Can't Tell Right from Wrong,* Kilpatrick (1992) maintains that there are two basic approaches to values education: character education and values clarification. The former is based on the identification of universal values that all young people should know. Teachers provide direct instruction regarding the importance of these values, offer examples from history and literature of individuals who exemplify the values, and expect students to practice the values in school.

Values clarification, also referred to as moral reasoning, presents students with dilemmas involving conflicting values. As they reason through the dilemmas and determine what they would do, students are supposed to arrive at a clearer understanding of what they value. Teachers are not expected to endorse particular values or inform students that the choice they would make is wrong.

Kilpatrick (1992, p. 16) is highly critical of values clarification, claiming that it has led to "wholesale confusion about moral values," undermined values taught at home, and reduced matters of right and wrong to the "merely subjective." It is, in fact, difficult to find contemporary advocates for an exclusive focus on values clarification. One of the approach's developers now endorses a "comprehensive" model of values education, one that includes direct instruction in particular values, modeling, and skill building (Kirschenbaum, 1995, pp. 8–11).

Kirschenbaum (1995, pp. 32–34) makes an important distinction between inculcation and indoctrination. Figure 5.1 contrasts these two approaches to values education. It is unlikely that indoctrination, as he characterizes it, will provide the

FIGURE 5.1 Inculcation versus Indoctrination

Inculcation	Indoctrination
■ Communicate what you believe and the reasons why you believe it.	■ Communicate what you believe solely on the bases of authority.
■ Treat other views fairly.	■ Treat other views unfairly.
■ Accord respect to those with other views.	■ Vilify, dehumanize those with other views.
■ Answer doubt with reason and respect.	■ Answer doubt with rigidity and scorn.
■ Partially structure the environment to increase likelihood of exposure to desired values and decrease likelihood of exposure to undesirable values.	■ Totally control the environment to increase likelihood of exposure to desired values and decreased likelihood of exposure to undesirable values.
■ Create positive social, emotional, learning experiences around the desired values—within limits.	■ Create positive social, emotional, learning experiences around the desired values—to an extreme.
■ Provide rules, rewards, and consequences—within reason.	■ Provide rules, rewards and consequences—to the extreme.
■ If someone disagrees, keep open lines of communication.	■ If someone disagrees, cut off communication.
■ Allow a certain latitude for divergent behavior; if beyond acceptable level, leave open possibility of change.	■ Allow no latitude for divergent behavior; if beyond acceptable level, ostracize totally and/or permanently.

Source: Howard Kirschenbaum, *100 Ways to Enhance Values and Morality in Schools and Youth Settings.* Boston: Allyn & Bacon, 1995, p. 33.

understanding or sensitivity to others' beliefs that a truly caring school community requires.

One constructive way to address issues of care and caregiving is offered by Lickona in *Educating for Character* (1991a). He contends that schools should teach "two great moral values": respect and responsibility (pp. 43–45). Lickona maintains that these values "constitute the core of a universal, public morality" and that they are keys to healthy personal development, caring interpersonal relationships, and a humane and democratic society (p. 43). It is difficult to imagine instruction on respect and responsibility that would not involve discussions of care and caregiving, but just to ensure that these matters are addressed, they should be added to Lickona's pair of core values.

Lickona (1991b, p. 68) elsewhere states, in fact, that elementary schools should develop a sense of community based on fairness, caring, and democratic participation. In addition, they should promote development away from egocentrism and help students (1) to judge what is right and (2) to care deeply about it. Toward these ends, he recommends that elementary educators strive to cultivate in every child the following qualities:

1. A self-respect that derives feelings of worth not only from achievement but also from prosocial behavior toward others
2. Social perspective taking ("How do others think and feel?")
3. Moral reasoning ("What is the right thing to do?")
4. Empathy, defined as the tendency to identify with and care about the welfare of others
5. The skills and attitudes needed for cooperative participation in human communities
6. Stable dispositions to respond to situations in moral ways—manifested in observable patterns of kindness, honesty, responsibility, and a generalized respect for others (Lickona, 1991b, p. 68)

When Duke and Jones (1985) reviewed best-selling textbooks on classroom management, they identified various ways that teachers in elementary and secondary schools can promote the acquisition of responsibility. The implication of these approaches is clear—responsibility must be practiced to be well-learned. Young people are unlikely to learn to be responsible if they are accorded few opportunities to exercise responsibility. The following represent opportunities for students to learn about and practice responsibility:

- Development of class and school rules and routines
- Review and assessment of rules and consequences
- Assessment of personal behavior
- Evaluation of academic progress
- Student-led conferences involving teachers and parents (to review academic and behavioral progress)
- Development of plans and contracts designed to correct behavior problems

- Academic and behavioral goal-setting
- Selection of learning activities and projects
- Group work
- Independent work
- Participation in activities to improve behavior of classmates
- Feedback to teachers on instruction and quality of classroom life
- Involvement in class meetings
- Assumption of roles related to upkeep and management of class and school

Although it is possible to teach students about respect and care, these dispositions may best be acquired as by-products of engagement in activities that call on students to assume meaningful responsibilities and work closely with others. Anyone who has played on an athletic team, participated in a dramatic production, or worked on the staff of a literary publication understands the bonds of caring that can develop as individuals collectively pursue a common and meaningful objective.

CASE IN POINT

The Hyde School in Bath, Maine, was founded in 1966 to help young people develop character. Hyde expects all students to develop the following traits:

- The courage to accept challenges
- The integrity to be truly themselves
- Concern for others
- The curiosity to explore life and learning
- Leadership in making the school and community work

The school's founder, Joseph Gauld, believed that most of what adults do in schools could and should be handled by the students themselves. Students at Hyde are responsible for maintaining the school environment, helping fellow students correct academic and behavioral problems, and enforcing the school's code of ethics.

Teachers are expected to teach by example, to model the core traits that they seek to develop in students. Seminars provide teachers with regular opportunities to help each other work on their own personal and ethical growth.

The Hyde School's impressive track record with troubled young people demonstrates that it is possible for almost anyone to learn how to be a contributing member of a caring school community.

The Need for Special Skills

Creating and maintaining caring school communities depends on more than an understanding of core values such as respect and responsibility. Students and staff members also need special skills for handling individuals and situations that threaten the well-being of the community.

> **Recommendation 3.2:** Provide opportunities for students and staff members to acquire and refine social skills.

It is never too soon to begin helping students to develop social skills. Young people who do not acquire social skills at home may have problems getting along with teachers and classmates and developing constructive friendships. Research suggests that students who fail to acquire social skills early in their schooling are more likely to experience behavior problems and academic problems (Hinshaw, 1992; Parker and Asher, 1987). Elementary educators should consider social skills instruction beginning in kindergarten.

Although opinions vary somewhat regarding the specific skills that are most important for caring school communities, general agreement exists that the ability to communicate effectively is crucial. Those who are unable to express their feelings to others often are compelled, as was Herman Melville's Billy Budd, to strike out physically. The results can be tragic. Kreidler (1984) identified five qualities that were central to a "peaceable classroom," and communication was involved in each one:

1. Cooperation. Children learn to work together and trust, help, and share with each other.
2. Communication. Children learn to observe carefully, communicate accurately, and listen sensitively.
3. Tolerance. Children learn to respect and appreciate people's differences and to understand prejudice and how it works.
4. Positive emotional expression. Children learn to express feelings, particularly anger and frustration, in ways that are not aggressive or destructive, and children learn self-control.
5. Conflict resolution. Children learn the skills of responding creatively to conflict in the context of a supportive, caring community.

Building on the work of Howard Gardner, Goleman (1995) has developed a framework for thinking about emotional competence. He contends that emotional competence is a function of personal competence and social competence. The former involves self-awareness, self-regulation, and motivation. The latter consists of empathy and social skills. Empathy represents awareness of the feelings, needs, and concerns of others, whereas social skills encompass the ability to induce desirable responses in others. Among the social skills identified by Goleman are communication (listening openly and sending convincing messages), conflict management (negotiating and resolving disagreements), and influence (wielding effective tactics for persuasion).

In *Waging Peace in Our Schools* (1996, pp. 27–28), Lantieri and Patti caution educators against expecting social skill development to be a smooth and speedy process. They refer to predictable stages in skill development, beginning with hesitancy or even resistance on the part of students. New techniques may seem "phony" or contrived because students are unaccustomed to using them and consequently feel awkward. Practice, persistence, role playing, and modeling by adults are essential if students are to benefit from social skills instruction.

Many instructional aides are available to educators interested in addressing social skills. Girard and Koch (1996, pp. 67–68), for example, offer a variety of exercises, including one to help students analyze anger. Several assumptions undergird the exercise. First, a key to conflict resolution involves how individuals deal with their own anger and that of others. Second, at the root of most anger lies fear.

The objective of Girard and Koch's exercise is to "identify and enhance communication skills that will improve conflict resolution processes." The exercise begins by asking students to form groups of eight. Each group is assigned a student or adult volunteer who has been trained as a facilitator. Using chart paper, each group generates a list of situations in which they have experienced anger. Once the lists have been made, group members review the examples and try to identify the fears that could have been involved in each one. The person who contributed each example is then asked to reflect on the validity of the fears identified by others. After analyzing several situations, the group facilitator asks members to look for common themes or fears in the examples. The facilitator reminds participants that the first step in anger management is understanding one's own fears and the fears of others.

The Council for Exceptional Children has published a compendium of dozens of lesson plans covering various social skills (Sargent, 1998). One of the lessons, for example, is designed to help middle school students avoid fights (pp. 157–158). It calls for students to discuss why they, or their classmates, get into fights and to identify the consequences of fighting. Then, students are asked to brainstorm various steps that might keep them out of fights. These could include reflecting on the reason for a fight and considering whether fighting would accomplish anything worthwhile.

Following the discussion part of the lesson, students are presented with a situation that could lead to a fight—such as having another student occupy someone's seat in the cafeteria when the initial occupant goes to get a napkin. Students are asked to model various ways they could deal with the situation without getting into a fight. The lesson continues with students role-playing how they would handle other situations in which they might consider fighting. The teacher provides feedback on the role-playing and encourages classmates to do the same. As a follow-up to the lesson, the teacher makes a point of checking with the students at a later date to see whether they have used any of the strategies and if they managed to avoid getting into fights.

A primary goal of social skills instruction is to provide young people with alternatives to harmful, hostile, and destructive behavior. By encouraging students to think before they act and by practicing ways to deal with difficult people and situations without becoming violent, educators can reduce the likelihood of impulsive conduct. A second, and equally important, goal is to teach young people how to understand, support, and care for each other. Educators must never assume that young people come to school knowing these skills.

Troubleshooting

When the Titanic struck an iceberg in the North Atlantic, another ship, the California, was close enough to have rendered assistance. Unfortunately, sailors on board the California did not heed the Titanic's distress signals. The result was a tragic loss of hundreds of lives.

Young people send out a variety of distress signals, but adults may not be alert to them or understand how they should be interpreted. Caring school communities must develop a capacity for troubleshooting, for anticipating problems before they grow too large. Every school needs the equivalent of a Distant Early Warning line, an early warning system designed to report signs of individuals' distress and situations that could result in threats to school safety.

> **Recommendation 3.3:** Encourage staff, students, and parents to recognize and report signs of trouble.

An effective system for troubleshooting requires developing the ability to recognize signs of trouble and the willingness to report them to an individual in a position to take action. Troubleshooters may include staff members, students, parents, and other community members who are aware of what is happening with young people. The last group includes social service agents, law enforcement and probation officers, representatives of the media, physicians, and mental health professionals.

For what early warning signs should concerned members of a caring school community be on the lookout? In 1998 the U.S. government published *A Guide to Safe Schools,* which included a section on what to look for as indications that a young person might become aggressive or violent. The list included the following:

- Social withdrawal
- Excessive feelings of isolation and being alone
- Excessive feelings of rejection
- Being a victim of violence
- Feelings of being picked on and persecuted
- Low school interest and poor academic performance
- Expressions of violence in writing and drawings
- Uncontrolled anger
- Patterns of impulsive and chronic hitting, intimidating, and bullying behaviors
- History of discipline problems
- Past history of violent and aggressive behavior
- Intolerance for differences and prejudicial attitudes
- Drug use and alcohol use
- Affiliation with gangs
- Inappropriate access to, possession of, and use of firearms
- Serious threats of violence (U.S. Department of Education, 1998, pp. 8–11)

However, whenever a list of warning signs is implemented, it is very important to recognize the potential for misuse.

> ### *Controversy*
> Should schools use lists of warning signs and risk factors to identify troubled students?

Recent years have witnessed criticism of law enforcement officials for "profiling" prospective lawbreakers. The profiles they use often target particular groups, such as minorities, and can result in false accusations, public humiliation, and violations of Constitutional rights. The potential always exists for a list of warning signs or risk factors related to school safety to be abused. Not every student who writes a story about an angry young person with a desire for revenge is a likely aggressor. Educators long have been warned about the Pygmalion, or self-fulfilling prophecy, effect with regard to academic performance. The same effect can apply to efforts to identify students with behavior problems. By labeling a student as a potential behavior problem, we may begin to treat him in ways that ensure he actually becomes a behavior problem!

Because of concerns about possible misuse of early warning signs, the experts who contributed to *A Guide to Safe Schools* (U.S. Department of Education, 1998, pp. 6–7) offered educators several cautionary guidelines. These included commitments to "do no harm," make a concerted effort to understand problems in context, and avoid stereotypes. In conclusion, the guide noted that troubled young people typically manifest multiple indicators. In other words, educators should resist the temptation to overreact to a single indicator.

In September 2000, the Federal Bureau of Investigation shared a compilation of data on school shooters. Although cautioning against profiling, the report urged educators to be aware of certain personality traits and behaviors found in recent cases of school shooting (Federal Bureau of Investigation, 2000, pp. 16–21). These traits and behaviors included the following:

- Hints at violent acts
- Low tolerance for frustration
- Poor coping skills
- Lack of resiliency
- Failed love relationship
- Tendency to nurse resentment over perceived injustices
- Depression
- Narcissism
- Alienation
- Tendency to dehumanize others
- Lack of empathy
- Exaggerated sense of entitlement
- Attitude of superiority
- Pathological need for attention
- Refusal to assume responsibility for personal actions
- Inappropriate humor
- Rigid and opinionated

Of all the individuals with roles to play as troubleshooters, students may be the most important. Students frequently know when other students are angry, depressed, or in trouble long before teachers or even parents. Students hear rumors that a fight is brewing or that a classmate is considering running away from home. The value of students as a source of early warnings is undermined in many schools, however, by what has been termed the "code of silence" (Halbig, 2000, pp. 34–36). Many students are afraid or unwilling to share information about classmates with school authorities.

The author encountered the code of silence when he and his colleagues conducted a needs assessment of school safety in an urban high school. Part of the assessment involved a survey of ninth graders. When asked whether they would report a student who brought a gun to school, only 36% of the ninth graders said that they would. Interestingly, students who reported feeling unsafe at school were *less* likely to say they would report a student with a gun than their classmates who felt safe at school.

It is hard to imagine a caring school community in which students, and others, are not provided with secure channels of communication for relating important information pertaining to school safety. Students are unlikely to share information unless they feel their anonymity will be protected. One Florida school district, for example, operates a Save-a-Friend hotline 24 hours a day, seven days a week, so that young people can report problems without revealing their identity (Halbig, 2000, p. 35). Troubleshooters also should receive training in what to look for as signs of trouble and the kinds of information that school authorities need in order to intervene effectively.

Positive Peer Influence

It is tempting for adults to assume that the influence of the peer group on young people invariably will be negative. In caring school communities, however, peer culture functions as a constructive force, reinforcing core values and supporting efforts to ensure the safety and well-being of students and staff members. Educators need to explore ways to capitalize on the peer group's potential for positive influence.

Recommendation 3.4: Develop opportunities for students to play an active role in creating and maintaining caring school communities.

Recommendation 3.2 called for students to be taught various social skills. The best way to ensure that these skills have been learned is to provide students with opportunities to use them on a regular basis. Two types of opportunity for the constructive use of social skills are peer-to-peer assistance and school and community service.

Peer-to-Peer Assistance

Numerous strategies have been used to encourage students to help each other. One of the oldest is the class meeting at which students are expected to help identify and solve classroom management problems and interpersonal disputes. In order for these meetings to function effectively, teachers need to develop a few guidelines. For example, students should not be allowed to interrupt each other. Those who are reluctant to speak should be permitted to submit written comments. Emphasis should be placed on first brainstorming and then evaluating a variety of possible solutions to problems. A good model for problem solving is offered by Thomas Gordon in *T. E. T.: Teacher Effectiveness Training* (1974).

Peer mediation is another time-tested strategy. Student volunteers receive training in how to arbitrate disputes among students and between students and teachers. Training covers such skills as active listening, generating nonviolent solutions, and problem solving. Once trained, peer mediators are "on call" when disagreements and conflicts arise. School authorities may offer students who get into disciplinary trouble the option of working with a peer mediator instead of receiving a punishment. Both class meetings and peer mediation were found to be used in schools designated by the U.S. Department of Education as "blue-ribbon schools" (Murphy, 1998, pp. 142–145).

Peers can play other kinds of constructive roles as well. Many schools have programs in which young people serve as peer counselors. An Arizona school system asked friends of chronic truants to take responsibility for seeing that they attended school regularly. An elementary school in Hawaii trained students to serve as Recess Refs, individuals responsible for handling playground misunderstandings. Figure 5.2 represents a survey of ways that students can affect the quality of their school environment. The survey was designed by the University of Virginia's Thomas Jefferson Center for Educational Design for use in school safety needs assessments.

One of the most ambitious peer-to-peer assistance programs was designed so that troubled young people could help each other. Positive Peer Culture, as the program has come to be known, involves single-sex groups of students, each of whom is experiencing problems in school or at home (Vorrath & Brendtro, 1974). Led by a trained adult facilitator, each group provides a safe environment in which young people are expected to assist each other to identify the sources of their problems and develop strategies to deal with them. One central goal of Positive Peer Culture is to provide a forum in which each participant can tell his life story. The program assumes that troubled young people have the capacity and the desire to help other troubled young people. In other words, it is not necessary for an individual to have resolved all of her problems before she can assist others. In some cases, in fact, an excellent way to work through one's own problems is by concentrating on the difficulties another person is experiencing.

FIGURE 5.2   Keys to School Success Survey, Thomas Jefferson Center for Educational Design

I. What do you do to make your school a better place? (Circle the number that best describes what you do.)

	Always	Most of the time	Occasionally	Seldom or Never
A. I help students who are new to my school	1	2	3	4
B. I offer suggestions about how to improve my school	1	2	3	4
C. When I see a stranger in school or on school grounds, I report it to the office	1	2	3	4
D. When I see students fighting, I report it to the office	1	2	3	4
E. I make fun of students who are different from myself	1	2	3	4
F. I try to discourage students from breaking school rules when I learn that they are planning to do so	1	2	3	4
G. I make an effort to keep my school clean	1	2	3	4
H. When I see students fighting, I stand around and watch	1	2	3	4
I. When I see a student cheating on a test or an exam, I report it to the teacher	1	2	3	4
J. I allow my friends to copy my homework	1	2	3	4
K. I treat other students with respect	1	2	3	4
L. I treat teachers and other school personnel with respect	1	2	3	4

School and Community Service

Another focus for constructive peer influence is service to school and community. A 1999 survey reported that nearly two out of every three public schools in the United States offered students some opportunity for community service (Galley, 1999). Such opportunities enable educators to underscore the fact that the purpose of an education is to contribute to society as well as advance one's own interests.

Students also can contribute to their schools in various ways. Recommendation 3.3 noted the importance of students as sources of information regarding classmates who are experiencing problems. Students can play a role in developing school rules, evaluating school safety programs and practices, and operating school honor systems. In some schools, students produce videotapes to orient new students to rules and safety procedures. Elsewhere, older students put on skits and give presentations to help younger students understand how to avoid unsafe situations.

Positive Peer Groups (PPG) is an award-winning, Ohio-based program that has demonstrated what alienated and disengaged students can do to help their schools become better and safer places to learn (Rosenberg, McKeon, & Dinereo, 1999). Based on the assumption that the best way to learn responsibility is to be given responsibility, PPG involves "negative" as well as "positive" student leaders in groups designed to address issues of schoolwide concern. Groups have developed and implemented programs to promote racial tolerance, prevent violence, and raise awareness of the dangers of alcohol abuse. PPG typically calls for a 25-week commitment to address one particular concern. Group members participate in every phase of a project, from initial data gathering to project design to postproject assessment.

The PALS program at Harrisonburg High School in Harrisonburg, Virginia, is an award-winning peer leadership program designed to promote responsible and caring behavior. PALS stands for Peers Assisting, Listening, and Sharing. The program, which is run by students and supervised by guidance counselors, asks participants to pledge not to use drugs or alcohol. Each member of PALS is assigned to an incoming ninth grader to facilitate a smooth transition from middle school to high school and provide freshmen with positive role models. The PALS program sponsors peer mediation and conflict resolution training, and members assume responsibility for warning their classmates about the dangers of drug and alcohol abuse.

Connecting to School

The ideas described in the preceding sections represent ways that students can forge bonds with their school. The value of *connectedness* in efforts to ensure safe schools for all students cannot be stressed too much. Connectedness has become the focus for considerable attention by educators, psychologists, and researchers in recent years. Bender (1999, p. 4) maintains that connectedness represents "the degree to which students are positively involved emotionally, academically, and socially with others in the school and/or home environment."

In one of the largest studies of adolescent health ever conducted in the United States, researchers interviewed more than 11,000 students, as well as parents and teachers, concerning their relationships (Resnick et al., 1997). Students who were more emotionally connected to their school were less likely to be involved in school violence. Connectedness to school and to parents was found to predict positive social behaviors in young people. In *A Guide to Safe Schools* (1998, p. 8) the U.S. Department of Education reported on research that indicates

> …when children have a positive, meaningful connection to an adult—whether it be at home, in school, or in the community—the potential for violence is reduced significantly.

Recommendation 3.5: Provide a variety of opportunities for students to feel connected to school and expect students to take advantage of them.

The key to connectedness is relationship. There simply is no substitute for constructive relationships between students and staff members and between students and their classmates. Unfortunately, there is no shortcut to building constructive relationships. They require time. Engagement in structured and meaningful activities can provide a solid basis for forming relationships. In some cases these activities may involve academic work, such as class projects, field trips, and cooperative learning activities. In other cases the activities entail extracurricular endeavors, including athletic teams, school clubs, theatrical productions, music groups, and school publications. A longitudinal study of 1,800 sixth graders from Michigan has provided convincing evidence that young people who participate in extracurricular activities generally do better academically, have lower rates of truancy, and feel a stronger attachment to school (Galley, 2000).

In *A Tribe Apart,* Hersch (1998, p. 78) noted that the number of students involved in school activities has shrunk dramatically in recent years. Whether this decline has resulted from lack of interest by young people, problems related to after-school transportation, or failure on the part of schools to provide interesting activities is unclear. What is clear is the fact that students who participate in school activities are less likely to cause problems or get into serious trouble. If they do encounter problems, their desire to participate in extracurricular activities often provides the incentive needed to overcome adversity.

In the wake of the Columbine High School tragedy, one suburban Virginia high school realized that it, too, could experience such violence at the hands of disaffected teenagers. Adopting the motto "A School Where Everybody Matters," the high school staff brainstormed various ways to reduce feelings of isolation and alienation among students. One effort involved the creation of a Gothic Club for the students who identified with nonconformist dress, music, and other countercultural symbols. Another Virginia high school, in an effort to promote connectedness for a diverse student body, initiated a campaign to involve every student in at least one extracurricular activity. A special effort was made to develop opportunities for students who held jobs or lacked after-school transportation.

It is tempting to think that opportunities for students to participate in school activities would be greater in larger schools. One classic study (Barker & Gump, 1964) found that larger schools did offer more activities, but that a greater percentage of students participated in school activities in smaller schools. Apparently, in larger schools only the "stars" earn places on teams and in plays and other productions, but in smaller schools every student who wants to participate is needed.

One important variable for caring school communities is school size. The Safe School Study Report to Congress (U.S. Department of Health, Education, and Welfare, 1978, p. 13) found that school size was linked to student anonymity and alienation, factors that in turn were associated with school crime. The report called for efforts to "personalize" schools by lowering teacher–student ratios and increasing the amount of continuous class time that teachers spend with groups of students.

It is much easier to promote constructive relationships and connectedness in small schools. How small should schools be? Although it is difficult to pinpoint a precise number, Raywid and Oshiyama (2000, p. 446) offer the following guidelines:

> Small enough so that people can know one another. Small enough so that individuals are missed when they are absent. Small enough so that the participation of all students is needed. Small enough to permit considerable overlap in the rosters from one class to another.

More will be said about the issue of school size when the design of school facilities is addressed in Chapter 8.

Even large schools can promote connectedness by using several proven strategies. Creating teams of teachers who work with the same group of students for a large portion of the school day is one approach that has been shown to be particularly effective in many middle schools. Teacher advisory programs that call for every teacher to meet periodically with the same group of students is another way to forge constructive relationships as well as encourage students to share their concerns in a safe setting. Looping represents a third strategy. When a teacher "loops," he moves with his students to the next grade, thereby providing an opportunity to cultivate stronger bonds with them. Looping is growing in popularity in elementary schools, but it also has the potential to ease the transition between schools. For example, a team of four eighth-grade teachers representing the four core academic subjects might move with their students to the ninth grade in the local high school, then "loop" back to the middle school to pick up another group of eighth graders.

Mentoring provides yet another way to promote caring relationships between students and adults. Mentors can be college students, employees from a school's business partner, senior citizens from a local retirement community, or parent volunteers. Mentors meet on a regular basis, either during or after school, with the students to whom they are assigned. Sometimes mentor and student may tackle academic work, and at other times they may attend a special event or just chat. Mentoring programs have proven to be effective ways to foster resilience in at-risk students (Clinton & Miles, 1999).

CASE IN POINT

Clinton and Miles (1999, pp. 33–36) describe the Tiger Pals Mentoring program at F. T. Corry Elementary School in Greensboro, Georgia. The school has designated a special room for adult volunteers—known as Tiger Pals—to meet with students. The room is colorfully decorated and inviting.

Mentors spend one hour or more each week with a needy student. After soliciting volunteers through newspaper announcements, radio spots, and appeals to community organizations, the school provided every mentor with approximately 10 hours of training. Students were referred to the program by teachers or parents. A kickoff dinner launched Tiger Pals. Every student was expected to give his mentor a tour of the school.

A program coordinator was assigned to operate Tiger Pals. Among other duties, she convened monthly meetings of the mentors to troubleshoot student problems before they got out of hand and provide encouragement and new ideas. Two mentor–student field trips were scheduled for the school year, and an appreciation dinner was held.

One unexpected by-product of Tiger Pals was that mentors became community advocates for Corry Elementary School. Many mentors continued to meet with their students after the school year ended.

Embracing Differences

To adults, the world of the young may seem to be characterized by bewildering conformity, but in reality this world is marked by extraordinary differences. How young people, and adults, respond to these differences is a key to the development of caring school communities. When students feel valued and cared for, regardless of their race, ethnicity, gender, socioeconomic status, sexual orientation, academic ability, religious beliefs, or disabilities, they are more likely to look forward to coming to school and to act in ways that promote the safety and well-being of others.

Educators are not always sure, though, of the appropriate position to take regarding student differences. Should schools strive to acknowledge, encourage, or reduce diversity? One traditional mission of public schools, of course, has been to take students from various backgrounds, including immigrant children, and socialize them to be Americans. Times, however, have changed. How should educators deal with gay students and students from non-Judeo-Christian families? Should schools urge students to respect cultures that oppress women or routinely violate human rights?

Although the topic of diversity cannot be addressed in all of its complexity in this chapter, it is important to recognize that many school safety problems can be traced to students who feel "different." Breggin (2000, p. 96) observes, for example, "Most perpetrators of sudden outbursts of violence turn out to be shy, withdrawn people who have for many years been harboring overwhelming feelings of hurt pride and injustice." He goes on to note that this profile fits most of the school shooters of the past decade. It is essential that educators do as much as possible to embrace student differences.

Recommendation 3.6: Encourage students and staff to understand and accept student differences.

A key to understanding differences is what Breggin (2000, pp. 95–109) refers to as "critical intelligence." Such intelligence leads individuals to listen to and try to understand others, rather than simply rejecting them because they are different. He puts it thusly (Breggin, 2000, p. 109):

> Genuine critical intelligence depends on recognition of the common human nature that we share. An empathic connection with human beings in general rips away the sham and hypocrisy that encourages us to feel superior. Generational, gender, racial, and cultural barriers melt before the insight that we are made of the same essential human stuff.

The first step toward helping young people embrace differences is to make certain that staff members embrace differences. When teachers, administrators, coaches, and other adults in school make jokes about and ridicule people based on their characteristics, they send a powerful signal to students. Luke (1996, p. 128) points out,

> Children learn from adult attitudes, words, and behavior what to fear and reject. Therefore, the first and most essential method [to encourage children to respect diversity] is through adult modeling. Young children will be more comfortable with diversity if adults themselves are comfortable with it.

Besides modeling acceptance, teachers can lead discussions of cultural and other differences, share cross-cultural success stories, invite guests to talk about how they have handled their differences, and use cooperative learning strategies that encourage students to work together to achieve common goals. Expectations also are an important component of a caring school community. Teachers should *expect* students to be accepting of their differences. In one elementary school program, educators formalized their expectations into a rule: "You can't say you can't play" (Sapon-Shevin, 1998, pp. 42–45). The rule was intended to discourage students from excluding classmates from playground activities. Students who frequently were excluded were taught how to ask to be involved in activities.

A variety of programs to promote acceptance of differences has appeared in recent years. One such effort is the Yes I Can Social Inclusion Program (Bender,

Franklin, & Johnson, 1999, pp. 59–71). Developed at the University of Minnesota, Yes I Can is designed to help students with disabilities establish bonds with other students and feel more a part of the school community. Aimed at adolescents, the program begins with lessons concerning what it means to have a disability. Disabled students and students without disabilities study together. The latter group become peer facilitators and, after six weeks of instruction, each peer facilitator is paired with one or more disabled students. Each pair remains together for the rest of the year, planning social outings and helping each other at school.

Programs such as Yes I Can offer constructive, proactive responses to the challenges of diversity. These programs, however, should not be regarded as a substitute for direct intervention when students bully or make fun of others because of their differences. At such times, it is up to staff members to tell students their intolerant behavior is wrong. Karen Franklin (Frankfurt, 1999, p. 26) made this point unequivocally with regard to the treatment of gay students, but it could apply equally well to other examples of intolerance:

> The majority of young people who harass, bully, and assault sexual minorities do not fit the stereotype of the hate-filled extremist. Rather, they are average young people who often do not see anything wrong with their behavior. And the reason they do not see anything wrong is simple—no one is telling them that it is wrong.

A Pervasive Sense of Psychological Safety

Much of this book has focused on physical safety and ways to reduce and eliminate disorder, disruption, and violence. In order for a school to be a caring community, however, all students must be assured psychological as well as physical safety. This means, among other things, that every student comes to school free of the fear that they will be subjected to verbal abuse, taunts, hazing, and sexual harassment.

When the American Association of University Women surveyed secondary students in the early nineties, it found an alarming level of sexual harassment in the nation's middle and high schools (American Association of University Women, 1993). Four out of five students in grades 8 through 11 had experienced some form of sexual harassment, ranging from suggestive comments to touching and grabbing. The impact of these acts was particularly great for female students. One out of three girls indicated that they did not want to come to school because of sexual harassment. One in five maintained that worry over sexual harassment had adversely affected their grades. Embarrassment, fear, and self-consciousness were other negative consequences.

CASE IN POINT

Karen said that Matt began to harass her when he tried to touch her breasts and genital area after class. He also made crude remarks and inappropriate propositions. Each time Matt harassed Karen, she reported his behavior to her teacher and her mother. Eventually the principal also was notified. No disciplinary action against Matt was taken.

Matt's conduct continued. His taunts were particularly threatening in physical education class. Karen kept telling her P. E. teacher, but still no disciplinary action was taken. Matt confronted Karen in the hall one day and rubbed his body against hers. Again she reported the incident, but no action was taken.

Karen's grades began to decline and she talked about suicide. After three months of complaints, Karen's teacher finally let her change seats so she would not be next to Matt. When Karen's mother asked the principal why nothing had been done to punish Matt, he replied that the school system lacked a policy on sexual harassment.

The Case in Point is based on an actual case that eventually reached the U.S. Supreme Court (Dowling-Sendor, 1999, pp. 16–17). For Karen, school was anything but a caring community. In the lawsuit, Karen's mother sued the school board over the failure of Karen's teachers and principal to deal properly with her reports of sexual harassment. Although the U.S. district court tossed out the suit, the Supreme Court agreed to review the decision. By a 5 to 4 vote, the Supreme Court reversed the lower court and ruled that school boards can be held liable under Title IX of the Educational Amendments of 1972. The school's failure to address Karen's complaints constituted, in the eyes of the highest court in the country, a form of sex discrimination.

Educators can be compelled to comply with federal and state laws, but they cannot be forced to care. Care derives from sincere efforts to put ourselves in other's places, to understand the impact of our behavior on other persons. Matt's harassment of Karen was bad enough, but its tragic effect was compounded when Karen's teachers and principal did not seem concerned enough to intervene.

Hazing, like sexual harassment, has been an area in which educators, until recently, have been reluctant to get involved. Defined as "the practice of seasoned veterans intimidating, humiliating, or physically punishing younger recruits as a rite of passage" (Bushweller, 2000, p. 19), hazing is found in fraternities and sororities, athletic teams, gangs, and school clubs. One national study reported that nearly half of the youthful respondents had experienced some form of hazing (Walsh, 2000, p. 14). Although certain types of initiation rituals have come to be accepted and even looked back upon with pride, other acts constitute gross invasions of an individual's privacy, assault, and blatant abuse. Fear of reprisals, embarrassment, and the desire to be accepted prevent many young people from disclosing their experiences with hazing.

Hazing has no place in schools in which young people are valued and cared for. Rather than ignoring the problem, educators must react swiftly to reports of hazing. Bushweller (2000, p. 21) urges every school to develop an antihazing policy, maintain continuous adult supervision of locker rooms, and educate teachers and coaches to recognize indications of hazing. He also acknowledges that current students may be reluctant to provide information about hazing incidents, so he suggests that educators periodically survey alumni to find out if hazing is practiced in school.

Students are not the only source of abusive behavior in schools. Unfortunately, teachers and other staff members on occasion have been found to mistreat the very young people for whom they are responsible. *Education Week* undertook a six-month investigation of sex abuse in schools that revealed numerous cases of sexual misconduct by staff members. As in Karen's case, the investigation also revealed that school authorities were reluctant to intervene on behalf of student victims. The reason often was attributed to "strong laws and union contracts that protect employees' job and privacy rights" (Hendrie, 1998, p. 1).

To protect students from abuse by school employees, school systems can take a variety of constructive steps. These include developing clear policies regarding how cases of alleged abuse should be handled and thorough training of staff members on how to recognize the signs of abuse. Students must be provided with safe channels of communication so that they can report when they, or those they know, have been victimized. School officials need to conduct systematic background checks on all school employees, including substitute teachers, to prevent the hiring of individuals with past histories of abuse and predatory behavior.

> **Recommendation 3.7:** Develop clear policies concerning the handling of cases of abuse by students and staff members.

> **Recommendation 3.8:** Conduct thorough background checks on all school employees.

A clear policy for handling cases of alleged abuse should specify the responsibilities of school authorities. One handbook (Cohan, Hergenrother, Johnson, Mandel, & Sawyer, 1996, p. 22), for example, recommends that these procedures be followed by building principals:

1. Notify the superintendent about the allegation. No one should interview the student before the superintendent takes charge of the case.
2. In the event of allegations, or even rumors, immediately contact parents or guardians of the children involved.
3. Remember that confidentiality of the allegations, as well as the people involved, should be of primary importance.
4. Investigations should be handled by professionals and supervised by the superintendent.
5. Document everything pertinent to the case.

Educators' obligation to protect students does not end at the closing bell. They also are expected to report cases in which they suspect students are being abused at home. For truly caring school communities to exist, students must know that their welfare, regardless of where they happen to be, is of paramount importance to those who educate them. Most states now have laws requiring educators to report any suspected cases of child abuse. Failure to report such cases can result in fines, litigation, and job loss.

The development of a pervasive sense of psychological safety is not just about preventing sexual harassment and reporting cases of abuse. It is also about eliminating the less dramatic sources of fear and anxiety that undermine students' feelings of trust and safety. Hyman and Snook (1999, pp. 54–55) list some of the "softer" sources of psychological mistreatment in schools and classrooms. These include:

1. Discipline and control techniques based on fear and intimidation
2. Low quantity of human interaction in which teachers communicate a lack of interest, caring, and affection for students through ignoring, isolation, and rejection
3. Motivational techniques for performance that are overly critical, excessively demanding, unreasonable, and ignore students' ages and abilities
4. Verbal assaults including the use of sarcasm, ridicule, humiliation, and denigration
5. Failure to intervene when students are teased, bullied, and scapegoated by peers

A review of these concerns suggests that the challenge of psychological safety is not limited to embattled urban schools. Many of the problems identified by Hyman and Snook can be found in prestigious suburban schools in which parents and teachers harbor high, sometimes unreasonably high, expectations for students. Before assuring all students that they will learn, educators must assure them that they will be cared for and safe.

Conclusion

The third standard of a school that is safe for all students calls for students to be valued and cared for. This applies as much to the pregnant 15-year-old girl as it does to the captain of the basketball team, to the student who struggles to earn average grades as well as the future Ivy Leaguer. Caring does not come automatically. It must be learned, nurtured, and reinforced. A caring school community is one in which the way people treat each other is given at least as much attention as how well they do academically.

The key to Standard 3 is recognizing that caring involves more than not harming others. Caring is proactive. It requires action—action on behalf of others' well-being and safety. Standard 3 is met when students and staff go out of their way to understand and support each other.

REFERENCES

American Association of University Women. *Hostile Hallways: The AAUW Survey on Sexual Harassment in America's Schools.* Washington, DC: American Association of University Women, 1993.

Barker, R. G., and Gump, P. V. *Big School, Small School.* Stanford: Stanford University Press, 1964.

Bender, William N. "Parameters of School Violence and the Available Options." In William N. Bender, Gregory Clinton, and Renet L. Bender (eds.), *Violence Prevention and Reduction in Schools.* Austin, TX: Pro-ed, 1999, pp. 1–14.

Bender, William N.; Franklin, Laura, M.; and Johnson, Sharon E. "Connectedness for Adolescents with Disabilities: Positive Effects of the Yes I Can Social Inclusion Program on Discipline and Violence Reduction." In William N. Bender, Gregory Clinton, and Renet L. Bender (eds.), *Violence Prevention and Reduction in Schools.* Austin, TX: Pro-ed, 1999, pp. 59–71.

Breggin, Peter R. *Reclaiming Our Children.* Cambridge, MA: Perseus Books, 2000.

Bushweller, Kevin. "High School Hazing Grows Violent and Humiliating." *American School Board Journal* (August 2000), pp. 19–23.

Clinton, Gregory, and Miles, Willie. "Mentoring Programs: Fostering Resilience in At-Risk Kids." In William N. Bender, Gregory Clinton, and Renet L. Bender (eds.), *Violence Prevention and Reduction in Schools.* Austin, TX: Pro-ed, 1999, pp. 31–45.

Cohan, Audrey; Hergenrother, Mary Ann; Johnson, Yolanda M.; Mandel, Laurie S.; and Sawyer, Janice. *Sexual Harassment and Sexual Abuse.* Thousand Oaks, CA: Corwin, 1996.

Dowling-Sendor, Benjamin. "Beyond Teaching," *The American School Board Journal,* vol. 186, no. 8 (August 1999), pp. 16–17.

Duke, Daniel L. "Adults Can Be Discipline Problems Too!" *Psychology in the Schools,* vol. 15, no. 4 (October 1978), pp. 522–528.

Duke, Daniel L., and Jones, Vernon F. "What Can Schools Do to Foster Student Responsibility?" *Theory into Practice,* vol. 24, no. 4 (Autumn 1985), pp. 277–285.

Educational Excellence Alliance. "Insult Culture Report" (unpublished two-page memo). Ithaca, NY: 1999.

Federal Bureau of Investigation. *The School Shooter: A Threat Assessment Perspective.* Quantico, VA: Federal Bureau of Investigation, 2000.

Frankfurt, Kate. "Countering a Climate: Gay Students." *High School Magazine* (May/June 1999), pp. 25–29.

Galley, Michelle. "Schools Offering More Service Opportunities, Study Finds." *Education Week* (October 6, 1999), p. 14.

Galley, Michelle. "Extra Benefits Tied to Extracurriculars," *Education Week* (October 18, 2000), p. 8.

Girard, Kathryn, and Koch, Susan J. *Conflict Resolution in the Schools.* San Francisco: Jossey Bass, 1996.

Goleman, Daniel. *Emotional Intelligence.* New York: Bantam Books, 1995.

Gordon, Thomas. *T. E. T.: Teacher Effectiveness Training.* New York: Wyden, 1974.

Grogan, Margaret. "Feminist Approaches to Educational Leadership: Relationships Based on Care." In B. Irby and G. Brown (eds.), *Women Leaders: Structuring Success.* Houston: Kendall/Hunt, 1999, pp. 21–29.

Halbig, Wolfgang W. "Breaking the Code of Silence," *The American School Board Journal,* vol. 187, no. 3 (March 2000), pp. 34–36.

Hendrie, Caroline. "Cost Is High When Schools Ignore Abuse," *Education Week* (December 9, 1998), pp. 1, 14–19.

Hersch, Patricia, *A Tribe Apart.* New York: Ballantine Books, 1998.

Hinshaw, S. "Externalizing Behavior Problems and Academic Under-Achievement in Childhood and Adolescence: Causal Relationships and Underlying Mechanisms," *Psychological Bulletin,* no. 111 (1992), pp. 127–155.

Hyman, Irwin A., and Snook, Pamela A. *Dangerous Schools.* San Francisco: Jossey Bass, 1999.

Kilpatrick, William. *Why Johnny Can't Tell Right from Wrong.* New York: Touchstone, 1992.

Kirschenbaum, Howard. *100 Ways to Enhance Values and Morality in Schools and Youth Settings.* Boston: Allyn & Bacon, 1995.

Kohn, Alfie. *Beyond Discipline: From Compliance to Community.* Alexandria, VA: Association for Supervision and Curriculum Development, 1996.

Kreidler, William J. *Creative Conflict Resolution.* Glenview, IL: Scott Foresman, 1984.

Lanier, Kirsten Olson. "A Metaphor for Parents," *Education Week* (May 12, 1999), pp. 48, 34.

Lantieri, Linda, and Patti, Janet. *Waging Peace in Our Schools.* Boston: Beacon Press, 1996.

Lickona, Thomas. *Educating for Character.* New York: Bantam Books, 1991a.

Lickona, Thomas. "An Integrated Approach to Character Development in the Elementary School Classroom." In Jacques S. Benninga (ed.), *Moral, Character, and Civic Education in the Elementary School.* New York: Teachers College Press, 1991b, pp. 67–83.

Luke, Bettie Sing. "Respecting Ethnic Diversity." In Sarah Miller, Janine Brodine, and Terri Miller (eds.), *Safe by Design.* Seattle, WA: Committee for Children, 1996, pp. 123–133.

Murphy, Madonna M. *Character Education in America's Blue-Ribbon Schools.* Lancaster, PA: Technomic, 1998.

Noddings, Nel. *The Challenge to Care in Schools: An Alternative Approach to Education.* New York: Teachers College Press, 1992.

Parker, J., and Asher, S. "Peer Relations and Later Personal Adjustment: Are Low Accepted Children at Risk?" *Psychological Bulletin,* no. 102 (1987), pp. 357–389.

Peterson, Kent D., and Deal, Terrence E. "How Leaders Influence the Culture of Schools," *Educational Leadership,* vol. 56, no. 1 (September 1998), pp. 28–30.

Pressley, Sue Anne. "Louisiana's Courtesy Call," *Washington Post* (March 5, 2000), p. A3.

Raywid, Mary Anne, and Oshiyama, Libby. "Musings in the Wake of Columbine: What Can Schools Do?" *Phi Delta Kappan,* vol. 81, no. 6 (February 2000), pp. 444–449.

Resnick, M. D.; Bearman, P. S.; Blum, R. W.; Bauman, K. E.; Harris, K. M.; Jones, J.; Tabor, J.; Beuhring, T.; Sieving, R. E.; Shew, M.; Ireland, M.; Bearinger, L. H.; and Udry, J. R. "Protecting Adolescents from Harm: Findings from the National Longitudinal Study on Adolescent Health," *Journal of the American Medical Association,* vol. 278, no. 10 (October 1997), pp. 823–832.

Rodkin, Philip C; Farmer, Thomas W.; Pearl, Ruth; and Van Acker, Richard. "Heterogeneity of Popular Boys: Antisocial and Prosocial Configurations," *Developmental Psychology,* vol. 36, no. 1 (January 2000), pp. 14–24.

Rosenberg, Steven L.; McKeon, Loren M.; and Dinero, Thomas E. "Positive Peer Solutions," *Phi Delta Kappan,* vol. 81, no. 2 (October 1999), pp. 114–118.

Sapon-Shevin, Mara. "Everyone Here Can Play," *Educational Leadership,* vol. 56, no. 1 (September 1998), pp. 42–45.

Sargent, Laurence R. *Social Skills for School and Community.* Arlington, VA: Council for Exceptional Children, 1998.

Selznick, Philip. *The Moral Commonwealth.* Berkeley: University of California Press, 1992.

U.S. Department of Education. *A Guide to Safe Schools.* Washington, DC: U.S. Department of Education, 1998.

U.S. Department of Health, Education, and Welfare. *Violent Schools–Safe Schools: The Safe School Study Report to Congress,* vol. I. Washington, DC: U.S. Department of Health, Education, and Welfare, 1978.

Vorrath, Harry H., and Brendtro, Larry K. *Positive Peer Culture.* Chicago: Aldine Publishing, 1974.

Walsh, Mark. "Hazing Is Widespread, Student Survey Shows," *Education Week* (September 6, 2000), p. 14.

Wuthnow, Robert. *Learning to Care.* New York: Oxford University Press, 1995.

6

Standard 4:
A Comprehensive
School Safety Plan

MAJOR IDEAS IN CHAPTER 6

- Multiple approaches to school safety are preferable to relying on one approach.
- To be effective, multiple approaches should be incorporated into a comprehensive plan for school safety.
- A comprehensive plan needs to address the encouragement of appropriate behavior as well as the handling of inappropriate behavior.
- Comprehensive plans should provide for data collection and management, communications, and staff development.
- The development of sound school safety plans requires time and broad-based participation.

Threats to school safety do not derive from a single source. They are the product of various conditions, including dysfunctional families, students' alienation and lack of academic success, peer pressure, jealousy, frustration, inadequate social skills, school overcrowding, teacher insensitivity, and poor school and community leadership. Unclear expectations as well as clear, but unreasonable expectations can play a role. What goes on outside of school as well as within school affects school safety. Because many factors contribute to unsafe schools, the quest for safe schools for all students must involve a variety of approaches. No one program, policy, or practice can address all of the reasons why young people harm themselves and others. No single strategy can prevent strangers or staff members from jeopardizing the well-being of students.

The most prudent course of action for all schools is to address safety comprehensively. This means developing policies, programs, and practices that promote safety and respond to unsafe conditions when they arise. The key to a sound school safety plan is a balanced approach.

> **Standard 4:** A balance exists between efforts to promote appropriate conduct, discourage misconduct, and effectively handle misconduct when and if it does occur.

An examination of the general components of school safety plans opens this chapter. These components encompass efforts to deal with problems when they arise as well as prevent problems from arising in the first place. The best way to ensure a balanced approach is to develop a comprehensive plan that addresses various dimensions of school safety. Several prescriptions for comprehensive plans are presented and analyzed in the next part of the chapter. An actual example of one such plan is provided. The chapter closes with a discussion of the steps required to develop a comprehensive school safety plan.

What Are the Goals of a Comprehensive School Safety Plan?

Gottfredson (1997), in a systematic analysis of research on what works in school safety, concludes that well-developed, comprehensive school safety plans involving multiple intervention strategies are more likely to curb school crime than single interventions. Reducing criminal activity in school clearly must be a central purpose of any school safety plan, but should such a plan also address other purposes? Experts have offered various judgments regarding what school safety plans should accomplish.

Blauvelt (1999), for example, maintains that school safety planning entails prevention and response components. Prevention aims to keep safety threats from occurring in the first place, and the response component is intended to deal effectively with problems when they do arise. Blauvelt offers suggestions for how each component can address various safety problems. When the objective involves extortion, for instance, a prevention strategy may be to ask teachers to collect younger students' lunch money as soon as they arrive at school and return it to them just before lunch (Blauvelt, 1999, pp. 38–39). A response procedure, on the other hand, assumes that an act of extortion already has taken place. In such a case, the victim should be asked to provide a detailed account of the episode, and an "incident report" should be prepared. Parents and police must be notified as soon as possible.

Perry (1999) differentiates between reactive and proactive measures. Reactive measures, such as metal detectors and locker searches, can reduce violence, she allows, but schools that rely exclusively on such measures risk losing "the hearts and minds of their students" (Perry, p. 9). Proactive strategies help students to be "responsible, respected and respectful, tolerant of differences and able to resolve conflicts in a peaceful manner" (Perry, p. 14). School safety plans that embrace proactive as well as reactive elements focus on teaching conflict resolution strategies, implementing character education, and building a caring school community. Stephens (1994, p. 205) endorses this balanced combination of measures when he defines a "safe schools plan" as "a continuing, broad-based, comprehensive and systematic process to create and maintain a safe, secure, and welcoming school climate, free of drugs, violence, and fear."

The author, in a prior book, identified three essential ingredients of a comprehensive school safety plan (Duke, 1980, pp. 16–31): A capacity for problem prevention, problem intervention, and problem management is critical for an effective plan. Examples of these three capacities were presented and discussed in Chapter 1. The first two correspond to Blauvelt's prevention and response components. Besides being able to prevent threats to safety and respond to threats when they do arise, every school also requires the capacity to manage problems. The focus of problem management rests more with the organizational conditions that give rise to safety than with particular individuals. As the author put it in *Managing Student Behavior Problems* (1980, p. 26):

> Problem management presumes that certain situations tend to give rise to behavior problems...and that certain organizational responses minimize the negative impact of these situations. By anticipating these situations and encouraging thoughtful organizational responses, school personnel may be able to "manage" many problems.

Managing problems differs from problem prevention, in that problems actually occur but they are handled in ways that keep them from unduly disrupting school operations or mushrooming into major concerns. Problem management is different from problem intervention because the latter focuses on individuals who get into trouble, not on the situations that may have contributed to or exacerbated their actions.

Lee, Pulvino, and Perrone (1998, pp. 61–77) offer a somewhat different way to characterize school safety measures. They differentiate between passive, assertive, and facilitative approaches. Passive approaches constitute a neutral conflict-management option. When using a passive approach, an educator adopts a wait-and-see position. Under certain circumstances, in other words, it may be better to avoid action because it only can make things worse. Passive strategies include doing nothing, withdrawing, "smoothing," and diversion.

Assertive approaches are described as confrontational. They are most appropriate when the tension between individuals prevents all parties from accomplishing what needs to be done. The goal of the educator using an assertive approach is to establish control over the situation. Because assertive approaches rely on an individual's ability to exercise power, the risk exists that the effort will fail and the person's credibility will be undermined.

The third approach, and the one generally preferred by the authors, is the facilitative approach. It is based on trying to resolve problems while maintaining constructive relationships between the parties involved. Facilitative strategies include problem solving, negotiating, and confluent responses.

It appears, then, that there are various ways to characterize the elements of a comprehensive school safety plan. This book contends that school safety depends on a balanced set of efforts aimed at promoting appropriate conduct, discouraging misconduct, and effectively handling misconduct if and when it does occur. Promoting appropriate conduct is a function of clear expectations (discussed in Chapter 3) and the development of a caring school community (discussed in Chapter 5). Discouraging misconduct is a function of meaningful consequences for rule violations (discussed in Chapter 4). Effective handling of misconduct is a function of the consistent, fair, and humane enforcement of school rules (discussed in Chapter 4).

In practice, the lines between these three components may blur. By effectively handling a rule violation, for example, an educator can discourage another student from violating the rule. Teaching social skills to students not only promotes appropriate conduct, it can discourage misconduct. Not every measure taken to discourage misconduct, however, necessarily encourages appropriate conduct.

Some observers may question the value of developing a comprehensive school safety plan. Planning obviously takes considerable time and energy. If a school has no major safety problems, a case can be made that a plan may alarm people unnecessarily. But is it preferable to wait until a tragic incident occurs to develop a plan? Should every teacher do her or his "own thing" when it comes to school safety? The potential for confusion, miscommunication, and counterproductive actions increases dramatically when no comprehensive safety plan exists. Some teachers, for example, may prefer to stress one approach, such as severe punishments, whereas other teachers may rely exclusively on more proactive approaches. Under such circumstances, students have difficulty determining what is expected of them or what will happen to them if they violate school rules.

Schools serve students with various needs, interests, aspirations, and attitudes toward safety and discipline. It is unlikely that a single approach to school safety will work equally well for all students. By developing a comprehensive school safety plan, a school can make certain that measures are in place to address a range of students.

> **Recommendation 4.1:** Develop a comprehensive school safety plan.

Once a plan is developed, it is important to realize that the plan should be reviewed on a regular basis. Schools are dynamic organizations, subject to changing demographics, policies, and local conditions. Particular strategies may work for a while, but then lose effectiveness. New safety problems emerge as others diminish. A primary responsibility of each school's School Safety Team should be the periodic evaluation of the school safety plan.

What to Include in a School Safety Plan

It is one thing to decide that school safety plans should promote appropriate conduct, discourage misconduct, and deal effectively with misconduct when and if it does occur. It is quite another matter to agree on the actual components of such a plan. Disagreement, for example, swirls around the desirability of mandatory drug tests for students and random searches for controlled substances and weapons. It is unwise to prescribe the exact makeup of a school safety plan without taking into account the problems facing a school, the feelings of the staff and students, community concerns, available resources, and other contextual matters.

Every school consists of personnel, policies, programs, and practices. At the very least, the components of a comprehensive school safety plan should address each of these dimensions of school operations.

CASE IN POINT

When the National Commission on Drug-free Schools (1990) issued its report, it recognized the importance of a comprehensive plan that addressed all aspects of school operations. Seven elements of a plan were identified:

1. Student surveys to determine the nature and extent of the drug problem, identify needs, and inventory results
2. Leadership training for key school officials
3. Clear, consistent school policies with responses to violations that include alternatives to suspension
4. Training for the entire staff on the effects of drug use, the school's drug policy and policy implementation, and interventions to be used with students
5. Assistance programs and support for students
6. Training for parents to assist them in understanding drug use prevention and related issues
7. Appropriate and factual curriculum on the dangers of drug use for students of all ages

---

Various experts have proposed models for comprehensive school safety plans. By examining several of these plans, it is possible to identify core components about which there is general agreement.

Systematic Management Plan for School Discipline

One of the earliest efforts to specify the elements of a comprehensive school safety plan was undertaken by the author (Duke, 1980). The Systematic Management Plan for School Discipline (SMPSD) consists of various policies, programs, and practices organized around seven central goals (Duke, 1980, pp. 166–172).

Goals of a Systematic Management Plan for School Discipline

1. Create an awareness on the part of all who work and study in the school that it is an organization governed by rules.
2. Collect, maintain, and utilize data on student behavior to improve school discipline.

3. Provide opportunities for those who work and study in school to express their concerns and problems in a supportive atmosphere.
4. In as many cases as possible, shift responsibility for diagnosing and managing serious behavior problems from individuals to teams.
5. Involve parents in the diagnosis and resolution of student behavior problems as well as in prevention programs.
6. Rather than trying to curtail behavior problems simply by increasing punishments, reinforce regularly those student behaviors that contribute to a healthy school environment.
7. Create opportunities for faculty and staff to assess local discipline problems and acquire the skills necessary for managing or reducing them.

A review of these goals suggests that the SMPSD entails a broad array of components. The foundation of the plan is a set of expectations, in the form of rules, and various mechanisms to ensure that students are aware of them. Data management also is important; thus provisions are made for reporting incidents, regularly analyzing disciplinary data, and using data analyses to improve school safety policies, programs, and practices. The SMPSD calls for the creation of different channels of communication to enable students and staff members to share their concerns regarding safety issues before serious problems arise. Heavy emphasis is placed on students assuming responsibility, along with school staff, for promoting a safe environment.

Teamwork is another key element, and the model calls for grade-level teams to engage in regular troubleshooting sessions in order to identify students who are experiencing problems. Parental involvement is needed to supplement and support the efforts of teachers and school administrators. The SMPSD provides for immediate notification of parents when their children are involved in disciplinary incidents.

In an effort to create a balanced approach to school safety, the SMPSD emphasizes the identification of ways to recognize and reward students for constructive behavior. Overreliance on punishments is discouraged. To ensure that the plan functions as smoothly as possible, regular staff development and faculty participation in the analysis of school safety data are prescribed.

Schoolwide Student Management Plan

Another example of a comprehensive approach to school safety is the Joneses' Schoolwide Student Management Plan (Jones & Jones, 1998, pp. 387–400). Although they believe that teachers and students hold the key to responsible behavior, the Joneses also recognize that teachers and students operate within an organizational context, and that this context either can help or hinder efforts to promote the well-being of those who work and study in the school. They consequently advocate a systems approach to managing student behavior. In order "to establish a clear, fair system that creates shared responsibility for helping students with behavior problems," the Joneses offer nine guiding concepts (1998, p. 389).

Key Concepts Supporting a Schoolwide Student Management Plan

1. School policies for responding to irresponsible student behavior will be most effective when they are supported by clear school-board policies and administrative regulations.
2. Teachers must initially assess their classroom management and instructional methods to determine whether they are consistent with the best, accepted practice.
3. The teacher has a responsibility to use behavior change methods aimed at altering students' behavior.
4. Teachers need to receive assistance from peers in examining their efforts to help youngsters who persist in their learning and behavioral difficulties.
5. Teachers will be more effective in helping students develop responsible behavior when the school has a clearly written and effectively communicated school-wide student-management plan.
6. An effective response to students who experience ongoing problems includes a procedure for holding staffings to develop specific plans to assist students.
7. Outside consultation should be provided when a student continues to have behavioral difficulties despite Concepts 1 through 6 being employed.
8. School personnel will better serve students with behavior problems when procedures are in place for coordinating with community resources.
9. Referral for special education services should be considered when interventions associated with Concepts 1 through 8 have been implemented.

A Schoolwide Student Management Plan (SSMP) consists of nine components, beginning with a philosophy statement and a set of school rules or expectations. Schoolwide procedures for handling routine activities, such as movement through the halls and arriving late to school or class, should be specified and taught to students. The roles and responsibilities of all individuals involved in managing student behavior need to be clearly stated and well understood.

The importance of a balanced approach to school safety is acknowledged in the Joneses' call for a variety of measures to create a positive school climate and reinforce students for desirable behavior. All students and staff should be taught a problem-solving approach that can be used when disagreements arise. A format for special plans of assistance is needed for students who experience serious behavior problems. The final components of the SSMP involve provisions for a schoolwide student management committee and continuing communication among teachers, administrators, and parents.

Schoolwide Discipline Plan

A third approach to comprehensive school safety planning is Walker, Colvin, and Ramsey's approach (1995, pp. 120–151), called the Schoolwide Discipline Plan (SDP). The SDP is based on research and practice that address antisocial and disruptive behavior in schools. The authors contend that a "sound discipline plan may reduce the need for developing a companion violence-prevention plan in many instances" (p. 122).

In their review of research on school discipline and their examination of "best practices," Walker et al. (1995, pp. 123–125) identify various keys to effective school-wide plans. These include the following:

- Proactive approaches
- Visible, supportive leadership from the principal
- Collegial commitment
- Staff development and effective teacher-training practices
- High expectations
- Clear communication between administration and staff
- Strong, positive school climate
- Interdisciplinary cooperation and collaboration
- Clear, functional rules and expectations
- Data management and evaluation

It is clear from this list that the authors believe a comprehensive plan needs to include provisions for effective teaching and administration as well as discipline. In their discussion of the "foundational phases" in the design of an effective SDP, Walker et al. (1995, pp. 126–147) identify five central elements.

Phase 1 involves the development of a clear sense of direction regarding expected behavior and the management of problem behavior. Aspects of this phase include the drafting of a mission statement for the school and a statement of purpose for the SDP. The specification of expected behaviors is the focus of Phase 2, and Phase 3 concerns the identification of procedures for teaching students about how they are expected to behave.

Phase 4 of the SDP calls for the development of measures for correcting problem behavior. These should address relatively minor problems that a teacher can handle alone, situations requiring the intervention of an administrator, and serious violations necessitating police involvement. The final phase of the SDP deals with procedures for record keeping, evaluation of disciplinary data, and dissemination of information on the plan.

Core Components
of a Comprehensive Plan

A review of the elements of the SMPSD, the SSMP, and the SDP reveals a set of core components around which any comprehensive school safety plan probably should be developed. Figure 6.1 presents a condensed version of the three models. Features common to all three models include the following:

- Clear expectations for behavior
- Teamwork

- Communication
- Proactive as well as intervention strategies
- Data management
- Staff development

Clear Expectations for Behavior

Much of what each model has to say about behavioral expectations reiterates the discussion in Chapter 3. Students cannot be expected to behave in ways that ensure their

FIGURE 6.1   Three Models of Comprehensive School Safety Plans

Duke[1]	Jones and Jones[2]	Walker, Colvin, and Ramsey[3]
■ Rules/expectations	■ Philosophy	■ Proactive approaches
■ Data management	■ School rules/expectations	■ Leadership
■ Opportunities for staff and students to share concerns	■ Procedures	■ Collegial commitment
■ Team approach to school safety	■ Clearly specified roles and responsibilities	■ Staff development
■ Parental involvement	■ Methods for promoting appropriate behavior and fostering a positive school climate	■ High expectations
■ Proactive approaches	■ Instruction in problem solving for staff and students	■ Clear communications
■ Staff development	■ Special plans for students with serious behavior problems	■ Positive school climate
	■ Communication among teachers, administrators, and parents	■ Interdisciplinary cooperation
	■ Schoolwide student-management committee	■ School rules/expectations
		■ Data management

[1] Daniel L. Duke, *Managing Student Behavior Problems.* New York: Teachers College Press, 1980.

[2] Vernon F. Jones and Louise S. Jones, *Comprehensive Classroom Management,* fifth edition. Boston: Allyn & Bacon, 1998

[3] Hill M. Walker, Geoff Colvin, and Elizabeth Ramsey, *Antisocial Behavior in School: Strategies and Best Practices.* Pacific Grove, CA: Brooks/Cole, 1995.

safety and the safety of others if no effort is made to convey such expectations to them. To do so first requires agreement among school staff concerning how students should behave. Because staff members come from diverse backgrounds, such agreement cannot be assumed. It must be developed through broad-based participation and patient discussion.

Once expectations have been developed, they need to be taught to students. As important as *knowing* these expectations is *understanding* why they are necessary. One central purpose of schools is to prepare young people for adult life. Because adults spend much of their lives in organizations, students need to learn why organizations are governed by rules. Chapter 3 even suggested that students should be tested on their knowledge and understanding of school rules and expectations. The Joneses (1998, p. 390) note that some schools

> ...begin the school year with an assembly in which key school rules and procedures are role-played. This is followed by classroom discussions in which students personalize the importance of these behavioral expectations.

Recommendation 4.2: Include in the school safety plan school rules and expectations along with provisions for teaching them to students.

As noted in Chapter 3, school rules need to be reviewed periodically. Conditions change, state and local policies are revised, and student behavior varies over time. Some rules become outdated, and new rules need to be added. Other rules prove to be ambiguous or difficult to enforce. One of the duties of the School Safety Team is to monitor school rules and make recommendations for changes.

Teamwork

The safety and well-being of students and staff members is too great a responsibility to assign to one individual. No matter how capable a principal, he or she cannot manage the complexities of a comprehensive school safety plan alone. For this reason, each of the models stresses the importance of teamwork. Chapter 4 acknowledged this point by calling for the formation of a School Safety Team. Besides reviewing school rules and recommending new safety policies, the team assists in determining what roles related to school safety should be played by various staff members, students, and parents.

Walker et al. (1995, p. 124) stress the necessity for all school staff "to be actively involved and committed in order to develop, implement, and maintain an effective schoolwide discipline plan." There is little value in a plan that large numbers of staff members feel has been imposed on them. The best school safety plans emerge from the deliberations of all members of the school community. In order for newcomers to feel a sense of ownership in the plan, the deliberations should be ongoing.

Recommendation 4.3: Include in the school safety plan provisions for a team-oriented approach at the school and grade levels.

Teamwork is important at the school level, but it is also necessary at the grade level. Determining which school safety responsibilities are best handled at each level is a key decision in the development of a comprehensive school safety plan. It is likely, for example, that identifying students with early signs of school-related problems may be best accomplished at the grade level. It makes sense that the teachers who come into regular contact with troubled students should participate in developing plans to assist these students.

The author's guidelines for a SMPSD include detailed recommendations concerning how teams should function (Duke, 1980, pp. 96–108). It takes team *work* for teamwork to succeed. This work should focus on the development of sensible procedures for handling safety-related issues. A grade-level team that is responsible for developing assistance plans for individual students, for example, may want to designate a staff member to oversee the implementation of each plan. Assistance plans should not be developed and forgotten. Each one needs to be monitored and adjusted, if necessary. Provisions for monitoring and adjusting, of course, are required for Individual Education Plans, but plans for non-special-education students also should encompass the same precautions.

Teams that deal with school safety issues may need, from time to time, to draw on expertise and insight that is unavailable on the team. When dealing with the needs of particular students, for instance, a team may wish to invite a parent, classmate, sibling, therapist, or community youth worker to participate. Chapter 9 will explore in greater depth the contributions to school safety efforts of parents and other community members.

Communication

Communication may seem too obvious a requirement to include as a special element of a comprehensive school safety plan, but the reality of many schools is that staff members are often busy from the moment they arrive until the moment they leave school. Information-sharing cannot be assumed. Nor can administrators and teachers assume that parents and students will provide timely information concerning possible threats to student well-being and school safety. Add to these concerns the challenge of effectively disseminating information regarding new policies and programs, and it is easy to see why every school safety plan should contain specific provisions for communication.

Walker et al. (1995, p. 124) give one example of the need for communication when they state, "Effective school discipline plans must have clear lines of communication between administration and staff in terms of which student behaviors warrant management by staff in the immediate context and which behaviors warrant office referrals." Disciplinary efforts can be undermined when some teachers refer every problem, no matter how minor, to the office. Students in these teachers' classes quickly get the impression that their instructors are unable to maintain an orderly environment without outside help. Other teachers, meanwhile, may get into serious trouble when they insist on handling problems that really do require assistance.

When administrators receive student referrals from teachers, it is important that they promptly communicate to teachers how they have dealt with these cases. Administrators may not always support teachers' claims regarding student misconduct, or their recommendations for punishment, but teachers deserve to be informed in a timely manner of how their referrals have been handled. Few things upset a teacher more than having a referred student return to class unpunished and with no explanation from the administration.

Communication between teachers and administrators is only one example of the importance of communication in efforts to promote school safety. The flow of information between administrators also is a key to school safety. Busy school administrators should set aside time during the school day to apprise each other of disciplinary cases they are handling and rumors they have heard. Students, too, should be encouraged to share rumors as well as actual instances of victimization with school authorities. To facilitate information sharing, some principals meet regularly with student advisory groups. Parents need to contact the school when they are concerned about their children, either at school or at home. An examination of serious incidents at school often reveals that crucial information was not conveyed in time to prevent the incident or, at least, limit its impact.

> **Recommendation 4.4:** Include in the school safety plan provisions for regular communication between students, parents, teachers, and administrators.

Jones and Jones (1998, pp. 393–395) recognize the fact that face-to-face communication is not always possible, or, in some cases in which emotions run high, desirable. They recommend developing forms that can be filled out when problems arise. When teachers, for example, record their thoughts regarding a student's persistent disruptions in class, they often are able to convey better quality information than when they march to the office and vent their frustrations to an administrator. Written forms also provide a record in the event that a challenge is later raised by a student or parent.

Proactive Strategies

The capacity to intervene when threats to school safety arise is crucial, but so, too, are efforts designed to prevent threats from occurring in the first place. For this reason, comprehensive school safety plans should incorporate proactive or preventive measures as well as interventions. A number of these measures were noted in Chapter 5. They included instruction in values and social skills along with various ways to help students "connect" with school. Proactive measures are not limited to students' beliefs and conduct, however. Efforts designed to address academic problems before they result in frustration, failure, loss of credit, and retention at grade level also play a vital role in promoting safe schools.

> **Recommendation 4.5:** Include in the school safety plan provisions for proactive strategies, including efforts to help students academically.

The author's model for the SMPSD stresses the value of providing reinforcing learning environments (Duke, 1980, pp. 120–134). Recognizing that outright rewards can be counterproductive, the SMPSD focuses instead on privileges earned through the demonstration of responsible behavior. Students who demonstrate an understanding of and respect for school rules, for example, should be allowed to exercise discretion in their use of nonclass time that less responsible students are denied.

Both the SSMP (Jones & Jones, 1998, p. 392) and the SDP (Walker, Colvin, & Ramsey, 1995, p. 125) emphasize the need to create positive school environments. The cause of school safety is hardly advanced when students do not look forward to attending school because it is a harsh and uninviting place. Effective discipline plans, according to Walker et al. (1995, p. 125), have "highly visible and creative structures to encourage appropriate social behavior, personal accomplishments, academic achievement, and general quality performance." Jones and Jones (1998, p. 392) rely a great deal on encouraging students to set their own improvement goals and subsequently recognizing them when they make progress.

Data Management

When educators are busy, communication may not be the only thing to suffer. They can lose track of what is happening under their very noses. It is not unusual to find teachers and administrators who cannot tell a school visitor the average daily disciplinary referral rate or the number of students who have been suspended in the past year for fighting. When members of the school community lose track of school safety data, they diminish their capacity to identify problems, set improvement goals, and celebrate successes. A comprehensive school safety plan should provide for the regular collection, analysis, and sharing of data on school safety.

> **Recommendation 4.6:** Include in the school safety plan provisions for the systematic collection, management, and dissemination of data on school safety and student well-being.

The SMPSD (Duke, 1980, pp. 63–78) calls for the development of standard procedures for reporting data related to school safety and the designation of one or two staff members as data managers. Data management requires receiving, compiling, and reporting regularly on school safety information. A key responsibility of the School Safety Team is to review school safety data, identify trends and troublespots, and share analyses of data with other members of the school community. School safety statistics should be used to set targets for improvement efforts.

Controversy
Should school safety data be shared with the general public?

School officials sometimes are reluctant to publicize safety statistics when they reveal cause for concern. Some officials harbor a legitimate fear that negative publicity can lead to loss of public support, copycat incidents, and withdrawal of students by anxious parents. Other officials may seek to conceal data in order to protect their reputations.

Although it is unwise to unduly alarm the school community or "cry wolf" by inflating statistics on school safety in order to secure more resources, it is also wrong to conceal data from parents, students, and other stakeholders. As Walker et al. (1995, p. 125) put it, "Schoolwide discipline should have the same features of accountability as any other school-based system that serves students or staff." The public has a right to know what is going on in their schools, regardless of whether the data is encouraging or alarming.

Withholding school safety data also can backfire. If safety problems reach a point at which school officials have no choice but to ask for public assistance, they may discover that citizens are unresponsive because they have been led to believe that the school had no problems. It is better to be honest from the outset about school safety conditions, even if it results in concern and criticism.

Staff Development

The last feature of a comprehensive school safety plan involves in-service training for teachers, administrators, and other staff members. It is a mistake to believe that skills related to school safety are ever "mastered." Circumstances change, new students arrive, policies are revised, and the latest research suggests better ways to handle problems. School leaders should take their cue from coaches of professional sports teams. No matter how talented their players, they begin each season by practicing the fundamentals of their sport. Skills related to discipline, classroom management, and school safety are the educational equivalent of these fundamentals.

Recommendation 4.7: Include in the school safety plan provisions for continuous staff development related to school safety.

A review of safety-related topics for staff development workshops in recent years reveals a wide array of subjects and skills. Besides traditional offerings related to classroom management and student discipline, educators now are learning about anger management, how to deal with difficult people, self-defense, conflict management, listening skills, problem-solving strategies, drug awareness, suicide prevention, and sexual harassment. Staff members are most likely to benefit from in-service training if they participate in the identification of workshop topics and if training is conducted over time in conjunction with regular school activities, rather than in a single workshop or class.

School safety is a collective responsibility. Staff development, therefore, should include bus drivers, cafeteria workers, secretaries, custodians, nurses, and teacher aides, as well as teachers and administrators. Because staff members always are being hired, provisions are needed for apprising newcomers of important training covered prior to their arrival. In this regard, it can be very helpful to videotape in-service programs for later viewing. Under certain circumstances, parents and school volunteers also may benefit from attending staff development programs.

Staff development related to school safety is most effective when it is regarded as a means for implementing and improving the comprehensive school safety plan. Training should be tied directly to the elements of the plan. Staff development may be discounted by teachers when it is perceived as a meaningless ritual rather than an integral part of a school's overall strategy for dealing with issues of general concern.

A Comprehensive School Safety Plan in Action

Because every school is, to some extent, unique, no two school safety plans are likely to be identical. Each must be developed with an understanding of the school's students, staff, history, resources, and pressing problems. Nonetheless, it may be worthwhile to examine a comprehensive school safety program that actually was implemented in a Baltimore, Maryland, junior high school. The following account is based on an evaluation of the program that found improvements in the organizational health of the school, students' sense of belonging, and student behavior (Gottfredson, 1987).

The junior high school was chosen because it had a history of disorder and discipline problems and required a program of assistance. The school was located in a high-poverty area and enrolled a high percentage of African American students. The unemployment rate in the community was high, as was the percentage of female-headed households.

After the school agreed to participate in the project, the principal formed a school-improvement team consisting of teachers, a counselor, a social worker, a school psychologist, a parent liaison, and school administrators. The team received training in organization development and spent a year planning a comprehensive program to address a variety of issues related to student safety and well-being. Data on school problems were analyzed, priorities identified, and goals set. Measures for each goal were developed so that the effectiveness of the plan eventually could be determined.

Project "CARE," as the comprehensive program came to be known, consisted of eight components, the strongest of which involved several systematic approaches to classroom management. Teachers were trained to implement Lee Canter's Assertive Discipline and William Glasser's Reality Therapy. Assertive Discipline helps teachers establish orderly classroom environments so that teaching can take place. Students learn what behavior is and is not acceptable and the consequences for unacceptable behavior. Appropriate conduct is recognized and reinforced through teacher encouragement and rewards. Reality Therapy focuses on developing student responsibility. Using structured classroom meetings, teachers help students discuss what is on their minds and how they can change behaviors that are unproductive. The meetings also promote positive peer influence and a caring classroom environment.

CARE called for closely monitoring the progress of each class in the junior high school. Classes with the best and the most improved attendance and behavior received rewards and public recognition. The nine classes with the most serious problems were targeted for special attention, including additional staff development for teachers and a positive reinforcement scheme. This scheme required teachers to specify the behaviors they wanted students to improve and what students needed to do in order to earn rewards. Charts were kept in each class so that students knew exactly where they stood in terms of earning rewards.

Another key component of CARE involved a systematic approach to instructional improvement. Reasoning that much of the school's disorder resulted from students' lack of academic success and subsequent frustration, the school improvement team agreed to implement Robert Slavin's Student Team Learning program. Student Team Learning involves techniques that engage students in academic competition for team rewards and recognition. Team members study together and coach each other in an effort to prepare for periodic tournaments and tests. All teachers were trained in Student Team Learning.

Besides programs to improve classroom management and academic instruction, CARE entailed an intervention to keep parents informed of their children's behavior and a parent volunteer program. Another component of the comprehensive plan sought to increase community support and advocacy for the school. Students were encouraged to participate in extracurricular activities as a way to foster more positive feelings about school and to give those who struggled academically an opportunity to experience success. A standard set of school rules, consequences, and disciplinary procedures were developed, and all staff members were required to implement them. Finally, students were provided with a career-exploration program that included career-oriented field trips and exposure to positive role models from various occupations.

A systematic evaluation of CARE found a number of encouraging outcomes. Teachers were able to benefit from staff development and change their instructional practice and classroom management. Disciplinary referrals declined, and the use of nonpunitive disciplinary techniques, such as parent conferences and removal of privileges, increased. Substantial improvements were reported in teacher morale and students' positive feelings about school. Student suspensions dropped, but the evaluator was reluctant to credit CARE alone for this decline because suspensions fell throughout the school system.

Turning around a troubled school is not a simple process. CARE did not achieve all of its goals. For example, students' educational aspirations did not increase, as hoped. What the CARE program demonstrated, however, is that important improvements can be made if they are approached in a comprehensive and carefully planned way. Those who find themselves in unsafe and low-performing schools should take heart from the experience of this Baltimore junior high school.

Steps in Developing a School Safety Plan

The history of educational innovation suggests that effective change is unlikely to result from hasty planning. Certain time-consuming steps must be taken if a comprehensive school safety plan is to stand a reasonable chance of succeeding. Figure 6.2 indicates the steps recommended by two leading texts. These schemes maintain that the work of developing a plan should be undertaken by a small and representative group, rather than one or two individuals or the school as a whole. Before the plan is approved, however, those who were not involved in drafting it should have an op-

FIGURE 6.2 **Steps in Developing a Comprehensive School Safety Plan**

Jones and Jones[1]	Walker, Colvin and Ramsey[2]
1. Select a committee.	1. Establish a commitment from all staff to work together on the plan.
2. Draft a document.	
3. Edit the draft in light of feedback.	2. Establish a building team and operating procedures.
4. Approve and celebrate the work.	
5. Communicate the plan.	3. Develop or revise a school discipline manual.
	4. Design and implement a staff development plan.
	5. Develop a data-management, feedback, and review system.

[1]Vernon F. Jones and Louise S. Jones. *Comprehensive Classroom Management,* fifth edition. Boston: Allyn & Bacon, 1998, pp. 397–398.

[2]Hill M. Walker, Geoff Colvin, and Elizabeth Ramsey. *Antisocial Behavior in School: Strategies and Best Practices.* Pacific Grove, CA: Brooks/Coles, 1995, pp. 147–149.

portunity to review and comment on its contents. Once the plan is approved, it needs to be communicated to all members of the school community, and those responsible for implementing it should receive appropriate training.

Combining these recommendations with findings from research on organizational change, an 11-step process for developing a comprehensive school safety plan is provided below. The steps include the following:

1. Official launching of planning effort
2. Creation of planning group
3. Identification of constraints
4. Visioning
5. Building awareness
6. Drafting of school safety plan
7. Feedback on draft plan
8. Development of revised plan
9. Approval of plan
10. Identification of resources and training needed to implement plan
11. Monitoring of implementation

Context and circumstances obviously exert influences on the actual course of school safety planning. Planning, for example, will be somewhat different in a brand-new school than in a well-established school. A school facing severe safety problems is likely to approach planning with a greater sense of urgency than a relatively peaceful school. Still, the 11 steps listed above probably should be part of the planning process undertaken by any school.

Launching School Safety Planning

How the planning process begins will go a long way to determining how the eventual product—a comprehensive school safety plan—will be received. It is crucial, therefore, that all stakeholders understand what is being undertaken *before* it begins. Surprise is the enemy of trust and credibility. The planning process should be announced at an open meeting to which staff, parents, community members, and the press are invited. Students also should be apprised of what is going to be done. Written announcements should be sent to those unable to attend the public meeting.

At the meeting, it is important to convey to people the fact that school safety planning is vital to the welfare of all those in the school community and critical to the creation of an effective learning environment. People should understand that there are no "hidden agendas" and that the essential features of the plan have not already been determined "behind closed doors." Those attending the meeting need an opportunity to express their feelings about safety in the school and community, share particular ideas that should be considered in drafting the plan, and reflect on how the planning process should be undertaken. Someone should be assigned the task of recording these comments for later review.

Forming the Planning Committee

One challenge in creating a planning committee is to constitute a group that is representative of the school staff, but small enough and sufficiently compatible to get its work done. Twelve members is probably as large as the group should be, lest group dynamics and the scheduling of meetings become major obstacles. Elementary school groups should include representatives from each grade level, a special education teacher, an administrator, and several individuals representing other role groups. Secondary school committees may consist of teachers chosen by department or grade level, a guidance counselor, a school resource officer, a school nurse, and one or more administrators. Although it is easier to get appropriate representation by appointing committee members, allowing some members to be elected ensures that the staff has a voice in the makeup of the committee.

Opinions vary about whether students, parents, and community members should be part of the planning committee. The Joneses note that the planning process tends to run more smoothly if nonstaff members do not participate in the early stages of the committee's work. They observe that the committee "needs to be able to discuss issues that are more personal in nature than is appropriate for students and community members to hear" (Jones & Jones, 1998, p. 397). Parents and students can join the committee at a later stage of planning, or focus groups can be convened to solicit reactions to the initial version of the plan.

Once the committee is formed, a number of organizational issues must be addressed before taking up the school safety plan itself. The following questions should be on the agenda for the committee's first meeting:

- Who should lead the committee?
- By what date should the committee's work be completed?
- How frequently should the committee meet?
- Should work be done by subgroups or the committee as a whole?
- Should decisions be made by consensus or a formal vote?
- If votes are taken, should a simple majority prevail?
- How will the committee make certain that members of the school staff and community are informed of its progress?
- Will there be only one official spokesperson for the committee?

Although these matters are important, the first order of business is to make certain that committee members are committed to the goal of developing a school safety plan. Dissent regarding particular aspects of a plan, of course, is to be expected, but individuals who oppose the very idea of developing a comprehensive school safety plan probably should not serve on the committee. Time is always a scarce commodity for educators, and it should not be wasted debating whether to have a plan in the first place.

Identifying Constraints

No committee has the luxury of working without constraints. Schools exist within school systems, which in turn are subject to various state and federal laws. Rather than pretending that planning can be undertaken unfettered, it is advisable for the planning committee, at an early date in its proceedings, to review the laws and policies that constitute the parameters within which it must work. It is a good idea to ask the school district attorney to address the committee on such issues as student rights, legal aspects of disciplining special education students, privacy issues, and guidelines for exclusion of dangerous students.

Resources also represent a constraint. No school has access to unlimited funds with which to promote safety. It is recommended, however, that resource issues be deferred until the committee has drafted an initial plan for review. A case always can be made that additional resources are needed in order to implement a promising new safety plan. A school is unlikely to change a law that constrains its plans, but it is possible that more money can be found if the plan is sound and widely supported.

Exploring Possibilities

Visioning involves the systematic identification of possibilities. Committee members adopt the role of educational designers, asking themselves what kind of school they want. As they create their "vision," they need to consider how school safety fits into it. Some approaches to safety may be more compatible with their vision than others.

To assist in the process of mapping school safety onto the committee's vision, it can be useful to raise questions about various aspects of educational design. These questions may include the following:

- How should students behave toward each other and staff members?
- How should unacceptable behavior be handled?
- What role should students play in school safety?
- What role should parents play in school safety?
- What kinds of data on school safety need to be kept?
- How can facilities be designed or improved to promote safety?
- How can school safety issues be addressed in the curriculum?
- How can new students and their parents be introduced to school safety and behavioral expectations?

Building Awareness

Once the committee has developed a vision of the kind of school it wants, investigating actual schools that mirror its vision can be helpful. Ideally, the committee can visit several schools and meet with staff members. Another way to build awareness is to consult the literature on school safety and school improvement. Research can help committee members refine their vision and identify promising programs and possible problems. A third source of valuable information is consultants. Inviting several school safety experts to address the committee can provide the external perspective necessary to evaluate the vision before it is translated into a school safety plan.

Drafting a Plan

The most difficult phase of the entire planning process entails developing the first draft of a school safety plan. It is challenging to capture a vision on paper. Often the enthusiasm that surfaced during initial deliberations is lost on paper. A good plan is written to inspire as well as guide. Despite the difficulty of drafting a plan, it must be done before the committee can proceed. Without a written version of the plan, it is hard to obtain the focused feedback necessary to fine-tune it.

Committees cannot write plans. Typically, several individuals or small subcommittees assume responsibility for composing parts of the plan. The plan should begin with a clear statement of goals. Without this statement, the success of the plan cannot be evaluated at a later date. Some committees also like to include a philosophical statement or set of guiding principles at the beginning of their plan.

The school safety plan should include sections dealing with the following topics:

- Expectations for student and staff behavior in school, going to and from school, and at school-sponsored activities
- Consequences for failure to meet expectations
- Procedures for teaching expectations
- Procedures for administering discipline
- Strategies for promoting appropriate conduct
- Strategies for discouraging misconduct and handling it when it does occur
- Procedures for ensuring due process and handling appeals and grievances
- Personnel responsible for various aspects of school safety and the nature of their responsibilities
- Crisis management or contingency plans for emergencies

Obtaining Feedback

Once a draft of the school safety plan has been developed, it needs to be shared with members of the school community—staff members, students, and parents. Older students may be given an assignment in one of their classes to read the plan and provide several pages of written reactions. Teachers of younger students may prefer to read parts of the plan to their students during a class meeting and solicit reactions. Hearings can be held as a way to obtain feedback from staff members and parents.

Because attendance at hearings may not be high, the committee also can invite representatives of different role groups in the school as well as local neighborhoods to participate in focus groups. Focus groups should be asked to react to specific aspects of the plan.

To ensure that the plan complies with laws and policies, it should be reviewed by the school district attorney. The committee also may wish to have the district business officer examine the plan for possible financial implications. Crisis management plans should be reviewed by the local police department or sheriff's office.

Revising the Plan

After reviewing feedback on the plan from staff members, students, parents, and others, the committee needs to make any revisions it feels are necessary. Before submitting the revised plan to the staff for final approval, the committee should ask the school district attorney to review any changes that have been made. In some school systems, the superintendent and school board also may need to approve the plan.

Obtaining Approval

It may not be legally necessary to secure the approval of the school staff, but doing so increases the likelihood that staff members will support the school safety plan. If the plan has been approved by a substantial majority of the staff, the principal has a solid basis for insisting that all staff members comply with the "will of the majority." Once the plan has been approved, it is important to notify the entire school community.

Planning Implementation

The committee's work is not done when the plan has been approved and disseminated. Plans have to be implemented, and implementation requires training and resources. In other words, implementing a school safety plan requires additional planning. The committee needs to consider what training is needed to put the plan into effect. It is possible, for example, that the plan calls for teachers to understand the process of conflict resolution so that they can teach it to students. Before the plan can be implemented, therefore, teachers would need to receive training in conflict resolution.

The need for training raises the issue of resources. Trainers must be hired and, in some cases, teachers must be reimbursed for time spent receiving training. The school safety planning committee should develop a budget to cover the costs of implementing its plan and a time line specifying the phases of implementation. Besides training, the plan may involve expenditures for new personnel, curriculum materials, incentives for students, printing and distribution of the plan, computer software for maintaining school safety data, data processing, and safety equipment such as metal detectors and two-way radios.

Monitoring Implementation

To ensure that implementation plans are carried out, a group should monitor the process and handle any questions that arise along the way. This group can be the original committee that drafted the plan, a standing committee on school safety, or the School Safety Team.

No plan is perfect, so it is important for the first year of the plan to be regarded as a pilot year. At the end of the year, the monitoring group should obtain feedback on the strengths and weaknesses of the implemented plan and make whatever revisions are necessary. The plan thereafter should be evaluated on a regular basis to make certain that it is achieving its goals.

Conclusion

Schools that are safe for all students do not rely on one particular approach or strategy. They instead offer a variety of prevention, intervention, and management measures aimed at promoting good behavior as well as discouraging misconduct. Although some students respond well to recognition and incentives, others need to know that negative consequences will result if they disobey school rules. Still other students will disobey rules despite the consequences. For these individuals, schools need structured interventions ranging from counseling and time-out to alternative placement.

To facilitate the development of a balanced set of school safety strategies, this chapter prescribed a comprehensive school safety plan. Such a plan should address all aspects of school safety, including expectations for student and staff behavior, proactive strategies, consequences for rule-breaking, programs for students who repeatedly threaten the safety of themselves and others, and a list of responsibilities for various role groups involved in school safety efforts. School safety plans need to be reviewed and updated on a regular basis.

REFERENCES

Blauvelt, Peter D. *Making Schools Safe for Students.* Thousand Oaks, CA: Corwin, 1999.

Duke, Daniel L. *Managing Student Behavior Problems.* New York: Teachers College Press, 1980.

Gottfredson, Denise C. "An Evaluation of an Organization Development Approach to Reducing School Disorder," *Evaluation Review,* vol. 11, no. 6 (December 1987), pp. 739–763.

Gottfredson, Denise C. "School-Based Crime Prevention." In L. W. Sherman, D. Gottfredson, D. MacKenzie, J. Eck, P. Reuter, and S. Bushway (eds.), *Preventing Crime: What Works, What Doesn't, What's Promising.* A Report to the United States Congress. (1997) (See www.preventingcrime.org)

Jones, Vernon F., and Jones, Louise S. *Comprehensive Classroom Management,* fifth edition. Boston: Allyn & Bacon, 1998.

Lee, James L.; Pulvino, Charles J.; and Perrone, Philip A. *Restoring Harmony.* Upper Saddle River, NJ: Merrill, 1998.

National Commission on Drug-free Schools. *Toward a Drug-free Generation: A Nation's Responsibility.* Washington, DC: Author, 1990.

Perry, Constance M. "Proactive Thoughts on Creating Safe Schools," *The School Community Journal,* vol. 9, no. 1 (Spring/Summer 1999), pp. 9–16.

Stephens, Ronald D. "Planning for Safer and Better Schools: School Violence Prevention and Intervention Strategies," *School Psychology Review,* vol. 23, no. 2 (1994), pp. 204–215.

Walker, Hill M.; Colvin, Geoff; and Ramsey, Elizabeth. *Antisocial Behavior in School: Strategies and Best Practices.* Pacific Grove, CA: Brooks/Cole, 1995.

7

Standard 5:
Crisis Management

MAJOR IDEAS IN CHAPTER 7

- Crisis management involves three levels of response.
- Responses to emergencies should be coordinated by a crisis team headed by the principal.
- The key to effective crisis management is understanding what needs to be done when an emergency arises.
- Crisis management requires plans for precrisis and postcrisis situations, as well as during an actual crisis.
- Backup plans should be developed in case of unforeseen problems such as power outages and the absence of key personnel.
- Communication during and after a crisis is critical to effective crisis management.

Practically everyone who has attended school has experienced a fire drill. Fire drills are an annual ritual across the United States. Although fire drills disrupt classes and schools rarely experience fires, few people propose eliminating fire drills. It is concern for what *might* happen that prompts emergency preparedness. Anyone who has ever witnessed the tragic results of a fire in which people lacked an evacuation plan and proper training understands the necessity of such precautions.

The years have proven that schools are not immune to crises. Students shooting other students. Adults holding students and teachers hostage. Abductions. Gang-related violence on campus. Strangers entering schools with weapons. Bomb threats. Natural disasters. Although such events are infrequent, they provide vivid testimony that the unexpected is always a possibility. Educators' inability to prevent emergencies must not deter them from being as well prepared as possible to handle such events when they do occur.

> **Standard 5:** School authorities anticipate and prepare for situations that could be disruptive or dangerous.

Crises need not result in disorder and chaos. By anticipating emergencies and developing contingency plans, educators can greatly reduce the likelihood of serious injury and loss of life. Yet until the past few decades, most crisis planning in schools occurred *after* a crisis, not before. Chapter 7 examines the kinds of emergencies for which schools should be prepared. Guidelines are offered for the operation of crisis management teams, and examples are provided to illustrate precrisis, crisis, and post-crisis planning.

The Nature of School Crises

A food fight erupts in the cafeteria after several students express dissatisfaction with the quality of their lunch. A noncustodial parent approaches his daughter on the playground and attempts to take her with him. Rumors circulate around school that a local gang plans to "get even" with several students in the parking lot after school. A distraught school employee holds a classroom full of students hostage and demands to meet with the superintendent. Are these crises?

There is no definitive answer to this question. Under certain circumstances, each might be regarded as a crisis. One person's crisis may be another person's concern. A study of principals found that their perceptions vary greatly regarding what constitutes a serious problem as opposed to a genuine crisis (Cohen, 1998, pp. 92–94). One principal, for example, considered poor attendance to be a crisis at his school. Another principal differentiated between minicrises and full-blown crises.

In its resource guide on crisis management, the Virginia Department of Education (1998, p. 3) characterizes a crisis as a "sudden, generally unanticipated event that profoundly and negatively affects a significant segment of the school population and often involves serious injury or death." Cohen (1998, p. 95) describes a crisis in terms of five criteria:

- The unexpectedness of the event
- The disruption of the normal school-day program
- The administrators' perception of loss of control over the school
- The need for instant action
- The threat or potential threat of danger

School administrators are fond of saying that they may not be able to define a crisis, but they know when they are faced with one. Crises seize our attention. "Business as usual" is impossible. Crises require response without the luxury of reflection. The forementioned resource guide for Virginia school administrators lists 29 situations that may require a crisis management plan (Virginia Department of Education, 1998):

Accidents at school	Aircraft disaster
Accidents to and from school	Allergic reaction

Angry parent/employee/patron	Injury
Assault by intruder	Intruder/trespasser
Bomb threat	Life-threatening crisis
Bus accident	Perceived crises
Chemical spill	Poisoning
Childnapping/lost child	Power failure/lines down
Death	Rape
Disaster (tornado, bomb)	Shooting/wounding
Disaster preventing dismissal	Suicide threats
Fighting	Vandalism
Fire/arson/explosives	Weapons situation
Gas leak	Weather
Hostage/armed	

When incidents such as these occur, members of the school staff may need to function in ways for which they are unprepared. Crises disorient people, leaving them uncertain of what to do. Resources for dealing with certain emergencies may not be immediately available. Careful planning is required to prevent a crisis from spawning chaos and compounding the impact of an already serious situation.

The Need for Crisis Management

An inadequate or inappropriate response to a crisis not only can sustain the crisis, it can generate a new crisis. We have seen what happens, for example, when the police overreact to an alleged crime. An overly aggressive response, particularly when it is considered to be motivated by prejudice, can lead to a violent counterreaction. In the "School Crisis Response Guide" distributed by New York's lieutenant governor to every school district in the state, Sergeant Michael Lynch's comments at a hearing on school violence are reproduced. Lynch (New York State, 1999) recognizes that the key to crisis management is good planning:

> To effectively combat school violence, it is essential that proper planning for violent type situations occur on a regular basis. Should a violent situation occur in one of New York State's schools it is imperative that each and every staff member know his or her role and how to react to protect themselves and their students. Plans should be familiar to all staff and be tested frequently utilizing whatever means possible. The plan should not merely be a document on a shelf collecting dust.

A carefully developed plan that is understood by those expected to carry it out may not avert a crisis, but it can reduce the likelihood of confusion and panic. Such conditions, of course, can prolong and intensify the impact of crises.

CASE IN POINT

An assistant principal was the first to notice Gary in the hallway. Gary had been suspended from school two days earlier for fighting. He was not supposed to return to school for eight more days. When the assistant principal approached Gary and told him he had to leave, Gary became verbally abusive and refused to go. As the assistant principal pulled out his two-way radio to call for help, Gary started running toward the stairs to the second floor.

The assistant principal looked at his watch as he waited for the principal to answer. The third-period bell would ring in three minutes. During the change of classes, Gary could get lost in the crowd or, worse, hurt somebody. The assistant principal did not know why Gary had returned to school or if he was armed. Remembering the school's plan for situations involving intruders, the assistant principal told the principal to give the signal for all teachers to keep their students in class when the bell rang and lock their doors. He also asked for the police to be notified.

Arriving within 10 minutes, the police were able to locate Gary easily because no students had been allowed to leave class. He was removed from the school, and trespassing charges were filed.

Based on an actual case, the Case in Point illustrates the benefits of planning for emergencies. Had Gary returned to school with malicious intent and had students filled the hallways when the bell rang, someone easily could have been hurt. Gary was a large and strong individual with a history of aggressive behavior. Because the teachers had been informed in advance of a code word that, when heard over the intercom, signaled the need to keep students in class and lock their doors, a potentially dangerous situation was averted.

A Guide to Safe Schools (U.S. Department of Education, 1998, p. 27) recommends that crisis management plans address two issues: (1) how to ensure safety during a crisis and (2) how to respond to the aftermath of a crisis. These two concerns also are recognized in the definition of crisis management used by the Virginia Department of Education.

> Crisis Management is that part of a school division's approach to school safety which focuses more narrowly on a time-limited, problem-focused intervention to identify, confront and resolve the crisis, restore equilibrium, and support appropriate adaptive responses. (1998, p. 3)

To meet Standard 5, school authorities should include plans for dealing with various crises and their aftermath. These plans are referred to as "crisis management plans" and "postcrisis plans." In addition, however, a need exists for "precrisis" plans. A precrisis plan deals with situations in which staff members are forewarned of an impending crisis. A student may notify a counselor, for example, that a classmate is considering suicide, or a teacher may overhear students talking about a fight that is planned after school in the parking lot. Precrisis plans call for verification of reports and rumors whenever possible, but even when verification cannot be obtained, caution dictates preparedness. Unlike crisis plans, precrisis planning assumes that school authorities have time to get organized.

Recommendation 5.1: Develop plans to handle precrisis, crisis, and postcrisis situations.

According to Blauvelt (1999, pp. 127–128), a comprehensive crisis management system includes plans for dealing with the following crises:

A. Accidents
   1. at school
   2. to or from school
   3. on a school bus
   4. after-school activity
   5. on a field/athletic trip
B. Serious (personal injury) assaults
   1. on a student
   2. on a teacher/staff member
   3. on an administrator
C. Bomb threats
D. Explosive device found
E. Explosive device detonated
F. Suspected child abuse
   1. occurred at home
   2. occurred at school
G. Kidnapping
H. Death at school
   1. natural causes
   2. accidental
I. Ethnic disturbances
J. Gang altercations
K. Student demonstration
   1. authorized
   2. unauthorized
L. Natural disaster
M. Riots
N. Suicide attempts/threats
O. Possession of a weapon
P. Violation of state laws
Q. Violation of school rules

Although no two crises are ever exactly the same, some of the steps that need to be taken in preparing for and dealing with different crises are similar. For example, no matter what the crisis, people who first learn of it need to know to whom to report. The next part of the chapter examines some common features of crisis management plans.

General Guidelines for Crisis Planning

Crisis management involves, in most cases, three levels of response (Virginia Department of Education, 1998, pp. 27–29). The focus of this chapter is building or school-level responses. Crisis management, depending on the emergency, also may necessitate responses by the central office of the school district and the community in which the school is located. A major crisis, such as the shootings at Columbine High School, required the concerted and sustained intervention of school, district, and community crisis intervention teams.

Blauvelt (1999, pp. 128–129) identifies 10 key elements of a school "Emergency Management Plan." The first element is an emergency management team consisting of staff members selected because of their training and responsibilities in the school. The plan must specify each team member's duties in a crisis, including who will be in charge in case the principal—typically the head of the team—is absent or incapacitated. Blauvelt recommends developing codewords or signals to alert staff members that an emergency exists and that it has passed.

The plan should designate a location at which all staff members without direct responsibility for student supervision can congregate. A school floor plan on which is located telephones, shut-off valves, and other key equipment should be included in the emergency management plan. The floor plan needs to indicate a command center, an evacuation site, and alternatives for both in case the specified locations are unavailable. Finally, the plan must provide for the assembling and storage of one or more "emergency kits." The kit should contain such items as portable telephones, flashlights, a camera, and first-aid supplies.

In thinking about the development of a crisis management plan, it may be helpful to consider seven questions that are likely to arise in a crisis.

1. *What should be done by the person or persons who first hear about or witness an emergency?*

This question raises a number of related questions that should be addressed in the crisis management plan. Under what circumstances, for example, should the observer try to intervene or render assistance? If the person is not an eyewitness, additional instructions may be needed. Guidelines distributed by New York State (1999, p. 1) urge individuals hearing of possible crises to treat all threats or reported emergencies as potentially real.

Assuming individuals are not members of the crisis management team, they should report the crisis to the principal, typically the head of the team. Because of their pivotal role, principals should always have an electronic link to the school office so they can be contacted quickly. If the principal is unavailable, a trained designee should be notified.

> **Recommendation 5.2:** Specify in each crisis management plan who should be contacted in the event of an emergency.

2. What should the emergency contact person do?

Once contacted, the principal must decide whether to convene the crisis management team. This decision is a judgment call based on a variety of factors, including the nature, severity, location, and timing of the emergency and the whereabouts of team members. In some cases, the principal, or the person designated to act in the principal's absence, may need to take action before the team can be convened. Action may include calling for assistance from law enforcement agents and emergency medical services and giving the signal to evacuate the school. All members of the crisis management team should be equipped with electronic pagers or two-way communication devices.

3. At what point should the crisis management team be convened?

In most cases, the principal should convene the team as soon after learning of a crisis, or potential crisis, as possible. Crises typically require more functions to be performed than one person can handle alone. Even if the actual crisis has passed by the time the team meets, postcrisis planning must be undertaken along with gathering as much information as possible about the incident.

> **Recommendation 5.3:** Specify in each plan the conditions under which the crisis management team should be convened.

4. Who should be on the crisis management team and what are their duties?

Schools may face a variety of emergencies, but to avoid confusion, it is best for each school to have only one crisis management team. Virginia's *Resource Guide for Crisis Management in Schools* (1998, p. 30) suggests that the team include the following members:

- Principal
- Principal's assistant or designee
- Guidance counselor

- Faculty member (who enjoys widespread respect among teachers)
- Security personnel
- School psychologist
- School nurse
- School social worker

Instead of focusing on team personnel, Blauvelt (1999, p. 117) emphasizes the responsibilities that team members may need to undertake during and immediately after an emergency. The team, therefore, should consist of individuals capable of performing the following duties:

- Leading the team and running the command center
- Providing first aid
- Coordinating activities at various sites involved in the emergency
- Coordinating contacts with police, fire, and medical personnel
- Coordinating three-person "sweep teams" to check areas in the school
- Coordinating contacts with the media
- Coordinating contacts with parents
- Recording the time that important notices were made and other critical information

Specific responsibilities, of course, are likely to vary somewhat depending on the nature of the crisis, but all crises require someone to serve as spokesperson for the team. This individual handles all inquiries, including those from the media, to ensure that correct information is conveyed and to limit the possibility of rumor and misinformation worsening an already difficult situation. One team member should serve as the coordinator of the command center, receiving incoming messages, logging them, and seeing that the appropriate individuals are apprised of the information.

> **Recommendation 5.4:** Specify in each plan the duties of members of the crisis management team.

5. Who needs to be informed of the crisis?

Assuming that outside communication is possible, certain offices and individuals may need to be notified as soon as possible. If the emergency requires medical attention and if it is safe for medical personnel to intervene, the rescue squad, fire department, or other group equipped to handle medical emergencies must be contacted. So, too, in most cases, must the police or another local law enforcement agency be notified. Many communities have an Office of Emergency Preparedness, or its equivalent, that should be contacted in the event of major crises. The superintendent of the school district also needs to be informed. A crisis management plan should include instructions regarding external communications in cases in which the regular phone lines are inoperative.

When the well-being of students has been jeopardized, parents must be notified as soon as possible. Because members of the crisis management team may be unable to handle such communication in the midst of, or during the immediate aftermath of, a crisis, it may be necessary to assign this responsibility to individuals in the central office or with the local news media.

> **Recommendation 5.5:** Specify in each plan the individuals and agencies that need to be contacted in the event of a crisis.

6. What should be done if outside assistance is unavailable?

It is possible to imagine situations in which outside help, either from medical units or law enforcement agencies, is unavailable during a crisis. Perhaps weather conditions do not permit an immediate response, or in the case of a widespread disaster, emergency units may be tied up elsewhere. Crisis management plans should anticipate such contingencies and specify what needs to be done and by whom until help can arrive.

> **Recommendation 5.6:** Specify in each plan what should be done when outside assistance is unavailable.

7. How should non-team members be informed about crisis management plans?

Because most crisis management teams have fewer than a dozen members, many school employees may lack familiarity with the details of crisis management plans. What is the best way to prepare staff members and students for emergencies? Schools frequently provide staff members with handbooks or looseleaf binders containing copies of plans. Is the distribution of written information sufficient to prepare a school for crises?

A Guide to Safe Schools (U.S. Department of Education, 1998) strongly recommends that members of school staffs regularly practice how to respond to various crises. All adults in a school should understand what they can do to prevent violence, secure assistance when necessary, and defuse potentially dangerous situations. They also should know who is responsible for supervising and assisting hearing-impaired students, students with limited vision, and students with limited proficiency in English during an emergency. Evacuation plans for nonambulatory students should be spelled out. These plans should include provisions for power outages when elevators may not be functioning.

> ***Controversy***
> Should schools conduct emergency drills so that students and staff members are prepared for crises?

Experts disagree regarding the involvement of students in practice drills for crises. One study, for example, has suggested that safety drills can cause students to feel less safe at school while doing little to reduce the rate of serious incidents (Portner, 2000). Experiencing a simulated emergency or lockdown may traumatize some students, particularly younger ones or those who already have experienced a crisis. Critics also note that the drills actually may give some students ideas about how to circumvent safety measures and foment disorder. Others, however, believe that students need to know what to do in the event that their school experiences an emergency. They feel that most students are capable of practicing emergency routines without becoming upset (Grech, 1999).

Until more is known about the costs and benefits of emergency drills, other than fire drills, it may be best to focus on training staff members how to respond to crises and notifying students that their teachers are prepared to give them instructions in the event of an emergency. If a crisis management team decides that students need to participate in drills, they should not disclose to students the actual code words or signals to be used to indicate an emergency.

The Importance of Communication

So critical to crisis management is effective communication that the subject requires its own discussion. Emergencies, of course, actually may be caused by miscommunication or lack of communication. Communication problems also may prolong an emergency or prevent a timely response to crisis conditions.

Prior to a crisis, staff members need to know the details of crisis management plans, including who to contact with information regarding possible emergencies. In her study of principals' experiences with school crises, Cohen (1998, p. 206) discovered that many teachers were unaware of their school's crisis management plans. Such plans may be of little value if only members of the crisis management team know about them. School administrators need to make certain that substitute teachers are apprised of crisis plans.

What should staff members know? They should know when to call 911 and when to contact the school office or another control center. Those on the receiving end of emergency messages need training in how to handle them. When, for example, should they make every effort to keep an individual on the phone line? Should they attempt to verify the message and, if so, how? Many schools, for example, are equipped with devices that allow staff members to determine the origin of incoming calls.

Once a crisis actually takes place, one of the first communication acts may involve convening the crisis management team. If possible, each team member should be equipped with a pager or two-way communication device. Otherwise, a telephone tree can be used. To prevent confusion, a brief, but clear message or signal regarding the need to meet should be used for all team members.

Every school needs access to a variety of communications equipment. The Virginia Department of Education (1998, p. 105) recommends that walkie-talkies and bullhorns or megaphones be available to members of the crisis management team. At least one phone line to the school should have an unlisted number so it can be used in the event other lines become jammed with incoming calls. Cellular phones should be on hand in case regular phones are inoperative or the school must be evacuated. In designing communications within schools, planners need to provide teachers with the means to contact the principal's office, either by two-way intercom or phone. The intercom also is important for issuing signals and instructions to the entire school. Some schools have installed special alarms for use in the case of fire or tornadoes and panic buttons connected directly to the police department and other emergency services.

Recommendation 5.7: Make available to members of the crisis management team a variety of means of communicating with each other, various parts of the school, and sources of assistance outside the school.

Because it may not be possible in all cases for educators to give directions orally, a simple set of hand signals is needed for use in certain emergencies. Signals should be developed for silently instructing students to stop moving forward, move backward, get down and cover up, and disperse quickly but in an orderly manner.

Communication is particularly crucial in the immediate aftermath of a crisis. Rumors are a frequent by-product of emergencies. To minimize the impact of misinformation and to calm those whose loved ones may have been involved in a crisis, selected members of the crisis management team should be designated to contact parents, issue press releases, and report to staff members who are not directly involved in the crisis. It is a good idea to have drafts of generic letters on hand so parents and students can be notified as quickly as possible and in order that everyone receives the same basic information. Figure 7.1 contains a sample letter that can be used after a student suicide.

Dealing with the media during and after a crisis can be an important responsibility of the crisis management team. Depending on the nature of the emergency, of course, a central office representative such as a public relations spokesperson may be designated to respond to all requests for information and to handle interviews with media representatives. In many cases, though, a member of the crisis management team will be expected to deal with inquiries. Kadel and Follman (1994, p. 145) recommend preparing an "official statement" about the crisis and the action that was or is being taken. Names of students and school employees should not be mentioned. The statement should be brief and free of jargon. A member of the

FIGURE 7.1   Student Suicide

To be read to the students by the classroom teacher.

TO: School Faculty
FROM: Principal
SUBJECT: (Crisis)
DATE:

John Doe committed suicide early Saturday morning. As a faculty we extend our sympathy to John's family and friends.

We encourage all students to consider the tragic nature of this death and to realize that death is final. John's death is a reminder to us all that the act of taking one's life is not an appropriate solution to any of life's problems nor is it an act of courage. Please let your teachers know if you would like to talk to a counselor or other staff member.

Funeral services for John will be held in _____ and there will not be a memorial service in this area. Expressions of sympathy may be sent to (name and address).

Source: Resource Guide for Crisis Management in Schools (Richmond: Virginia Department of Education, 1998), p. 110.

crisis management team either can read the written statement or distribute copies to media representatives.

Once a crisis has passed, the media may desire a press conference that enables reporters to ask specific questions. The crisis management team should assign one member to handle press conferences, and this individual should confer with other team members as well as legal counsel to anticipate the questions that may be asked and to determine what information should and should not be shared. In the event that an unexpected question is asked, the spokesperson should indicate that he needs to get back to the questioner with an answer. It is always preferable to check first rather than provide information that may be inaccurate, misleading, or privileged.

In the aftermath of a crisis, it is important for the crisis management team to meet with staff and students to review what happened and to permit the healing process to commence. Acting as if a crisis never happened is not an appropriate response. Whether staff and students meet separately or together, postcrisis gatherings provide an opportunity to share what is known about the situation and review what steps will be taken to return school operations to normal. Those who require special assistance or counseling should be informed of how to obtain it. A meeting with parents and community members also may be necessary, depending on the nature of the crisis.

One of the last communication acts in a crisis involves the preparation of a detailed "incident report." In this report, the crisis management team is expected to recount the crisis as best it can and what was done to respond to it. Because the incident report constitutes an official document that eventually may be used in litigation, the accuracy of information is of paramount importance. Each crisis management team should identify one member whose primary purpose is to keep an ongoing record of the crisis. This individual may find it easier to speak into a tape recorder than to maintain a written record in the midst of an emergency.

> **Recommendation 5.8:** Designate one member of the crisis management team to maintain an ongoing record of the crisis and the team's response.

Representative Responses to Selected Emergencies

Crises come in various shapes and sizes, and they may be characterized in different ways. Some crises, for example, are contained within a specific area of the school, but others involve the entire school. Still other crises, such as a leak at a nuclear power plant, may affect the school, though they occur away from campus. Depending on the source of an external crisis and the location of students' homes, students either may have to be evacuated or kept in school and not allowed to go home.

CASE IN POINT

Fluvanna Middle School in rural Virginia developed three codes for use in emergencies.

"Code Red" means that everyone must evacuate the school. Students understand that they must go to designated areas on the playing fields or directly to waiting school buses. Teachers are expected to take roll once students have assembled and determine if any individuals are missing. A "Code Red" may be used in the event of a bomb threat.

"Code Blue" refers to a lockdown situation, such as when an intruder is in the school. Students and teachers must remain in their rooms. Each teacher takes roll and reports missing students to the office. Paper is placed over the glass on each door so that an intruder cannot see inside classrooms. Teachers are advised not to open their door, but to wait until it is unlocked by a school administrator.

"Code Yellow" pertains to weather-related problems, such as a tornado. Instructions vary depending on the nature of the problem and the amount of preparation time available.

Crises may be precipitated by natural disasters, mechanical or electrical failures, the actions of one individual, or the actions of a group. Weapons may or may not be involved. If the weapon is a firearm or a bomb, it has to be handled differently than if the weapon is a pen knife. In certain instances, school authorities receive advance warning of a crisis; in other cases, the crisis is "in process" or over before they learn of it.

To deal with these contingencies, crisis management teams need more than one plan. They do not need dozens of different plans, however. Plans are only useful when individuals can recall them easily and understand what they are supposed to do with relatively little preparation. Fluvanna Middle School, in the preceding Case in Point, had three basic plans. This part of Chapter 7 discusses representative responses to several types of emergency. The responses are referred to as "representative" rather than exemplary or effective because virtually no empirical data are available on the comparative benefits of different crisis management plans. The responses presented here have been gathered from well-regarded experts and government guidelines dealing with crisis management (Blauvelt, 1999; New York State, 1999; Poland, 1994; U.S. Department of Education, 1998; Virginia Department of Education, 1998). The selected emergencies include a situation in which an individual has a firearm in school, a fight during school, a bomb scare, and a threatened suicide.

Armed Individual

It could be a student or a stranger. The firearm could be a pistol or a semiautomatic rifle. The fact is that the office receives a report that someone with a firearm is in school. The first step is to contact the local law enforcement office and request immediate assistance. School personnel typically are not prepared to deal with situations involving firearms.

Once help has been requested, the individual in charge (let us assume it is the principal) must ascertain, to the best of her ability, where the armed individual is located. As it so happens in this case, the individual is a student, he has a pistol, and he is threatening students in the gymnasium, where physical education classes are in progress. The principal checks her watch to determine when the next bell for changing classes will ring. Realizing that the bell will ring in 10 minutes, she turns off the bells, gets on the intercom, and gives the prearranged signal for teachers to keep students in their rooms and lock the doors. The signal is this notice: "The school bell system is not working."

While the principal is giving the signal to secure classrooms, her secretary has been instructed to convene the crisis management team in the office. A call also is placed to the central office informing the superintendent of the situation. When the crisis management team arrives, one individual is assigned to watch the front door and prevent anyone other than law enforcement officers from entering. Because school is scheduled to end in less than an hour, the principal notifies the district transportation office of the situation. A request is made for the superintendent to notify parents that school may not be dismissed on time and the reason why.

The police arrive and are briefed by the principal, while another team member drafts a statement to be read to anyone phoning the school for information regarding the crisis. Although it is not yet known whether any students or staff members have been injured, another team member contacts the local rescue squad and asks them to come to the school and await further instructions. Once the police have been briefed, they coordinate any actions related to the armed student in the gymnasium. The focus of the crisis management team's efforts is protecting the rest of the school by keeping students and staff in class, apprising them of developments if it can be done safely, and handling phone inquiries. The police cordon off the school soon after arriving on the scene, so no visitors are allowed to enter.

First Steps When Someone with a Firearm Is in School

1. Contact the police and the rescue squad.
2. Do not confront the armed person.
3. Shut off the bell.
4. Signal teachers to keep students in class and lock their doors.
5. Convene the crisis management team unless it is unsafe to do so.
6. Notify the superintendent and make arrangements, if necessary, to alert the transportation office and parents.
7. Prepare a brief message for those making phone inquiries.
8. Brief police when they arrive.

Fight

Not all fights constitute a crisis. Under certain circumstances, however, a fight involving two or more students, or a student and a nonstudent, should be treated as an emergency. If the combatants represent rival gangs or feuding families, for example, the situation quickly can escalate into a threat to general safety. Upon learning about or encountering a fight in school or on school grounds, the administrator in charge must make a judgment call regarding the seriousness of the altercation. Factors to consider in making such a judgment include the number, age, and size of the combatants, whether they are armed, whether they are gang members, the size of the audience, and the location of the fight. If the fight is judged to be serious, meaning it has the potential to involve serious injury or to escalate, the administrator needs to contact the local law enforcement office or school security office. Otherwise, the administrator should enlist the assistance of several staff members who have received training in how to handle aggressive behavior.

Because the presence of an audience can transform a containable fight into a melee, it is advisable to disperse the audience (Poland, 1994, p. 183). Several staff members will be needed to facilitate this process. They should escort onlookers back to class or to a supervised location where they cannot observe the fight.

For the staff members who remain with the combatants, it is important to determine who they are and to call the students by name. While avoiding the middle of the conflict, a staff member should present the combatants with choices. Poland (1994, p. 183) advises against threatening them with consequences as long as they are agitated. Virginia's crisis manual (Virginia Department of Education, 1998, p. 62) recommends giving specific commands in an authoritative voice and reminding the combatants of the rules. If the opportunity presents itself, and staff members understand how to protect themselves, they should try to position themselves between the fighters, but not use physical force. This strategy, of course, assumes the fighters do not possess weapons.

If staff members succeed in separating the individuals, they should be guided to neutral locations and given an opportunity to calm down. As long as they are upset, no effort should be made to impose penalties or punish them. Medical assistance may be required, but even if it appears that the combatants did not sustain injuries, it is a good idea to have the school nurse meet with each individual. The nurse should make a record of the examination and any comments made by the fighters. It may be advisable to take photographs of the students and any visible injuries they recieved.

Eventually it will be necessary to invoke the school district policy regarding fighting and contact the students' parents. District policies concerning fighting vary considerably. Some districts distinguish, for example, between assailants and individuals defending themselves. Only the former is subject to punishment. Other school systems punish all students involved in a fight. A police report may be required, but even if it is not, the administrator in charge should describe the incident in writing. Students involved in fights typically are subject to suspension or expulsion, but in some places, such as Houston, Texas, students charged with fighting also must appear in court and pay a fine (Poland, 1994, p. 183).

First Steps in Dealing with a Fight in School or on School Grounds

1. Dispatch trained staff members to the fight scene.
2. Determine whether the fight is sufficiently serious to require the involvement of law enforcement officers.
3. Disperse any onlookers and assign staff members to escort them away from the fight scene.
4. Address the combatants by name and inform them that they are breaking a rule and tell them what their choices are.
5. If the opportunity presents itself, separate the combatants without using force.
6. Remove the combatants to separate locations and wait for them to calm down.
7. Debrief the combatants separately on the circumstances of the fight and record their comments.

Bomb Threat

One of the most difficult judgments a principal may have to make is whether to evacuate school in response to a bomb threat. Although evacuation is the most prudent course of action, it disrupts the school day and interferes with learning. In the year after the Columbine High School tragedy, an estimated 5,000 bomb threats were received by schools in the United States (Blair, 2000, p. 22). Most of the bomb threats turned out to be false alarms, pranks played by students solely for the purpose of interrupting school activities, but a small percentage were legitimate warnings. So bothersome and costly have bomb threats become for schools that a number of states have passed laws that require harsh penalties for those found guilty of making threats. Penalties include loss of driving privileges, expulsion, and reimbursement by parents for damages.

Many school bomb threats are received over the phone. A procedure, therefore, is needed for those who normally receive calls to the school. It is critical, for instance, that individuals obtain as much information as possible. Blauvelt (1999, p. 156) recommends listening to the entire message without interrupting the caller, writing down the message, and noting the time of the call, the estimated age of the caller, and any background noises. Keeping the caller on the line as long as possible is important. Once the initial message has been delivered, the person who received the call should attempt to find out as much information as possible about the bomb, its location, and the reason for planting it. After the caller has hung up, an effort should be made to trace the call. Many schools have Caller ID, which displays the phone number of incoming calls. If not, in many parts of the United States, the person receiving the call can lift the receiver and press #57 to trace the call.

The information recorded by the person taking the call serves as the basis for the principal's decision regarding evacuation. Assuming the principal decides that evacuation is necessary, the Virginia Department of Education (1998, pp. 149–150) suggests that 911 be called, along with the central office. The public address system should not be used to notify staff members. Instead, available staff members or, preferably, members of the crisis management team, should be sent throughout the school to deliver a signal to teachers and other staff members. The school bells should be shut off.

If the bomb threat indicated a time when the device was set to detonate, the principal may choose to conduct a confidential building search prior to evacuation. A plan should be worked out in advance that assigns staff members to search all parts of the school. The plan should include normally unsupervised areas like restrooms, custodians' closets, and outdoor storage facilities. Staff members must be instructed to report, but not to handle, any suspicious objects. The principal needs to deliver a signal over the public address system so that the school can be evacuated in an orderly manner. The Virginia school crisis manual (Virginia Department of Education, 1998, p. 151) suggests announcing that a fire drill will be called 15 minutes before the threatened time of detonation.

Once the school has been evacuated, no one other than the police or designated members of the crisis management team should reenter the building until the authorities have given the "all clear" signal. If the bomb threat is received late in the school day, the principal may decide to dismiss students while they are still outside the school. Before such a decision can be made, however, permission must be obtained from the superintendent. The superintendent then notifies the transportation office.

The principal should make certain that she has access to a cellular phone while outside the school building.

First Steps in Dealing with a Bomb Threat

1. Gather as much information as possible from the person making the bomb threat (if the threat is received by phone).
2. Determine whether the threat warrants a confidential building search by staff members and evacuation.
3. If evacuation is called for, contact 911 and alert the central office.
4. Shut off the school bells.
5. Notify staff members to evacuate the school by using a prearranged signal.
6. Evacuate the school and do not permit anyone except authorized persons to reenter until the "all clear" signal has been given.

Suicide Threat

Each year in the United States thousands of young people take their own lives. The suicide of a student, particularly if it occurs in school during regular hours, constitutes a serious emergency. But so, too, does a suicide threat. It is critical that staff members take such threats seriously. Training is needed to help staff members recognize the signs of suicidal ideation, and each school should develop a protocol for handling such emergencies.

CASE IN POINT

In May 1995 a U.S. District Court in Tampa ruled that a Florida school district was partly to blame for the suicide of a 13-year-old student. Under state law Florida educators are required to supervise and protect students with "reasonable care." The jury in *Carol Wyke v. The Polk County School Board* determined that educators failed to exhibit reasonable care when they failed to respond appropriately to an attempted suicide by the plaintiff's son, Shawn Wyke.

Shawn tried to hang himself in the school's restroom the day before he died. When he was found, the school administrator read passages to him from the Bible, but he did not notify Shawn's mother or take any other action. The following day, Shawn hanged himself from a tree in his backyard. (Portner, 1995)

Poland (1994, p. 184) points out that the key issue in cases of suicide is not whether the school *caused* the suicide, but whether the school took reasonable steps to prevent it. What might be judged "reasonable steps," of course, can vary with the situation, but at the very least school authorities have an obligation to notify at least one of the student's parents or, in certain instances, a representative of social services. Regarding students at risk of suicide, the Virginia Code clearly states what action must be taken:

> Any person licensed as administrative or instructional personnel by the Board of Education and employed by a local school board who, in the scope of his employment, has reason to believe, as a result of direct communication from a student, that such student is at imminent risk of suicide, shall, as soon as practicable, contact at least one of such student's parents to ask whether such parent is aware of the student's mental state and whether the parent wishes to obtain or has already obtained counseling for such student. (Stapleton, 1999, p. 17)

In cases in which a student indicates, or it is suspected, that the reason for threatening suicide involves parental abuse or neglect, the school is obligated to notify the local department of social services instead of the parent.

An actual attempt to take one's life is the most obvious indication that a young person is at risk of suicide. Are there less-obvious indicators for which educators should be on the alert? According to Poland (1994, p. 184), the "most common factors in youth suicide are depression, substance abuse, conduct problems, recklessness, impulsivity, and gun availability." Teachers should be attuned to suicidal thoughts and feelings of hopelessness that students express in their assignments. Often at-risk students will convey feelings of not wanting to live and of profound despair to someone they know. Students and staff should understand that such comments need to be taken seriously. Every student in the school should know someone to whom they can immediately report telltale comments and suspicious behavior by classmates.

Staff members who have concerns or hear about students who might be at risk of harming themselves should contact a member of the crisis management team. The team needs to be convened as soon as possible to consider the student in question. Because it may take a while to arrange a meeting, a designated member of the team should contact the student's parents or the local social services department after meeting with the student to discuss the situation. The staff member must decide if the student needs an immediate referral to a mental health clinic or, at least, continuous adult supervision until the team can meet and make a decision.

Deciding what to say to a parent is not easy. Some parents may deny that their child could be suicidal; others become agitated and angry. The person designated to contact a parent should consider the type of message most likely to elicit cooperation and understanding. In some states, if a parent refuses to seek help for their child and forbids the school to do so, state law allows trained professionals, such as physicians and psychologists, to help the young person anyway (Poland, 1994, p. 184).

When the crisis management team meets to discuss the student, one member should be selected as the case manager. This person is responsible for monitoring whatever plan to help the student is developed by the team and for reporting back to the team on the success of the plan. The case manager is the individual who establishes and maintains primary contact with the student.

First Steps in Dealing with a Student Who May Be Suicidal

1. Contact a member of the crisis management team.
2. Meet with the student to assess the seriousness of his condition.
3. Decide whether immediate referral to a mental health clinic is required.
4. If immediate referral is not required, determine whether the student needs direct supervision.
5. Convene a meeting of the crisis management team as soon as possible (the same day as the report is received).
6. Contact the student's parents or the local social services department, if parental abuse or neglect is suspected.
7. Develop a plan for helping the student, and assign a member of the crisis management team to monitor the plan.

Postcrisis Planning

The discussion thus far has focused on what to do before, during, and immediately after an emergency. Crisis management also involves planning for the postcrisis period, which may range from a week to the remainder of the school year.

When the members of a school community experience a traumatic event such as the suicide of a student or a hostage-taking incident, the aftermath may be marked by anxiety, fear, and depression. Students and staff members can find it difficult to express their feelings or return to their regular routines. Opportunities to discuss feelings and concerns often are a crucial part of the healing process. *A Guide to Safe Schools* (U.S. Department of Education, 1998, pp. 28–30) recommends that schools make the following provisions to deal with the aftermath of a crisis:

- Help parents understand children's reactions to violence.
- Help teachers and other staff deal with their reactions to the crisis.
- Help students and faculty adjust after the crisis.
- Help victims and family members of victims reenter the school environment.
- Help students and teachers address the return of a previously removed student to the school community.

In recent years, grief counseling has become an important component of postcrisis intervention. Most school systems now have a team of individuals who are "on call" in case of an emergency. The team may consist of counselors and psychologists employed by the school district who have received special training. Private psychologists and representatives of local churches and youth organizations also may be involved. Grief counseling allows individuals to express their sadness over the loss of a classmate or a traumatic event and share their fears regarding personal safety and their own mortality. Members of an intervention team can help clarify the facts surrounding a crisis and dispel any rumors that may be circulating. Another important function that team members can perform is the identification and referral of individuals who require intensive postcrisis assistance.

Postcrisis plans often include schoolwide meetings to discuss incidents and, when lives have been lost, memorial services. The American Association of Suicidology, in its guidelines for schools dealing with a student suicide, counsel, however, against a large-scale memorial service or assembly when students take their own lives (Poland, 1994, p. 185).

Once a crisis ends, the crisis management team should meet to debrief the incident, gather facts, and assess the effectiveness of the school's response. No crisis management plan is perfect, and team members should be encouraged to raise concerns and make suggestions about how to improve crisis and postcrisis interventions. Following a thorough analysis of the crisis and the team's response, the crisis management team needs to prepare and file an official report with the superintendent.

Beyond grief counseling, schoolwide meetings, and team debriefing are the actions of individual staff members in the wake of a crisis. All the careful planning in the world may come to naught if teachers ignore the emotional needs of students or administrators deal with parents in an insensitive and unsympathetic way (Kadel & Follman, 1994, p. 146). Staff members should receive training on how to deal with the aftermath of a crisis. Such training must emphasize the fact that the negative consequences of a traumatic event may take weeks or months to surface. A year after the Columbine High School tragedy, a student who had witnessed it took his own life. Although his reasons were not fully understood, it is possible that depression related to the violent loss of classmates played a key role.

Staff members themselves are not immune to the delayed effects of a traumatic incident. In a caring school community, adults look after each other as well as students. Postcrisis plans may include small support groups for staff members who need opportunities to discuss their feelings.

Conclusion

The fifth standard of a school that is safe for all students requires that school authorities develop plans for dealing with emergencies. It may be impossible to prevent a random act of violence or a natural disaster, but by having clear guidelines regarding what to do when a crisis arises, school personnel can reduce the likelihood of miscommunication, confusion, injury, and possible loss of life. Guidelines should cover such matters as who receives word that an emergency exists, the responsibilities of members of the crisis management team, and when outside assistance needs to be sought.

Crisis management involves planning what to do in the aftermath of a crisis as well as during it. The residual effects of traumatic events may be almost as harmful as the actual events. Educators need to be alert to signs of anxiety, fear, and depression. Provisions for special counseling, school meetings to reflect on crises, and contacts with parents frequently are part of postcrisis planning. School authorities also must be prepared to deal with media representatives regarding the details of emergency situations and the school's efforts to handle them.

REFERENCES

Blair, Julie. "States Seek to Defuse School Bomb Scares," *Education Week* (May 10, 2000), pp. 22, 26.

Blauvelt, Peter D. *Making Schools Safe for Students.* Thousand Oaks, CA: Corwin, 1999.

Cohen, Sheryl. *Principals' Experiences with School Crises.* Ph.D. Dissertation, University of Virginia, May 1998.

Grech, Daniel. "Security Drills, or Scares?" *Washington Post* (September 13, 1999), pp. B1, B5.

Kadel, Stephanie, and Follman, Joseph. "Crisis Management and Response." In Phillip Harris (ed.), *Violence and the Schools.* Palatine, IL: IRI/Skylight Publishing, 1994, pp. 139–159.

New York State. "School Crisis Response Guide," Albany, NY: Author, Office of the Lieutenant Governor, 1999.

Poland, Scott. "The Role of School Crisis Intervention Teams to Prevent and Reduce School Violence and Trauma," *School Psychology Review,* vol. 23, no. 2 (1994), pp. 175–189.

Portner, Jessica. "Florida District Is Partially Responsible for Student's Suicide, U.S. Judge Rules," *Education Week* (May 17, 1995), p. 9.

Portner, Jessica. "School Violence Down, Report Says, But Worry High," *Education Week* (April 12, 2000), p. 3.

Stapleton, Paul D. "Superintendent's Memo No. 182, October 1, 1999," Virginia Department of Education.

U.S. Department of Education. *A Guide to Safe Schools.* Washington, DC: Author, 1998.

Virginia Department of Education. *Resource Guide for Crisis Management in Schools.* Richmond: Author, 1998.

8

Standard 6: School Facilities Designed for Safety

MAJOR IDEAS IN CHAPTER 8

- Behavior is influenced by the physical environment.
- Student movement into and out of school and from class to class is a major source of safety problems.
- School facilities can be designed in ways that reduce the likelihood of safety problems and enhance student and staff well-being.
- Safety problems can result when schools grow too large or become overcrowded.
- A major goal of school design should be to facilitate adult supervision of student activities.
- A variety of security technology is available to safety-conscious educators.

Anyone who has driven on a new interstate highway and an old country road is likely to understand the relationship between the design of physical space and safety. The old country road may have sharp turns, blind entrances, unbanked curves, no shoulders, and other conditions that make safe driving a challenge. The new interstate, on the other hand, has been designed with safety in mind. The highway is divided to prevent head-on collisions. Access roads are limited to control traffic flow and reduce accidents. Curves are lengthened and often banked to allow drivers to maintain a constant rate of speed without the fear of losing control. Shoulders are provided in case drivers need to pull over in an emergency. Signage is clear and displayed well in advance of exits.

Schools, like roads, can be designed to promote the safety and well-being of students and staff. Corridors, for example, can be wide and well lit, reducing the likelihood that students bump into each other and permitting easy visual supervision by staff members. Older schools, unfortunately, often have narrow corridors and poor lighting, making the change of classes and hall supervision more difficult. These schools need extensive renovation to eliminate hazards and reduce the likelihood of safety problems. This chapter explores various aspects of school facilities that can affect safety.

> **Standard 6:** The physical environment of the school has been designed to promote the safety and well-being of students.

The chapter opens with a discussion of safety problems that may be caused, or at least affected, by the physical design of schools. Ways that schools can be designed, or redesigned, to reduce these problems is the subject of the next part. Ideas regarding traffic flow, supervision, controlled access, and outdoor safety are presented. The last part of the chapter considers how good design can go beyond addressing problems to creating pleasant and inviting surroundings for young people.

The Impact of Physical Environment on Behavior

No one disputes the fact that human beings are incredibly adaptable. Learning can occur virtually anywhere and under an infinite variety of conditions. Just because some people can learn in harsh and hostile settings does not mean, though, that no thought should be invested in designing safe and comfortable schools. The goal of educational design is to discover optimal ways to arrange the physical environment in order to promote effective and meaningful learning. Because people have a right to feel safe in school and because learning is enhanced by a certain degree of order, good educational design must attend to safety matters as well as instructional needs.

Reviews of research (Duke, 1998; Irwin, 1978; McGuffey, 1982) have identified a variety of environmental factors that may affect how young people learn and behave in school. These factors include the size of the physical setting and how crowded it is, the condition of the facility, and the relationship between form and function. Lighting, ventilation, and acoustics play a role, as do aesthetics and the location of the facility. Because individuals are affected in different ways by particular design features, sweeping generalizations about the impact of the physical environment on behavior may be risky. Still, it is important to understand how particular individuals may be helped or hindered by the nature of the space they occupy.

In what ways may the physical features of schools adversely affect the behavior of some individuals, thereby reducing the likelihood of a safe and orderly learning environment?

Students must spend a portion of their time in school moving from one place to another. Movement presents opportunities for confusion, jostling, rushing, and disruption. When movement takes place in overcrowded schools or schools where corridors, stairways, and entrances have been poorly designed, the potential for problems is multiplied. One principal of a large suburban high school refers to the negative consequences of such conditions as "hall rage." She explains the phenomenon in the following way: "People are in a cramped situation. Everyone needs space around them. Good kids, nice kids, lose their temper when they've been stepped on for the 100th time, get elbowed or bumped, or drop stuff and can't pick it up." (Nakamura, 1998, p. A1)

The physical environment of school also can contribute to fear and anxiety by reducing the effectiveness of adult supervision. Supervision depends on visibility, for example. When schools are characterized by lengthy corridors, nooks and crannies, poor lighting, inadequate stairways, and barriers to good vision, staff members find it difficult to monitor student conduct. Students sometimes do not feel safe in certain parts of the school. A survey of school safety by the U.S. Departments of Education and Justice (Kaufman et al., 1998, p. 32), for example, found that 9% of the students aged 12 through 19 reported avoiding one or more places at school.

In one of the few studies of the relationship between safety at school and the physical environment, Astor, Meyer, and Behre (1999, p. 18) asked students in five high schools to locate on school maps where violent incidents occurred. The two least-safe areas by far were hallways and cafeterias. Interestingly, when teachers were interviewed, they tended to feel that it was not their professional responsibility to monitor these and other unsafe locations or to intervene and stop violent acts.

School safety may be adversely affected by uncontrolled access to school grounds and the school itself. When strangers and suspended or expelled students can enter school undetected, the potential for trouble increases greatly. Access is, to a substantial degree, a matter of design. Suggestions for improving access control will be discussed later in the chapter.

In many parts of the United States, students spend some time each day outside of the school building. They may congregate at the main entrance before or after school, socialize in a courtyard after lunch, visit the playground for recess, or have class outdoors in good weather. A variety of safety problems can occur during these times. When the locations of places for disembarking from and boarding school buses and automobiles are not well planned, the possibility of accidents increases. Dense foliage close to a school affords hiding places for potentially dangerous individuals. Play areas that are not well maintained and carefully designed can lead to injuries.

One way to handle safety problems related to the physical environment of the school is to hire more staff members, thereby increasing the capacity for direct supervision. Although such a strategy may be desirable, it is very expensive. The remainder of this chapter addresses ways to enhance school safety through thoughtful design and renovation of physical space and the application of appropriate security technology.

Safer Movement in and around School

In most cases, the likelihood of students sustaining injury is greater when they are moving than when they are stationary. Every day students move into and out of school buildings, from one class to another class, and around classrooms. They travel to and from the restroom, cafeteria, media center, computer lab, gymnasium, and athletic fields. In designing the physical environment of the school, it is important to address the following questions related to movement:

- How can the likelihood of safety problems resulting from movement within the school be reduced?
- How can adult supervision of student movement in school be facilitated through design?
- How can security technology be used to increase safe movement in school?
- How can students with physical disabilities be assured safe movement in school?
- How can the likelihood of safety problems arising from movement into and out of school and around campus be reduced?

Hallways and corridors are the arteries handling most student traffic in school. Campus-style schools have breezeways and pathways connecting permanent buildings as well as portable units. When these routes must handle large numbers of students, the potential for unintended as well as premeditated confrontations increases. It is difficult for staff members to supervise crowded corridors and detect when students are in trouble. Safe movement is hampered when lockers are located in corridors, and students must stop between classes to pick up books and materials. To promote safe movement and better supervision, schools need wide corridors free of lockers and other obstacles.

Recommendation 6.1: Design schools with wide corridors free of lockers and other obstacles.

In existing schools, it may not be possible to widen narrow corridors. Under such circumstances, school officials faced with crowded conditions may need to consider an alternative bell schedule. With more than 3,000 students, Centreville High School in Fairfax County, Virginia, decided to have 9th and 10th graders change classes on a different bell schedule from 11th and 12th graders. As a result, fights and disruptions between classes were reduced substantially (Nakamura, 1998, p. A1).

To deal with the challenge of lockers, some new schools are designed with locker "bays" located off corridors. Although it cuts down on traffic problems in corridors, this arrangement does not eliminate problems associated with students having to retrieve books during a brief period of time between classes. Locker bays can become just as congested and hard to monitor as crowded corridors.

Lockers can be located in homerooms as a way to reduce congestion. Another possibility is to eliminate lockers entirely. The need for lockers would be lessened substantially by purchasing an extra set of textbooks for every classroom and installing coathooks in every classroom. Students could leave their books at home and use the classroom text. Coats could be carried from class to class and hung up during instruction. An added benefit of eliminating lockers is the removal of hiding places for weapons, drugs, and contraband. What school administrator would not welcome relief from locker searches and the distribution of locker combinations?

Stairways represent another potential problem area. Building codes specify the key dimensions of school stairways (Castaldi, 1982, pp. 256–257), but additional considerations also may be necessary. Some schools are designed with stairways that are divided by railings into up lanes and down lanes. In other cases, stairways are designated either as "up" or "down" routes during class changes. These measures reduce the possibility of traffic congestion and accidents. Where railings are provided on stairs, they should be high enough to prevent students from being pushed against them and falling over.

No physical design, of course, can substitute for direct supervision by trained personnel, but good design can make the job of supervision much easier and more effective. It is important, for example, that hall monitors have unobstructed views of long corridors. If one monitor can stand at a central point and have clear sightlines down two corridors, the need for additional monitors is reduced.

Many schools supplement on-site supervision with remote monitoring of corridors. The use of security technology to enhance supervision of student movement will be addressed in the next part of the chapter.

Cafeterias present a special challenge for safety-conscious educators. Students must move through cafeteria lines, check out with a cashier, find a table at which to eat, consume their lunch, return their trays and dirty dishes, and exit within a relatively short period of time. Once again, good design can help reduce the likelihood of problems. Cafeterias should have more than one access point, so that departing students do not have to contend with students entering the cafeteria. In many new schools, cafeterias are designed as large open spaces, like the food courts found in shopping malls. Creekland Middle School, a middle school of more than 3,000 students in Gwinnett County, Georgia, deals with cafeteria congestion by designating traffic lanes. Students who have finished lunch, for instance, must drop off their trays and walk along the perimeter of the cafeteria to exit (Jacobson, 2000, p. 1). In this way they do not clog up the middle of the cafeteria where other students are eating.

Movement around a school, particularly a large and crowded one, is difficult enough for an able-bodied student, but the challenge becomes truly daunting for students with physical disabilities. The Americans with Disabilities Act and related legislation ensure that people with disabilities are accorded the same opportunities and access to services as other citizens. Barriers in the physical layout of a school that prevent disabled students from taking advantage of opportunities and services must be removed or access to a comparable learning environment must be provided (Earthman, 2000, p. 174). Schools need to provide ramps and elevators for wheelchair users, Braille labeling for students with poor vision, and visual warning systems for the hearing impaired. To reduce the possibility of injury during class changes, some students with disabilities may need to leave class a few minutes early or be accompanied by an aide or classmate.

> **Recommendation 6.2:** Provide disabled students with safe and ready access to all parts of the school.

Movement into and out of school, as well as around campus, presents designers with additional challenges. Signage must be clear for those unfamiliar with school facilities. Lighting should be sufficient to allow safe passage and effective supervision. One of the greatest threats to student safety outside of school involves vehicular traffic. Schools designed in recent years tend to separate bus unloading and loading areas from parking lots for staff and students. By directing those who arrive by bus and by car or on foot to different entrances, schools can reduce the likelihood of accidents and injuries.

> **Recommendation 6.3:** Provide different routes into and out of school for bus riders and students who arrive by car or walk to school.

Better Supervision through Design

When serious safety threats occur in school, they are unlikely to take place in occupied classrooms (Kaufman et al., 1998, p. 32). This is because a teacher is present to provide direct supervision, and the number of students to be supervised is relatively small. Safety problems tend to occur in places where adult supervision is absent or where the ratio of students to staff members is relatively high. These places include restrooms, corridors, cafeterias, and locker rooms.

Good design can help reduce threats to safety in nonclassroom space. The strategic location of administrative offices and teacher workrooms, for instance, is one way that design can improve supervision. Instead of clustering offices and workrooms in a central administration area, they should be distributed throughout the school at points where students need to be monitored. The New American School Design Project at the Massachusetts Institute of Technology developed the following recommendation (Strickland, 1994, pp. 49–50).

> To help assure that schools are safe spaces, administrative offices overlook courtyards and school entrances, teachers' offices are distributed throughout the buildings and have glass walls looking into stairwells and corridors, and corridor windows encourage the informal monitoring of indoor and outdoor spaces.

> **Recommendation 6.4:** Design offices, classrooms, and workrooms with large windows or glazed walls and distribute them throughout the school at key locations.

The new high school in Manassas Park, Virginia, was designed with teacher workrooms opposite student restrooms. The Grafton Middle and High School complex in York County, Virginia, has an assistant principal's office overlooking the atrium where students gather for breaks and lunch. Many secondary schools locate attendance, guidance, or administrative offices at each primary entrance to the school. Because workrooms and offices typically have staff members present throughout the day, they can serve as the basis for continuous supervision of places where students congregate.

If offices, classrooms, and workrooms are to be effective sources of indirect supervision, they should have large windows or glazed walls that permit clear views of the areas requiring monitoring. Teachers can watch activity in corridors during class. In addition, windows and glazed walls allow administrators, as they walk through the school, to ascertain quickly when teachers are having classroom management problems or need help.

Locker rooms can be the scene of fights, hazing, thefts, and vandalism. To improve locker room supervision, a glass-walled office for coaches, physical education teachers, or the athletic director should be located adjacent to each locker room. Lockers should be aligned so that someone sitting in the office can monitor every row of lockers. It is also helpful if lockers are relatively short so that visibility across the entire locker room is unimpaired.

The school clinic or nurse's complex also should be designed with supervision in mind. Because most schools have only one nurse or health clinician on duty, the individual must be able to observe students in the waiting area while attending to other students requiring medical assistance. Privacy needs may prevent the use of glazed walls, so the design of the clinic should permit direct supervision of waiting areas and examination areas from a central location. The clinic also must be equipped with a secure storage area for medications. The storage area should have an alarm system to ensure that it is not opened when the nurse is away from the clinic.

Restrooms are another area where safety problems frequently are reported. In some schools, many students suffer throughout the day because they are afraid to go to the restroom. To curtail the use of restrooms for purposes other than those for which they were intended, doorless entrances, such as those found in airports, should be provided. The absence of doors allows monitors to detect more readily cigarette smoke, calls for help, and raucous behavior.

To supplement supervision-enhancing designs, an increasing number of schools are turning to surveillance technology. This option is not without controversy, however.

Controversy
Should closed-circuit television and video cameras be used to monitor school facilities?

Today it is possible to install closed-circuit television systems (CCTV) and video cameras to monitor activities in parts of the school where on-site supervision is lacking or where problems frequently occur. Video surveillance may be considered for hallways, entry areas, parking lots, gymnasiums, and places where valuable equipment or money is kept, such as science laboratories, computer centers, cafeterias, and main office complexes. Monitoring can be scheduled for times when students are present, times when facilities are supposed to be unoccupied, or on a random basis. Video surveillance also can be arranged for school buses.

Proponents of video surveillance maintain that it fits well into a systematic approach to school safety, an approach that begins with deterrence and detection and extends to delay and response (Green, 1999, pp. 7–8). The mere presence of video cameras throughout the school, for example, may deter many students and intruders from carrying out their plans. If they do decide to proceed, surveillance equipment can detect and record their actions. Videotapes can be reviewed by security personnel as part of their investigations of incidents and eventually used as evidence in a trial.

Despite their obvious benefits, CCTV and video cameras are not without problems. Civil rights activists warn that the potential for invasion of privacy and misuse of video surveillance is great. Others contend that the presence of security technology "sends the wrong message" to students and undermines efforts to create a culture of caring and responsibility. A comprehensive review of research on school security technology commissioned by the National Institute of Justice (Green, 1999, p. 25) identified additional problems of a technical and practical nature:

- CCTV systems are expensive. Installation can also be expensive, as well as logistically difficult.
- Choosing the correct camera equipment requires some technical knowledge.
- A single camera can effectively view a smaller area than would be intuitively expected.
- Cameras can be stolen or vandalized.
- Ongoing maintenance and operational support are required.
- Insiders with full knowledge of the installed video system's capabilities can possibly circumvent the system to their advantage.
- If it becomes well known where cameras are being used at a school, students may simply move their misbehaviors to a different part of campus.

Another limitation of CCTV involves the challenge of continuous monitoring. Hylton (1996, p. 81) points out that prolonged observation of a television screen can have a hypnotic effect on a viewer. Research at the Sandia National Laboratories found that the attention span of most viewers will fall below acceptable levels after only 20 minutes of monitoring (Green, 1999, p. 30). Kosar and Ahmed (2000, p. 26) add, "A single person can be expected to effectively monitor no more than eight pictures from closed-circuit cameras at one time on a continuous basis."

Experts suggest that video surveillance is better suited to some security purposes than others. Green (1999, p. 25) does not recommend CCTV and video cameras as a means to prevent fights or weapons from being brought into school. She believes, though, that video technology is useful for determining who started a fight in the hall or stole a computer from the media center.

When incorporating video surveillance into a comprehensive design for school safety, educators need to attend to several key details. Lighting must be adequate, for instance, or else images will be too dark to be identifiable. Cameras should be housed in enclosures that are vandal-resistant and that offer protection from the elements (if located outdoors). It is important that cameras can be adjusted from a remote location, such as a monitoring center. Rather than assigning individuals to monitor CCTV on a continuous basis, viewing should be scheduled for times when problems are most likely to occur. If fights are a concern, for example, the best times for viewing may be when students are arriving at and leaving school and during class-changing times.

School Safety through Controlled Access

Much of this book has focused on ways to reduce the likelihood that students will harm themselves and their classmates. Schools are not impervious to threats from outsiders, however. Gang violence spills over onto campus. Intruders enter schools to steal property and take students hostage. Noncustodial parents attempt to remove children without permission. To protect students and staff members from unwanted visitors, it is important that schools are designed to control access to campuses and buildings.

Controlling access to school buildings is easier and more straightforward than controlling access to school grounds. The foci of efforts to control building access are doors and windows. During school hours, doors tend to be used more than windows by those entering school without permission. Windows can be equipped with alarms that indicate when someone is trying to enter or leave. If necessary, they can have bars to prevent entry. Doors, however, present a greater challenge, because they must be used on a regular basis and cannot be locked from the inside because of fire code regulations. Access can be controlled through a combination of direct supervision by school personnel, limited points of entry, and security technology. The latter include video surveillance of entry points, remote entry systems, metal detectors, motion sensors, and intruder alarms.

> **Recommendation 6.5:** Control access to school buildings and grounds by using a combination of direct supervision, limited points of entry, and security technology.

In order to prevent people who might threaten school safety from entering school buildings, it is helpful if staff members are able to distinguish unwanted strangers from those who have a legitimate reason to be in school. Uniforms and identification badges can be useful in identifying students, though these measures are not foolproof or without controversy. Visitors can be required to check in at the main office and receive a badge to indicate that they have done so. Probably the most reliable design strategy for facilitating recognition of strangers, however, is to limit the size of schools. It is much easier to determine who does and does not belong in a school of 400 than a school of 4,000. More will be said about the issue of school size later in the chapter.

For purposes of quick evacuation in the event of a fire, schools are required to have a specified number of doors leading outside. Additional doors may be needed so that students can go to playing fields and custodians can receive shipments of supplies. It is impossible for staff members to supervise every door on a continuous basis during the school day. Video surveillance can help determine when someone enters by a door other than the main entrance, but a video camera cannot prevent entry. The most effective way to prevent entry is to install doors that cannot be opened from the outside and equip them with alarms and electronic security panels. Panels can be networked and linked to a console that is monitored, either by school personnel or an outside agency. Outside hardware should be removed from all doors to make forced entry more difficult. Designated staff members should be assigned to check doors that are not equipped with alarms to make certain that they have not been propped open.

Another crucial element of access control involves key security. One staff member should be designated as the distributor of keys. A record should be kept of every individual to whom keys are given. All keys should be stored in the same place, and this storage place must be secure. Access to keys needs to be limited to the principal and the distributor of keys. Hylton (1996, pp. 211–212) recommends that only one duplicate key be kept on hand and that duplicate keys must never be checked out as a matter of convenience. Because rekeying an entire school is very expensive, master keys should be available to only a small number of individuals.

Many schools that have experienced security problems or that are located in high-crime areas require all students and staff members to carry an identification (ID) card. The ID card must be shown to individuals who are assigned to monitor main entrances to the school. Visitors have to report to the main office, display appropriate identification, sign in, and receive a special badge. Anyone who does not display a proper ID card or visitor's badge is reported immediately to school security personnel.

The technology now exists to combine access clearance with attendance-taking (Jennings, 2000). Students move their ID cards through a processing machine as they enter school. The machine automatically compiles an attendance list. It also can indicate which students cut class the previous day, thereby providing a quick way to identify attendance problems. Schools that adopt ID cards should avoid magnetic-strip cards, because they are relatively easy to duplicate. Kosar and Ahmed (2000, p. 25) recommend fixed-foil patterns in ID cards because they are very difficult to copy.

In the wake of fears that weapons are being brought into schools, metal detectors at main entry points have grown in popularity. Metal detectors include stationary, portal-type devices and handheld scanners. A comprehensive guidebook on security technology (Green, 1999, p. 65) reports that metal detectors can be effective at preventing most weapons from being brought into school, but only when they are used by properly trained individuals. Contrary to popular belief, metal detectors do not detect only metal; they reveal any material that will conduct an electric current. For this reason, training is required to distinguish weapons from other objects. Where there are a large number of conductive objects, such as a backpack, a metal detector may be less effective than a physical search. Searches, of course, take time and may constitute an invasion of privacy. If searches are done, they should be conducted randomly, so as not to delay student entry to school, or as a follow-up when a walk-through metal detector produces a signal. Handheld scanners may be more useful than stationary metal detectors, because they are portable and can be used at different entrances or elsewhere on campus.

Anyone who has gone through an airport metal detector knows that there is a routine that must be followed. Students and staff members must be clear about the procedures to be used with school metal detectors. If a portal-style detector is used, the entry area should be arranged so that traffic is directed to the metal detector and there is no way to circumvent the entry point. In large schools, several devices may be required in order to prevent unreasonable delays. Such delays can produce gridlock, frustration, and disruptive behavior.

Controlling access during times when students and staff members are arriving presents one set of problems, whereas controlling access during the rest of the school day is another matter entirely. School officials must decide whether to station a security officer at the main entrance at all times, provide a receptionist in the entry area, or rely on remote access control. Remote access control involves the use of CCTV outside the main entrance to the school. Someone in the main office can check on who wishes to enter the school before releasing the door lock.

Remote access control may not be practical in a large school that receives many visitors during the day. In such schools, locating a security officer's or receptionist's desk at the entrance probably makes more sense. The desk should be equipped with a concealed duress alarm or "panic button" in case the person monitoring entry to the school is confronted by a dangerous visitor (Green, 1999, pp. 113–119).

It is also important for others in the school to be able to call for help quickly. This is especially true for teachers in portable classrooms and other isolated parts of the school and campus. Duress alarms may not be as useful as pager devices with built-in panic buttons for staff members in these settings. Because pagers are portable, they can be used in situations when a stationary duress alarm may be unreachable. Signaling devices should provide the person receiving the call for help with the location of the individual requiring assistance.

Controlled access is more than a matter of monitoring entry to school buildings. Access also is a safety issue *within* school buildings. Schools should be designed so that sections that are not in use can easily be closed off. If the gymnasium or auditorium, for example, is used at night or on weekends, the rest of the school should be closed to visitors. Metal grates that descend from the ceiling or accordion-style barriers can be used to achieve this purpose when it is inappropriate to install locking doors. Areas that are likely to be used during nonschool hours should be equipped with restrooms and water fountains to eliminate the need to enter other parts of the school.

Recommendation 6.6: Design schools so that sections that are not used during nonschool hours can be closed to visitors.

Another good idea is to lock classrooms and other rooms when they are not in use. This provision cuts down on theft, vandalism, and the misuse of school facilities.

Figure 8.1 depicts the floor plan of a school that has been designed with safety and security in mind. The main entrance is flanked by glass-walled offices so that movement into and out of school can be monitored. In addition, a reception desk has been placed inside the main entrance so visitors can obtain information and permission to remain on the premises. Both the gymnasium and the auditorium can be used without opening up the rest of the school. Restrooms are individual units rather than communal facilities. The covered patio area is bordered by screening and glass to prevent access without limiting natural light and pleasing views. Classrooms have windows to permit views of hallways and exterior areas.

Safety on School Grounds

To ensure that all students are safe from the time they arrive at school until they leave, educators must attend to what goes on outside of school buildings as well as inside. Students spend considerable time milling around school entrances, walking between buildings and to portable classrooms, playing outside during recess and physical education classes, and receiving instruction in good weather. Can school grounds be designed to reduce threats to student safety?

Good design can help promote outdoor safety in various ways, depending on the nature of the school site. Rural and suburban schools with large tracts of open land, of course, present different challenges from urban schools with limited space. Fencing, for example, may be a more practical means to control access to school grounds for urban schools because the borders of school property are well defined and they can be more easily monitored by supervisory personnel. Schools with sprawling campuses may have fencing or natural barriers, but they are unlikely to be as effective at controlling access. Whenever a barrier is used to restrict access, Hylton (1996, p. 48) recommends that an unobstructed area, or "clear zone," be maintained on both sides of the barrier to permit easier visual surveillance.

Several issues arise regarding controlled access to school grounds. These issues relate to times when access control is desired and whether access control should

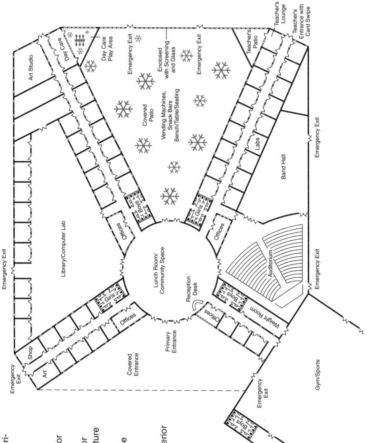

- Interior walls of administrative offices are primarily glass
- If school grows, extend classroom "wings"
- Restrooms are individual units
- Covered patio outer wall can be enclosed for winter
- Primary entrance can be easily enclosed for contraband detection if necessary in the future
- Emergency exits are alarmed
- Windows in classrooms where possible; use narrow glazing and glass block
- Avoid a flat roof that is easily accessible
- Minimize hiding places around building exterior

Not to Scale

FIGURE 8.1 A School Design That Incorporates Various Safety Features.

Source: Reprinted with permission of the National Institute of Justice. From Mary W. Green, *The Appropriate and Effective Use of Security Technologies in U.S. Schools.* Washington, DC, National Institute of Justice, U.S. Department of Justice, 1999, p. 20.

include vehicular as well as pedestrian traffic. Controlled access to school grounds during school hours generally requires the presence of supervisory or security staff, because gates and other barriers generally cannot be locked. It is also helpful if the main office is designed so that visual surveillance of parking lots and the main entrance is possible. After hours, security can be achieved by locking gates, providing perimeter lighting to help reveal intruders, and removing foliage near the school that might conceal individuals. Security patrol vehicles should be able to reach all parts of the campus as well as circumnavigate school buildings. Some schools also permit one or more mobile homes to be located on campus so that occupants can report trespassers. If the school is located in a neighborhood, a "Neighbor Watch" program can be initiated to encourage residents to report suspicious activity around the school.

If schools are isolated, intruders may have to rely on a vehicle. Controlling vehicular access, therefore, must also be a component of school security. Landscaping should prevent vehicles from reaching the immediate vicinity of the school except by established routes. These routes should be controlled by gates that can be locked when necessary. Many high schools that allow older students to drive to school require them to park in fenced and gated areas. During school hours these areas are locked to discourage students from leaving school without permission. A parking lot monitor is available to unlock the gate when necessary and to monitor student activities.

Recommendation 6.7: Design school grounds to control access to pedestrian and vehicular traffic.

Courtyards provide an excellent location for outdoor activities during school hours. Surrounded by one or more buildings, courtyards limit access and facilitate supervision. Students are less tempted to wander away or get into trouble. For maximum benefit, courtyards should be attractive, well maintained, and well lighted.

Play areas are a vital part of the elementary school program. To protect young children from strangers and discourage them from wandering off, play areas should be fenced. Playground equipment should be selected with student safety in mind and inspected frequently for damage that could result in injuries. Dunklee and Shoop (1993, pp. 89–90) recommend that surfaces under playground equipment consist of resilient materials such as bark, wood chips, or shredded tires. To facilitate supervision, play areas should include a mound or raised area from which activities in all locations can be viewed by monitors.

Designing Special Facilities

School systems sometimes must provide learning environments for students who require special supervision. These students may have been expelled from regular school or found to have serious behavioral and emotional problems. For whatever reason, their presence in a regular school is considered to pose a threat to other students' safety. Facilities for these students involve a variety of design challenges.

CASE IN POINT

The Ivy Creek School in Charlottesville, Virginia, serves as a regional alternative school for emotionally disturbed students. Previously located in a collection of unappealing trailers adjacent to a vocational–technical center, the new school was designed with considerable input from staff members. They understood how a poorly designed facility can undermine safety and effective learning.

Located on a woodsy lot, the $3 million facility looks less like a "lock-down" school than an attractive residence. High ceilings and lots of glass create an open feeling. The unbreakable glass serves a second purpose, providing supervisors with clear views of activities inside classrooms.

Access from one suite of classrooms to another is purposely limited so that students cannot wander off or disturb other classes. Each suite contains a time-out room for students unable to control their conduct. Light switches for time-out rooms are located outside of the rooms.

Other special safety features include recessed coat hooks, so students cannot be injured if they are pushed against them. Ceilings have no exposed beams, a suicide-prevention precaution. Furniture was selected because it lacked sharp edges.

It is not unusual to find alternative schools located in unattractive buildings such as abandoned elementary schools and warehouses (Duke, Griesdorn, & Kraft, 1998). Not only can these facilities contribute to safety problems through poor design, they reinforce the notion that those who attend them are "losers." The Ivy Creek School represents a different approach. Just because young people have behavioral and emotional disorders does not mean that they should be condemned to unpleasant settings. Providing these students with attractive and comfortable surroundings may be therapeutic and facilitate the work of their teachers.

When the author and his colleagues studied the design of alternative schools in Virginia, the most effective schools were found to pay close attention to the design of physical space (Duke, Griesdorn, & Kraft, 1998; Duke & Griesdorn, 1999). Study carrels, for example, were provided for students who were easily distracted by their classmates. Small meeting rooms were available for individual tutoring and teacher–student meetings requiring privacy. Space was provided for students to take a break, eat lunch, and get some exercise. Individual restrooms, rather than communal facilities, cut down on the need to supervise students.

Controversy
Can schools be designed to be too secure?

The preceding discussion raises a question. If alternative schools for troubled students can be designed to be pleasant and comfortable environments, why is it necessary to create schools that feel like prisons? There are people, of course, who feel strongly that students who are uncooperative or dangerous should not be "rewarded" by being sent to inviting environments. Others, however, argue that these young people should be given every opportunity to improve their behavior by being placed in secure, but not prisonlike settings.

Is it possible for designers to focus too much on safety and security? Can educators reach a point where their emphasis on supervision and behavior control is self-defeating?

These questions cannot be answered conclusively with the present corpus of research on school safety. It would be necessary, for example, to track schools for long periods of time in order to determine whether a point is reached when additional safety and disciplinary measures become counterproductive. Most studies of school safety initiatives assess impacts for a relatively brief period. Programs aimed at reducing the likelihood of violence, substance abuse, and behavior problems are notorious for being short-lived.

In designing schools that are safe for all students, educators should remember that the vast majority of students are rule-abiding and cooperative. They do not pose a threat to their own well-being or the well-being of others. Efforts to protect these students from harm should not so limit or restrict them that they have little incentive to behave responsibly.

As for facilities intended for students with a track record of behavior problems and dangerous activities, there are ways to minimize safety threats without creating an overly harsh environment. Instead of eliminating windows, for example, safety-conscious designers can use unbreakable glass. Graffiti-resistant surfaces and recessed fixtures in restrooms can be used to reduce vandalism without conveying a sense of restriction. Students who may be tempted to disturb each other can be separated if instructional space is not cramped and poorly furnished. If prisons can be air-conditioned to reduce discontent among the incarcerated, why cannot schools be equipped with effective cooling units? Good design may not prevent all threats to safety, but it can reduce the likelihood of problems and minimize their impact when they do arise.

Environmental Enhancement through Design

The discussion so far has concentrated on ways that design can address specific safety concerns such as student movement and access to school buildings and grounds. Design, though, is not just a way to reduce problems. At its best, good school design can create settings that enrich, inspire, and promote effective teaching and learning. To conclude this chapter, let us examine several ways that the quality of life in schools can be improved through design.

If one design idea has attracted attention in recent years, it concerns downsizing schools. Research has found that larger schools are more likely to experience serious discipline problems (Duke, 1998, pp. 22–23). When problems do arise, school size may affect how they are handled. Administrators in large schools must cover more territory, for example, thereby slowing their response time when problems occur. It is more difficult to recognize students by name or to distinguish between students and strangers in a large school.

School size also can have social and academic consequences. The likelihood that students will feel isolated, alienated, and disengaged increases in larger schools (Lee, Bryk, & Smith, 1993, p. 188). School size also has been found to be inversely related to student achievement as measured by standardized tests (Keller, 2000; Lee & Smith, 1997). A large study of the impact of school size found that the optimal size of high schools was between 600 and 900 students (Lee & Smith, 1997).

One way to limit school size is to build small schools from scratch. This option may not be available, however, in many school systems that already have large high schools. A second design strategy is to subdivide existing schools into subunits, variously known as houses, academies, or schools-within-a-school. Subunits may be organized by grade level or academic theme; although in many cases they are made up by random assignment of students. Typically consisting of 300 to 500 students and a team of teachers representing different disciplines, each subunit enjoys a measure of spatial and administrative integrity. They often are defined by corridors, wings, or floors. Each subunit may be headed by its own assistant principal and include a guidance counselor. Subdividing large schools into smaller units allows a team of teachers to get to know a group of students very well, reducing the chances that some students will feel isolated and that their particular needs will be overlooked.

CASE IN POINT

When concerns about overcrowding in the high school arose in the mid-nineties, the central administration of Danville City Public Schools (Virginia) considered building a second high school but decided such a project was unrealistic. That is when the idea of creating focus schools surfaced as an alternative strategy for reducing overcrowding.

The school system converted a nearby junior high school that was no longer in use to a satellite campus for the focus schools. Teachers in the district were invited to propose ideas for focus schools. The first four focus schools included the Business Partnership Academy, Global Village School, Global Studies through Arts and Technology School, and EXCEL, a school offering a rigorous academic curriculum. Each school consisted of between 100 and 160 students and 8 to 12 teachers.

A two-year study of the focus schools (Butin, 2000) found that student achievement on state tests improved, attendance climbed, dropping out was curtailed, and serious behavior problems declined. In addition, overcrowding at the main high school was alleviated.

Focus-school operations are coordinated by an administrator who reports to the principal of George Washington High School.

School size is less of a problem for elementary and middle schools than high schools, but when these schools grow too large, design solutions also are available. Middle schools can be organized into pods or teams consisting of four core academic teachers and approximately 100 students. Each team shares a common section of the school so that teachers can regroup or combine students for different purposes. Large elementary schools can be subdivided into "families" and "neighborhoods" using existing corridors and wings. A "family" consists of several contiguous classrooms for students at the same grade level, and a "neighborhood" may involve one each of first-, second-, third-, fourth-, and fifth-grade classrooms, all located on the same corridor. These arrangements facilitate cooperation and joint planning among teachers and provide a more personalized learning environment for students.

Recommendation 6.8: Build or subdivide schools so that students feel they are members of a personalized learning environment.

Besides downsizing schools, designers can help create classrooms that enhance learning and reduce the likelihood of behavior problems. Classrooms that are arranged into different areas for different types of learning activities, for example, reduce the possibility that students engaged in noisy activities will disturb students requiring quiet for focused attention. Designers can provide storage areas that allow students to retrieve books and materials without disrupting instructional activities. Good lighting, acoustics, and temperature control enhance learning and cut down on behavior problems. It is helpful if every classroom has an area where the teacher can meet with a student in relative privacy.

It may sound strange to say that physical space communicates, but people do, in fact, receive "messages" from their surroundings. In *Savage Inequalities*, Kozol (1991) poignantly describes the message conveyed to students who inhabit poorly maintained, rundown schools in impoverished urban school systems. The message is painfully direct: "You don't matter." It has been estimated that 14 million students attend schools in need of extensive repairs and replacements (U.S. Department of Education, 1998, p. 4).

How can young people feel valued if they are compelled to attend schools that are unsightly, poorly ventilated, and deteriorating? It stands to reason that students are more likely to obey school rules and behave appropriately when they learn in attractive, well-kept environments. Pride in one's school can translate into heightened self-esteem. Schools constitute a community's tangible commitment to the next generation. How schools are designed and maintained, therefore, speaks volumes concerning how adults feel about young people.

Conclusion

School safety involves more than clear expectations, contingency plans, and trained personnel. This chapter has explored various ways in which the design of physical space and security technology can promote the well-being of students and staff members. Because students often feel more safe in some parts of the school than others, educators need to consider environmental improvements in places such as corridors, stairways, restrooms, locker rooms, and cafeterias, where problems tend to occur.

School facilities can be designed in ways that reduce the likelihood of problems resulting from student movement to and from class. Design enhances supervision through better lighting, unobstructed spaces, glazed surfaces, and the location of administrative offices. Hard-to-supervise nooks and crannies can be eliminated. Where design cannot reduce threats to safety, security technology may be of assistance. Available to safety-conscious educators is a variety of sophisticated equipment, including metal detectors and scanners, closed-circuit television and video surveillance cameras, duress alarms, and special locking systems for doors.

School facilities can be designed in ways that enhance the quality of daily life in school as well as address specific security problems. Well-designed and well-maintained schools convey to students in very concrete ways that they are valued by their community. By designing smaller schools and redesigning large schools into smaller units, educators can reduce feelings of isolation and foster more caring learning environments. Classrooms, too, can be designed to be more functional, orderly, and inviting.

R E F E R E N C E S

Astor, Ron Avi; Meyer, Heather Ann; and Behre, William J. "Unowned Places and Times: Maps and Interviews about Violence in High Schools," *American Educational Research Journal,* vol. 36, no. 1 (Spring, 1999), pp. 3–42.

Butin, Dan W. *Rethinking High School: A Study of Focus Schools in Danville, Virginia.* Charlottesville, VA: Thomas Jefferson Center for Educational Design, University of Virginia, 2000.

Castaldi, Basil. *Educational Facilities,* second edition. Boston: Allyn & Bacon, 1982.

Duke, Daniel L. "Does It Matter Where Our Children Learn?" Charlottesville, VA: Thomas Jefferson Center for Educational Design, University of Virginia, 1998.

Duke, Daniel L., and Griesdorn, Jacqueline. "Considerations in the Design of Alternative Schools," *The Clearing House,* vol. 73, no. 2 (November/December 1999), pp. 89–92.

Duke, Daniel L.; Griesdorn, Jacqueline; and Kraft, Mike. "A School of Their Own: A Status Check of Virginia's Alternative High Schools for At-Risk Students." Charlottesville, VA: Thomas Jefferson Center for Educational Design, University of Virginia, 1998.

Dunklee, Dennis R., and Shoop, Robert J. *A Primer for School Risk Management.* Boston: Allyn & Bacon, 1993.

Earthman, Glen I. *Planning Educational Facilities for the Next Century.* Reston, VA: Association of School Business Officials International, 2000.

Green, Mary W. *The Appropriate and Effective Use of Security Technologies in U.S. Schools.* Washington, DC: National Institute of Justice, U.S. Department of Justice, 1999.

Hylton, J. Barry. *Safe Schools: A Security and Loss Prevention Plan.* Boston: Butterworth-Heinemann, 1996.

Irwin, F. Gordon. "Planning Vandalism Resistant Educational Facilities*," Journal of Research and Development in Education,* vol. 11, no. 2 (Winter 1978), pp. 42–52.

Jacobson, Linda. "Huge Middle School Has Big Job in Feeling Smaller to Its Students," *Education Week* (May 10, 2000), pp. 1, 16–17.

Jennings, Mark. " 'Attendance Technology' Easing Recordkeeping Burden," *Education Week* (May 10, 2000), p. 7.

Kaufman, P.; Chen, X.; Choy, S. P.; Chandler, K. A.; Chapman, C. D.; Rand, M. R.; and Ringel, C. *Indicators of School Crime and Safety, 1998.* Washington, DC: U.S. Departments of Education and Justice, 1998.

Keller, Bess. "Small Schools Found to Cut Price of Poverty," *Education Week* (February 9, 2000), p. 6.

Kosar, John E., and Ahmed, S. Faruq. "Building Security into Schools," *The School Administrator,* vol. 57, no. 2 (February 2000), pp. 24–26.

Kozol, Jonathan. *Savage Inequalities.* New York: Crown, 1991.

Lee, Valerie E.; Bryk, Anthony S.; and Smith, Julia B. "The Organization of Effective Secondary Schools." In Linda Darling-Hammond (ed.), *Review of Research in Education,* vol. 19. Washington, DC: American Educational Research Association, 1993, pp. 171–267.

Lee, Valerie E., and Smith, Julia B. "High School Size: Which Works Best and for Whom?" *Educational Evaluation and Policy Analysis,* vol. 19, no. 3 (1997), pp. 205–227.

McGuffey, C. W. "Facilities." In H. J. Walberg (ed.), *Improving Educational Standards and Productivity.* Berkeley: McCutchan, 1982, pp. 237–288.

Nakamura, David. "At Crowded Suburban Schools, Frustration Turns to 'Hall Rage'," *Washington Post* (April 25, 1998), pp. A1, A10.

Strickland, Roy. "Designing the New American School: Schools for an Urban Neighborhood," *Teachers College Record,* vol. 96, no. 1 (Fall 1994), pp. 32–57.

U.S. Department of Education. "America's Schools Are Overcrowded and Wearing Out." Washington, DC: Author, 1998.

9

Standard 7:
School Safety and
Community Support

MAJOR IDEAS IN CHAPTER 9

- School safety efforts depend, to a great extent, on parent and community support.
- The breakdown of families has had a major impact on school-based efforts to promote safety.
- Agencies and groups that serve young people may not necessarily work together effectively to promote safety.
- Successful school–community initiatives address safety issues in a comprehensive way.
- By supporting the well-being of families, schools and communities can contribute to safe schools.

School safety is more than a matter of what goes on in school. Every school exists within a community, and what happens in the community can have a substantial impact on the well-being of students and staff members. Communities may be supportive of, indifferent to, or resistant to school-based efforts to protect students. Many of the resources upon which safety-conscious educators rely are derived from community expertise, energy, and pocketbooks. Problems in communities, from youth gangs to drugs, spill over into schools, disrupting learning and destroying young lives.

With community support, there is much that educators can do to promote safe schools for all students. Across the United States, alliances between educators and parents have raised awareness of the need for safer schools and communities. Partnerships between schools and various community agencies, from police departments to hospitals, are addressing specific safety needs. Programs have been created to help young people when they are not in school and to assist parents in doing a better job of raising their children.

> **Standard 7:** Parents and community members are involved in and committed to efforts to create and maintain safe schools.

This chapter begins with a brief overview of the changing community context of public education in the United States and how these changes can affect school-based safety efforts. The discussion then shifts to community resources that can assist educators concerned about the safety and well-being of young people. These resources range from parents and policy makers to youth groups and businesses. The obstacles that may need to be overcome in order to gain community support are addressed. The chapter closes with examples of how communities and educators can work together to combat threats to school safety.

The Changing Community Context of Schools

To understand schooling requires an understanding of the communities in which schools exist. The relationship between schools and communities is complex, for the community is simultaneously a source of threats to school safety and a wellspring of material and moral support in the campaign for safer schools. Whatever changes a community experiences are sure to impact its schools and their efforts to safeguard young people.

Evidence strongly suggests that communities in the United States are changing in important ways. Perhaps the most profound change involves the character and composition of the American family. Other changes range from the increased availability to young people of drugs and firearms to media-induced desensitization to violence. Garbarino (1997, pp. 13–14) contends that today's youth grow up in a "socially toxic environment," a social world that is "poisonous to their development."

Popenoe (1994, p. 95) observes that the family is the bedrock of civil society, the primary source of instruction regarding such crucial civic values as honesty, trust, self-sacrifice, and personal responsibility. Parents serve as their children's first teachers and as powerful role models during childhood. When the welfare of the family is jeopardized, the potential adverse effects on schools and communities are enormous. The past half century unfortunately has witnessed the steady erosion of the family as a stable and constructive social asset.

From 1985 to 1995, the percentage of families with children headed by a single parent increased from 22% to 26% (Annie E. Casey Foundation, 1998, p. 23). In some poor urban areas, the percentage exceeds 50%. Add to the number of single-parent families those with two parents who have experienced divorce and remarried, and it becomes clear that a substantial number of young people in the United States have had to cope, or are coping, with stresses and strains at home. These stresses and strains become manifest in various ways, including school absenteeism, acting-out behavior, withdrawal, and declining academic performance.

In a review of changes in the American family, Yankelovich (1994, p. 33) noted that approximately 70% of the households in the 1950s "consisted of a male bread-winner, a female homemaker, and two or more children under the age of 18 living at home." Although this image of the family still lingers in the public imagination, fewer than 1 out of 10 families fit the image today (Yankelovich, 1994, pp. 33–34). A substantial number of adults, for example, live together without children. Many families consist of two parents, both of whom work outside the home.

Along with these changes in families have come shifts in beliefs. From the middle to the late 1980s, for example, the number of Americans who felt that "the family is the place where most basic values are instilled" fell from 82% to 62% (Yan-kelovich, 1994, p. 35). A study by the National Opinion Research Center in 1999 found that having an obedient child was less important to adults than it had been a decade earlier (Cohn, 1999). The director of the research center noted that "strictness and discipline have given way to a more liberal approach to raising and guiding chil-dren" (Cohn, 1999). This change comes as no surprise, given the number of families in which the parent or parents work. It is difficult for parents to impose strict disci-pline when children come home to empty houses.

As welfare rolls were pared in the 1990s, many parents who had stayed at home found themselves forced to enter the workforce. One consequence of this change has been to increase the number of young children in need of day care for all or some portion of the day. In 1998 the Annie E. Casey Foundation (1998, p. 6) estimated that almost 29 million American children under the age of 13 required child care. Regret-tably, many of these children are not receiving any consistent type of before-school or after-school care. The National Survey of America's Families, conducted in 1997, estimated that 4 million children between the ages of 6 and 12 were routinely caring for themselves while their parents were working (Jacobson, September 13, 2000).

Homelessness has long been a concern in the urban centers of the nation, but until recently it involved mostly adults. In contemporary society, an increasing number of families with children are compelled to live on the streets. Other families with modest means regularly relocate as they find themselves unable to afford rent. Homelessness and transience deprive young people of the stability they need to de-velop constructive relationships with peers and school personnel. The overall strong economy in the United States in the 1990s concealed a substantial number of families who failed to benefit from a decade of growth.

Communities are changing in other ways as well. A majority of Americans no longer reside in cities, for example. Suburbs now are home to the largest percentage of Americans. For many working parents, this shift means longer commutes to and from work and less time at home with children. Some studies indicate that the amount of time parents spend with their children in constructive activities has declined in recent decades by as much as 50% (Garbarino, 1997, p. 14).

Once predominantly white and middle class, suburbs are beginning to resemble cities in their economic, racial, and cultural diversity. Between 1980 and 1990, the percentage of Latino/Hispanics in the United States rose by 53%, and the number of Asian and Pacific Islanders more than doubled (Soriano, Soriano, & Jimenez, 1994, p. 217). Spanish no longer can be considered a foreign language in the United States. Diversity, of course, can be a great asset, but it also can produce tensions as individuals from different backgrounds try to adjust to living together. Sometimes these tensions are manifested in the formation of gangs based on race and ethnicity.

Schools Feel the Impact of Changing Communities

Changes in the family along with other changes in the composition and character of communities have affected public education and the quest for safe schools in various ways. Although some of the impacts have been constructive, many have not. Perhaps the most damaging effects have resulted from the destabilization of the family. Elliott, Williams, and Hamburg (1998, p. 380) conclude from a review of research that many young people are raised in "environments that provide neither consistent structure nor a basic sense of safety and, therefore, these children lack the internal psychological structure necessary for achieving a sense of autonomy, competence, and pride in academic, social, and personal endeavors." The seriousness of this problem was brought home when a six-year-old boy from Mount Morris Township, Michigan, brought a gun to school and fatally wounded a first-grade classmate (Claiborne, 2000). When police checked out the boy's living situation, they discovered that he was forced to live in a rundown crack house with his uncle, who was wanted by the police. The boy's father was in jail for parole violation, and his mother had abandoned him. The importance of very young children developing attachments to caring adults has been demonstrated in numerous studies. Young people who go through childhood without these attachments are much more likely to experience intellectual, emotional, social, and moral problems (Popenoe, 1994, p. 99).

When family instability results in separation, divorce, single parenting, loss of income, and child abuse, schools suffer the consequences (Loeber & Stouthamer-Loeber, 1998, pp. 111–115). Children miss school more frequently and do less well in their schoolwork. Displaced frustration and anger over family problems results in acting out and disruptive behavior at school. When children are forced to switch schools because of family changes, their established bonds with teachers and friends are severed. Moving to a new school is a challenge under the best of circumstances. When the move is accompanied by problems at home, the challenge may be too great for some children to manage.

The increase in families in which the only parent or both parents work outside the home presents schools with additional concerns. So-called "latchkey" children who leave school and go home to empty houses are more likely to get into trouble than children who are supervised after school. A report published by the National Institute of Justice (Sherman et al., 1997) indicated that the largest proportion of delinquent and antisocial acts by school-age children were committed between the hours of 3:00 P.M. and 6:00 P.M., hours when many young people are relatively free of adult supervision. In communities in which neighborhood crime is high, some children may be so afraid to go home that they try to remain at school (Lorion, 1998, p. 299).

As the number of working parents increases, schools find it harder to involve parents in their children's education. Exhausted after a day's work and still facing household chores, parents are less available for school functions, after-school conferences, parent-education classes, PTA meetings, and other activities. When students violate school rules and must be sent home, it is difficult to reach working parents and arrange for them to pick up their children.

One of the most disturbing consequences of these changes in families and communities is the growing gulf between generations. When adults spend less time listening to and interacting with young people in general, as well as their own children, the prospects for cross-generational understanding and collective action for the sake of young people decline. Hersch (1998, p. 20) puts it bluntly when she writes:

> It is a problem not just for families but for communities when the generations get so separated. The effects go beyond issues of rules and discipline to the idea exchanges between generations that do not occur, the conversations not held, the guidance and role-modeling not taking place...How can kids imitate and learn from adults if they never talk to them?

Changes in the family are undeniably affecting schools and their ability to provide safe havens for young people. It is also the case, however, that families are products of the communities in which they reside. As Schorr (1997, p. 307) succinctly puts it, "The research makes clear...that the capacity of families to do their child-rearing job is powerfully dependent on the health of their communities." When streets and neighborhoods are unsafe, adults are less likely to supervise and become involved with young people. Parents have fewer sources of support readily available. Young people who are exposed to violence where they live may be more prone to emotional distress, aggressive behavior, and academic difficulties (Lorion, 1998, pp. 302–304).

Given the close relationship between what goes on in school, at home, and in the community, it is unlikely that significant progress in school safety can be made without carefully planned and collaborative efforts involving educators, parents, and other citizens. It is of little long-term benefit to address threats to safety at school and ignore them in the community or to focus solely on crime and violence in neighborhoods and leave schools to fend for themselves. The ultimate goal is to create safe communities in which young people can learn, grow, play, and contribute. If communities are safe, schools will be safe.

Recommendation 7.1: Develop plans that address safety in school, at home, and in the community, and that involve educators, parents, and various community organizations.

Sources of Support in the Safe School Campaign

Efforts to make schools safe for all students involve two kinds of initiatives. The first aims directly at reducing dangerous activities at school. The second focuses on reducing dangerous activities in the entire community. To be effective, both initiatives require collective action among educators and other community members. Important contributors to these safety efforts include parents, community leaders, law enforcement agencies, courts, youth organizations, social service agencies, churches, higher education institutions, hospitals, businesses, and the media. In what ways can these "human resources" and organizations help to achieve safe schools and communities?

Parents

Just because more parents are working outside the home does not mean that they are always unwilling or unable to work with educators concerned about safe schools. It does mean, though, that educators must be more creative and flexible in their requests for help. Wuthnow (1998, p. 77) finds that the rate of individual volunteering in the United States actually has been increasing, a sign that civic responsibility has not fallen prey to busy schedules.

Parents may contribute individually and collectively to school safety. On an individual basis, for instance, parents can familiarize themselves with the code of conduct at their children's school and stay in touch with teachers so they know when their children are experiencing problems. Parents can request school conferences and attend them when invited. Parental support for school-based discipline is crucial to the success of these efforts. Some schools have found that an effective antidote to persistent disruptive behavior is to require that parents come to school and observe their child.

The U.S. Department of Education's *A Guide to Safe Schools* (1998, p. 15) contains a lengthy list of ways that parents can help create safe schools. Among the tips are the following:

- Discuss the school's discipline policy with your child. Show your support for the rules, and help your child understand the reasons for them.
- Involve your child in setting rules for appropriate behavior at home.
- Talk with your child about the violence he or she sees—on television, in video games, and possibly in the neighborhood. Help your child understand the consequences of violence.
- Help your child find ways to show anger that do not involve verbally or physically hurting others. When you get angry, use it as an opportunity to model these appropriate responses for your child—and talk about it.

The primary contribution that parents make to school safety, of course, is to raise their children to respect others and value good behavior, safety, and rules.

Parents also can affect school safety by helping their children do well academically. Research indicates that student achievement is enhanced when parents help organize and monitor their child's time, assist on homework assignments, and discuss school matters with their child (Finn, 1998, pp. 20–21). Young people who meet academic expectations are less likely to get into trouble at school or pose a threat to their classmates.

Parents can further the cause of school safety through collective action as well as individual efforts. By banding together in PTAs and ad hoc organizations, parents can raise awareness of safety issues, put pressure on educators and policy makers to allocate resources to safety initiatives, and become directly involved in school-based efforts to reduce violence, drug and alcohol use, and other problems. Teams of parent volunteers provide additional assistance by escorting children to and from school, monitoring halls and playgrounds, and phoning parents when their children miss school.

Recommendation 7.2: Encourage parents individually and collectively to become involved in school and community safety initiatives.

CASE IN POINT

Parents in Pelham, New York, became concerned about the safety of their middle and high school students after hearing reports of alcohol and drugs at weekend parties. Joining with educators and community leaders, they formed Parents and Community Together (PACT) and developed an action agenda to reduce risks to young people.

PACT compiled a drug and alcohol awareness handbook for parents and sponsored speakers on various topics related to the welfare of young people and families. An e-mail address was created to promote sharing of concerns among parents. One concern that attracted PACT's attention was the willingness of some parents to allow their children to host parties at which alcohol was served and adult supervision was absent. The organization raised awareness of these parties and encouraged parents to know where their children were going in the evening and on weekends.

Besides working on a safer community, PACT joined with the Pelham School District to promote safer schools. A student-assistance counselor was hired as a result of PACT lobbying, and a districtwide effort to create caring school communities was initiated.

Nonparents

Although parents play a pivotal role in community-based efforts to protect young people, other individuals in the community also can contribute a great deal. Grandparents, married adults without children, and single adults often have a keen interest in the well-being of local young people. These individuals can serve as mentors, Big

Brothers and Sisters, school volunteers, and sources of special expertise concerning the problems faced by young people. Nonparents can sponsor safety programs, participate in planning comprehensive school and community safety initiatives, and help in locating resources. Because adults without children in public schools generally outnumber those with children in schools, educators must have the support of the former if they are to generate the political pressure necessary to improve safety policies and increase allocations for safety initiatives.

Community Leaders

It is impossible to mount a large-scale campaign for school and community safety without adequate leadership. Such a campaign requires funds, direction, and the mobilization of human energy. Educators need to become skilled at enlisting the support of community leaders, including elected and appointed officials. These individuals are in a position to know where to look for funds and expertise, both within the community and outside. They can be instrumental in sponsoring new or revised policies related to safety. Such policies may include curfews, bans on private parties without adult supervision, and weapons buyback programs.

A trend over the past few decades has been for localities to create youth commissions representing various agencies and groups that serve the needs of young people. One central task of such bodies is the development of a comprehensive strategic plan for addressing the needs of young people. Such plans may cover a variety of issues, including educational opportunities, teenage health problems, youth employment, social services, juvenile justice, and recreation. Community leaders must ensure that provisions concerning the safety of young people in school and elsewhere are included in these plans.

> **Recommendation 7.3:** Enlist community leaders in efforts to secure funds for, and sponsor policies that promote school and community safety.

Law Enforcement Agencies

In Chapter 7 the role of local law enforcement agencies in school-based crisis management was discussed. School officials have to call on the expertise of police officers when emergencies arise. But what about other times? A growing number of school systems are placing uniformed officers in secondary schools. Partnerships between schools and law enforcement agencies permit cooperation in such areas as background checks on school employees, monitoring of athletic events, after-hours patrolling of school grounds and facilities, and consultation on safety-related issues.

Relations between schools and law enforcement agencies are not without controversy. Some people worry that the presence of police officers in schools is inconsistent with the mission of education and that officers may become overzealous about apprehending wrongdoers. The NAACP in Montgomery County, Maryland, for example, expressed fear that placing police officers in schools would lead to arrest records for more young people (Schulte, 2000). On the other hand, parents have voiced criticism when the police failed to provide adequate protection for students. After the Columbine shootings, parents of murdered students filed lawsuits alleging that local law enforcement did little to help students who were trapped for hours in the school library (Portner & Richard, 2000). Littleton police also were criticized for being unfamiliar with the physical layout of Columbine High School (Portner, 2000). Crime in New York City public schools dropped when the New York City Police Department assumed responsibility in 1999 for managing the school system's 3,300 security officers (Coles, 2000).

Local law enforcement contributions to school safety can be divided into efforts by uniformed officers—school resource officers (SRO)—who are assigned to schools during regular school hours and other forms of support, including backup in the event of a crisis and technical assistance. Figure 9.1 represents an actual memorandum of understanding between the police department and the public schools of Danville, Virginia. The document describes roles and responsibilities of SROs as well as the school's obligations related to the SROs. Each SRO is expected to respond to calls for assistance, report criminal activities, make arrests, and help the principal develop and implement school safety plans. In addition, officers participate in conferences, counsel students, and provide instruction on safety-related topics. On the school's part, principals agree not to assign officers to routine hall, cafeteria, and bus duty. Furthermore, school staff members are obliged to report all violations of the law to the SRO.

Because local law enforcement may be called on during emergencies, it is important for school officials to make certain that the police or sheriff's office has detailed maps of all school facilities and grounds. Guidelines should be developed governing such sensitive issues as student interrogation and the arrest of students at school. Under what circumstances, for instance, should a school administrator be present? When do parents have to be called and required to come to school? When should law enforcement officers be asked to investigate thefts and vandalism at school or to search for drugs and contraband? Clear guidelines on these and related matters reduce the likelihood that the rights of students will be violated in the process of police intervention.

> **Recommendation 7.4:** Develop guidelines governing the responsibilities of school resource officers and the circumstances under which law enforcement agencies become directly involved in school safety efforts.

The Court System

The quest for safe schools may bring educators into contact with the court system, particularly juvenile and domestic relations courts (J&DR). J&DR courts typically have jurisdiction over delinquency, status offenses including truancy, petitions related

FIGURE 9.1   Danville Public Schools & Danville Police Department

MEMORANDUM OF UNDERSTANDING (MOU)

The following MOU is a joint understanding of the Danville Police Department and the Danville Public School System concerning the position of a School Resource Officer or a D.A.R.E. Officer working within the Danville Public School System.

CHAIN OF COMMAND

All Danville Police Officers working in the position of a School Resource or D.A.R.E. Officer will be under the command of the Captain of Patrol in his everyday activities. However, each officer working as either an SRO or D.A.R.E. Officer will be assigned to a specific Captain at the Police Department for days off, vacation days, evaluation purposes, etc. If the Captain of Patrol cannot be located for one reason or another, the chain of command would be followed with the Assistant Chief being next, and then the Chief of Police.

LAW ENFORCEMENT'S ROLES AND RESPONSIBILITIES

All officers working as either an SRO or D.A.R.E. Officer will first and foremost be a law enforcement (LE) Officer on campus. He or she will wear the uniform in accordance with the policy of the Danville Police Department, which will include their duty weapons. All officers will act as role models to all students in their everyday activities. Each officer will have the responsibility to be a resource to the school administrators, teachers, parents and students for conferences or counseling, and present specialized educational programs such as Class Action, D.A.R.E. Core lessons, etc. The SRO/D.A.R.E. Officer will implement reactive methods of SRO policing: reporting procedures, police reports, arrests, intervention, and respond to calls on campus. The SRO/D.A.R.E. Officer will gather intelligence information on gangs, burglaries, juvenile crimes, etc. The SRO/D.A.R.E. Officer will determine whether law enforcement action is appropriate and will take action as required. As soon as possible the SRO/D.A.R.E. Officer will make the principal of the school aware of the situation or action. The SRO/D.A.R.E. Officer will assist the principal in developing plans and strategies to prevent and/or minimize dangerous situations on or near the campus. The SRO/D.A.R.E. Officer will be responsible to fill out and maintain a copy of all School Safety Assessments, which will be filled out twice within a school year. Recommendations concerning school safety issues will be forwarded to the school principal as soon as possible. It will also be the responsibility of the SRO/D.A.R.E. Officer to fill out a Student Incident Report on each incident and send this form to the Department of Criminal Justice Services each month as ordered in the policy of the Danville Police Department. The SRO/D.A.R.E. Officer will be consistent and fair, use good judgment and discretion, show respect for students and faculty, and show sincere concern for the school community.

SCHOOL'S ROLES AND RESPONSIBILITIES

It will be the responsibility of the principal of each school where a School Resource Officer or D.A.R.E. Officer works, to inform him or her as to problems occurring in and around their school. However, no SRO/D.A.R.E. Officer shall be used for regularly assigned lunch room duties, bus duties, hall monitors, etc. If there is a problem area, the officer may assist the school until the problem is solved. It will be the responsibility of *all* faculty members to report *all* violations of the law to the SRO/D.A.R.E. Officer. This will assist the officers with

(continued)

FIGURE 9.1   Continued

the type of programs that they need to emphasize as well as assist the police with problems that occur after school hours. It will be the responsibility of the principal to assist the officers working their schools in school safety assessments as required by HB 1851. This will be done twice within a school year. All school administrators and police officers will work together to make a safe school environment conducive to learning.

TIME LIMIT OF REVIEW

The Memorandum of Understanding will be reviewed by the Police Department and the Danville Public School System every two years.

---

to abused or neglected children, traffic offenses, and some domestic relations issues such as custody and visitation rights. Under certain circumstances, juveniles may be transferred to a circuit court and tried as adults. Offenses for which juveniles may be tried as adults include drug sales, robbery, burglary, and murder.

Young people who are apprehended for an offense are not necessarily brought before the court. Law enforcement officers have two basic options: diversion and arrest. If they choose diversion, they can handle the case informally and release the young person to the custody of parents, refer the young person for counseling or treatment, or release the individual with a warning. The courts become involved only when law enforcement officers opt to arrest. In most states, public school systems continue to be responsible for educational services until such point as a young person is placed in a juvenile or adult correctional center. Educators and representatives of the court must work together to determine the most appropriate way to deliver educational services unless or until a young person is referred to a correctional center. Those who are not judged appropriate for a regular school may be placed on homebound instruction or in an alternative school. In Marion County, Indiana, the juvenile court system partnered with the school district to develop the New Directions Academy, a school for students who could not be accommodated in a regular educational setting.

One important focus of the J&DR court is the enforcement of compulsory-attendance laws. School officials increasingly are working with local law enforcement officers to apprehend students who are truant. When students repeatedly miss school, a school district must decide whether to file a petition with the court. If the district elects to file, it has to decide whether to file the petition against the parents or the student. In cases in which parents claim they have no control over their child, the petition usually is filed directly against the young person. Once a petition is filed, the court may schedule a meeting with the parents and student and draft an attendance contract, or it can order them to appear before a judge. In either case, a representative of the school system may be expected to appear and present an up-to-date record of attendance and other pertinent information.

Another area of concern for J&DR court is drug- and alcohol-related offenses. Recognizing that young people involved in drug use pose a special challenge, some localities have created drug courts that handle only problems related to repeat drug-related offenses (Gore, 1999). Rather than trying offenders and referring them to a correctional facility, drug court may require young people to come to court on a regular basis for urine testing and counseling sessions. Offenders listen to each other's life stories and struggles with drugs. Those who successfully complete the program can have their charges erased from the court record.

Realizing that incarceration is not always a useful consequence, courts have begun to explore a variety of alternatives, or what is referred to as "graduated sanctions." One option that has attracted great interest is community service. Performed either at school or elsewhere in the community, such service provides young people with opportunities to accomplish something constructive instead of "doing time." For community service to be effective, however, work supervision must be continuous and involve trained supervisors (Toby & Scrupski, 1990, p. 279). A comprehensive list of graduated sanctions is likely to include the following options:

1. Counsel and release programs
   a. intake diversion program
   b. police counseling
2. Informal adjustment
   a. anger-control training
   b. substance abuse program
3. Court supervision program
   a. probation
   b. electronic monitoring
   c. house arrest
   d. restitution/restoration
   e. community service
   f. alternative school
4. Intensive supervised program
   a. intensive probation
   b. outreach detention
5. Residential placement
6. Secure detention
   a. juvenile facility
   b. adult facility

Youth Agencies and Organizations

Most communities provide a variety of agencies and organizations whose primary function is to serve young people. They range from social service units such as Child Protective Services to the YMCA and YWCA. Efforts aimed at improving the safety and well-being of young people can be strengthened by involving these groups.

Youth agencies and organizations can assist in direct and indirect ways. A direct contribution to youth safety, for example, may involve sponsoring a crisis hotline or a shelter for young people unable to remain safely in their homes. Investigations of reported child abuse and neglect are another illustration of a direct service. Indirect contributions to youth safety often take the form of constructive alternatives to getting into trouble. After-school, weekend, and summer programs have been developed in communities across the nation to reduce youth isolation and engage young people in enjoyable and productive activities.

Heath and McLaughlin (1996) spent five years conducting field research on more than 60 community-based youth organizations (CBOs) in three major urban areas. Serving as links between young people and the adult world, these CBOs provided opportunities for urban youth to acquire valuable skills and participate in meaningful activities reflecting youth interests and culture. CBOs included theater groups, dance teams, and athletic organizations. More than merely places to hang out, they constituted "intentional learning environments" in which the voices of young people were listened to and valued. The young people served by the CBOs in the study benefited in various ways from their participation. They tended to have higher academic achievement and aspirations and greater self-confidence and optimism than their uninvolved peers (McLaughlin, 2000, pp. 4–5). They also were more inclined to give something back to their communities.

When Heath and McLaughlin (McLaughlin, 2000, pp. 8–18) investigated the qualities that helped make CBOs successful, they found many of the same characteristics that were associated with effective schools. Young people were cared for and provided personal attention. Efforts were made to respond to a broad range of talents, skills, and interests. Adults in CBOs concentrated on identifying and building on the strengths of young people rather than dwelling on their shortcomings. Young people were provided with a variety of feedback and plenty of recognition. They were expected to assume significant responsibilities for maintaining and improving their CBOs.

Organizations such as those studied by Heath and McLaughlin offer young people safe and supervised places to go when they are not in school. They also provide opportunities for individuals to pursue a "passion" and develop a sense of pride in personal and collective achievement. CBOs may be located at school or elsewhere in the community, but in either case it is important that young people regard them as something other than an extension of regular academic work.

Recommendation 7.5: Develop opportunities for young people to undertake meaningful activities in a supervised and safe setting after school, on weekends, and during the summer.

Other Community Organizations

Every community includes organizations that may not be intended primarily to serve children and adolescents, but that nonetheless are willing and anxious to help promote the safety and well-being of young people. Among these organizations are businesses, higher education institutions, religious groups, hospitals, and the media.

Crowson and Boyd (1996, pp. 142–143) were impressed with the Minneapolis Youth Trust, a "citywide collaborative organization involving Minneapolis employers, schools, and a number of youth-serving agencies." With leadership from the Mayor's Office, the trust helps young people acquire employment skills and obtain job experience. These functions indirectly contribute to community safety by diverting young people from unproductive activities and helping them build a promising future. Minneapolis businesses are asked to provide financial support for the trust, create jobs so that young people receive practical experience, and contribute mentors to guide program participants. The trust includes a set of partnerships between local schools and businesses.

Institutions of higher education also are playing important roles in community-based youth programs. The University of Illinois, for example, took the initiative in forging an alliance among four Chicago elementary schools, parents, and various community agencies (Crowson & Boyd, 1996, p. 143). Referred to as the Nation of Tomorrow project, this collaboration has striven to improve the academic development, child care arrangements, and health of children from poor neighborhoods. The university provides technical expertise to help with project organization, parent education, and fundraising. Higher education institutions can help school safety efforts in other ways as well. They offer specialized training for educators, conduct school safety audits, design and administer needs assessments, and undertake research on safety-related issues.

In many poor neighborhoods, the most stable organizations besides public schools are churches. Church members typically reside in these neighborhoods and share a deep commitment to helping local young people. From Atlanta to Los Angeles, churches and other religious organizations have raised funds and provided volunteers for youth initiatives. Churches also provide space for child care and after-school programs.

Health organizations increasingly are taking an interest in the safety of young people. Besides helping schools and youth-serving agencies to assess the health needs of young people, hospitals are providing free and reduced-fee services to poor children and sponsoring safety-awareness programs. Health workers often volunteer to mentor young people who lack constructive adult role models and to screen students for risk factors.

Local media organizations also play an important role in community-based efforts to help young people. By refusing to cover only negative news about youth, reporters encourage the public to adopt a balanced view of young people. Stories that describe young people who contribute to their community and who successfully overcome obstacles can be potent antidotes to feelings of hopelessness. By refraining from sensationalizing violence and by raising awareness of threats to youth safety and how to resist or handle them, the media can lessen the impact of toxic environments.

It is difficult to imagine any person or organization in the community who could not contribute in some way to the safety and well-being of young people. Individuals can help by volunteering their time, raising funds, and putting pressure on political officials. Organizations can generate resources, provide jobs for young people, encourage employees to give their time to helping young people, offer space for youth-related activities, share technical expertise, and raise public awareness of important issues related to safety. Contributions by individuals and organizations can make a great difference, but only when they are carefully coordinated. What must communities do to address youth safety and well-being in a thorough and integrated way?

The Challenge of Collaboration

If collaboration in the service of youth were simple or easy, there would be no reason for this discussion. The fact is, however, that collaboration across agencies, organizations, and individuals occurs less frequently than prudence and practicality would dictate. This part of the chapter examines some of the obstacles in the path of well-coordinated youth safety initiatives.

One obstacle is reflected in the lack of agreement about the term that best captures the nature of the desired relationship among youth-serving groups. Crowson and Boyd (1996, pp. 140–141) refer to a continuum from cooperation to coordination to collaboration, each being distinguished by such criteria as the amount of autonomy maintained by participating organizations and how decisions are made. They note that some youth programs simply are "co-located"—they share the same space, but little else.

To avoid confusion, the term "collaboration" will be used to characterize the desired relationship among community groups. What this term means in practice, of course, has to be worked out by local participants. For present purposes, collaboration refers to any relationship among groups and organizations in which a concerted effort is made to support common goals, share resources, avoid duplication of services, exchange information, and coordinate decisions and policies. A collaborative initiative to reduce truancy, for instance, might bring together schools, police, and the court system. Police officers would be expected to pick up young people who were not in school during regular school hours and return them to school. Young people who were repeatedly truant would be brought before a special court designed to handle school attendance problems. The court would be empowered to require parents or guardians to see that children attended school. School administrators and counselors would participate in court proceedings and help draft individual contracts designed to assist each truant student in attending school more regularly.

A variety of barriers stand in the way of successful collaboration. Youth-serving organizations, for instance, do not always share the same views of problems. Schools may be seen as the cause of, or the cure for, threats to youth safety. Opinions may vary regarding the best ways to address particular concerns, such as drug use or antisocial behavior. A religious group may see prayer in schools as a cure for incivility, whereas a teacher organization calls for greater parent education. One way to accommodate these differences, of course, is to endorse multiple approaches to solving problems. Implementing multiple approaches, however, can require more resources than are available to a community. In addition, some groups may oppose particular interventions for religious, philosophical, or political reasons. A civil rights organization, for example, may not support a requirement that all students wear uniforms to school on the grounds that it infringes on a young person's freedom of expression.

Another barrier to collaboration involves interorganizational jealousy. Community groups sometimes are reluctant to work closely with school systems because they do not feel like equal partners. Educators who sincerely desire to engage the community in efforts to promote the safety and well-being of young people must be willing to share expertise and resources without insisting on controlling the agenda.

Fear of losing organizational identity is another impediment to collaboration. "Collaboration requires a rearrangement of turf," according to Maeroff (1998, p. 299). "Agencies that have struggled to establish their domains may not readily overlook territorial demarcations." Working together to eliminate duplication of services can threaten the very existence of some smaller youth-serving organizations. They may prefer to go it alone, even if such a course of action means diminished effectiveness, rather than being overshadowed or possibly absorbed by larger organizations.

It takes time to collaborate. Organizations must meet together, assess needs, become familiar with how each other operates, and build trust. There are no shortcuts in this process. Unfortunately, time is a scarce commodity for virtually every organization. Given the fact that many youth-serving groups have small staffs, it may be difficult to secure the commitment of time necessary to mount a successful communitywide initiative.

Although daunting, these hurdles are surmountable. Ample evidence exists that community groups can work together effectively for the sake of young people (Elliott, Williams, & Hamburg, 1998; Maeroff, 1998; Perry, 1999; Schorr, 1997). Let us look at several examples of successful collaborative efforts related to the safety and well-being of young people.

The Promise of Collaboration

Safety-oriented collaborative efforts may take two basic forms. One type deals with a particular threat, such as gangs or drugs. The second type is comprehensive in nature, attempting to address various threats to youth safety. Examples abound of successful initiatives of both types.

In the case of Amesbury, Massachusetts, an initiative that focused initially on the prevention of teen dating abuse eventually grew into a comprehensive program to reduce violence in general (Hildt, 1996). The murders of several teenage girls by their boyfriends triggered concern in Amesbury that resulted in a public meeting in June 1993. Those who attended the gathering lamented that the community no longer felt as safe as it once did. Besides the murders, numerous examples of disputes that quickly escalated to fighting were cited. An action plan that called for a "community-wide violence prevention summit" was drafted.

When citizens came together in October 1993 for the summit, they heard reports from the police chief, a representative of the district attorney's office, and a worker from the battered women's shelter. Young people as well as adults were involved in discussion groups. The result of the summit was an "Amesbury Violence Prevention Plan" that called for a multifaceted approach. Schools were called on to offer parenting classes, violence prevention curricula, and peer-mediation programs. A campaign was mounted to lobby the state legislature for laws aimed at preventing violence. A policy was drafted that condemned violent entertainment in local theaters and video arcades. Plans were initiated for a community center with constructive activities for youth. Support groups to improve communication between adults and teenagers were formed.

As more public attention began to be focused on the issue of youth violence, adults began to take a look at their own behavior. Members of Amesbury's Board of Selectmen, for instance, came under criticism for the uncivil way in which they conducted local business. Plans were made to sponsor a violence prevention week. Activities scheduled for this time included a boycott of violent televisions shows, community awareness-building about racism, and instruction in school on sexual abuse and conflict resolution. Churches were asked to acknowledge the accomplishments of young people and reiterate the value of peace. Amesbury eventually institutionalized its communitywide efforts by forming a violence prevention committee consisting of adults and young people. The committee promotes collaboration on safety matters among schools, churches, and other community organizations.

Broward County, Florida, is the site of another communitywide effort to address youth safety. The Broward County school board obtained a Florida Community Juvenile Justice Partnership Grant in 1993. The grant enabled the school system to create the Coalition for Community Empowerment (CCE), a project "designed to reduce disciplinary referrals and suspensions in eight targeted schools in high-crime, high-poverty areas of the country" (Hernandez, 1999, p. 369). CCE involved a variety of local organizations, including the police, boys and girls clubs, and the National Education Association's Center for the Revitalization of Urban Education.

The primary objectives of CCE were to improve support systems for families and to increase access for young people to community resources. Focusing on students with a history of absenteeism, disruptive behavior, disciplinary referrals, and suspensions, the program called for the development of one-year "contracts" between parents, schools, and young people. Contracts called for family counseling with a community mediator trained in the conflict-resolution program developed by the Peace Education Program (Hernandez, 1999, p. 371). The intention was to help students and their families learn to handle disputes at home and in school without fighting or anger. Students also received academic assistance from retired teachers and participated in recreation programs offered by CCE partners.

In addition to working directly with young people and their families, CCE called for training the faculties of the eight schools in the Peace Education Foundation's conflict resolution program. In this way, teachers and administrators could reinforce the skills that students were learning in their family counseling sessions. Law enforcement agencies agreed to monitor the three housing projects in which participating families lived and to provide the families with crime prevention instruction. School resource officers from the police department helped keep an eye on students when they were at school.

Funding for CCE lasted for five years, allowing the program to serve approximately 400 young people between the ages of 10 and 17. An evaluation of the program indicated that disciplinary referrals, suspensions, and arrests for breaking the law were reduced in the participating schools (Hernandez, 1999, p. 372). The success of CCE prompted an initiative aimed at reducing threats to youth safety throughout South Florida.

The experiences of Amesbury and Broward County demonstrate that obstacles to communitywide initiatives can be overcome. Researchers who study collaborative efforts have identified various elements of successful programs. In *Common Purpose,* Schorr (1997, pp. 360–368) cites four key elements:

1. Successful initiatives combine action in the economic, service, education, physical development, and community-building domains.
2. Successful initiatives rely on a community's own resources and strengths as the foundation for designing change initiatives.
3. Successful initiatives draw extensively on outside resources, including public and private funds, professional expertise, and new partnerships that bring clout and influence.
4. Effective initiatives are designed and operated on the basis of one or more plausible theories of change.

The fourth element harkens back to the discussion in Chapter 2 of different perspectives on school safety. Each perspective encompasses one or more theories of change. An educational perspective, for example, assumes that changes in behavior are learned. Promoting safe schools and communities, based on this perspective, requires creating opportunities for people to learn how to be safe and how to deal with threats to safety. It is important to note that both the Amesbury and the Broward County initiatives provided such opportunities.

Strong Families: The Cornerstone of Safe Schools and Communities

The preceding pages of this book have contained various references to the central role of parents in promoting the safety and well-being of young people. Capable and committed parents are the bedrock on which strong families are built. Earlier in this chapter, some ways that parents can contribute to collaborative safety initiatives were presented. In the concluding part of this chapter, it is necessary to discuss what schools and communities can do to help parents in their efforts to build strong families. It is worth noting that many of the most successful collaborative programs include a parental support component.

> **Recommendation 7.6:** Include in collaborative school safety initiatives a component designed to strengthen families and support parents.

One of the most important forms of parental support is quality child care. With more working parents than ever before, communities need to provide reasonably priced day care centers, preschools, and after-school programs. Research clearly indicates that the availability of quality child care helps reduce the likelihood of aggressive behavior and violent acts by young people (Elliott, Williams, & Hamburg, 1998, p. 386). Some schools have begun to provide day care as a way to strengthen families and encourage parents with toddlers to volunteer at school.

Another way that schools and communities can help parents is by offering parent education programs. The relationship between parenting and such youth-related problems as delinquency and aggression is well established (Laub & Lauritsen, 1998). Parents need to understand how to monitor and supervise their children, set limits, provide structure, and respond to inappropriate conduct. Instruction in anger management and conflict resolution helps parents learn to model the kinds of behaviors their children need to acquire in order to handle life's difficulties. Classes on infant stimulation and cognitive development provide parents with tips on how to promote effective learning.

When parents experience problems with their children, they may benefit from various types of outside assistance, including family therapy and parent support groups. It is comforting for parents to know that they are not alone in having problems raising children. One approach to parental assistance with documented effectiveness in reducing the likelihood of youth violence is Functional Family Therapy (FFT). Refined over four decades, FFT targets dysfunctional behaviors in family situations (Alexander, Pugh, & Parsons, 1998). Instead of encouraging reliance on the therapist, FFT focuses on parents and children assuming responsibility for behavior change. The duration of FFT treatment ranges from 8 to 30 hours of family contact.

Kentucky, as part of its omnibus Kentucky Education Reform Act of 1990, established a network of family resource centers designed to serve families with children up to 12 years of age (Smrekar, 1996). A model for communities everywhere, these centers provide full-time child care for two- and three-year-olds, after-school child care for children from 4 to 12, health and education services for new and expectant parents, education to enhance parenting skills, support and training for child day care providers, and health services and referrals. Family resource centers are located at or near schools with relatively high percentages of children from poor families.

An increasing number of secondary schools are housing various services for adolescents. Dental and health care, mental health counseling, and social services are provided at school, thereby relieving working parents of the need to miss work in order to take their children to these providers. Were it not for school-based health facilities, many young people from poor families would not receive any routine or preventive medical attention.

When it is necessary for parents to come to school and meet with counselors and school administrators, extended hours can be of great help to those who work outside the home. Some schools stagger the schedules of counselors, for example, so that the school guidance office is open in the late afternoon and evening. School systems have begun to operate satellite centers in, or send mobile units to, housing projects and poor neighborhoods so that parents and children can receive assistance without having to find transportation to school.

Conclusion

Schools do not exist in isolation. They are surrounded by neighborhoods and communities, and what goes on in these places has a direct bearing on school safety. Family problems, feuds between neighbors, and gang activities spill over onto campuses, disrupting school activities and placing students and staff members at risk. To reduce these threats and to promote the well-being of young people, educators need to build effective alliances with parents, youth-serving agencies, and other community organizations.

A cornerstone of any school safety initiative must be strong ties between home and school. This chapter explored ways that parents can assist educators in addressing safety problems and ways that educators and other community groups can help parents deal with the challenges of childrearing. Child care, family counseling, and parent education are some of the services that can reduce domestic dysfunctions.

Other entities with crucial roles to play in school and community safety include law enforcement agencies, courts, youth agencies, businesses, churches, health organizations, and the media. Achieving effective collaboration among these bodies requires considerable planning and commitment. The chapter included a discussion of some of the obstacles to collaboration and several examples of local initiatives that managed to overcome them in the process of making schools and neighborhoods safer for all young people.

REFERENCES

Alexander, James; Pugh, Christie; and Parsons, Bruce. *Functional Family Therapy.* Boulder, CO: Center for the Study and Prevention of Violence, University of Colorado, 1998.

Annie E. Casey Foundation. *Kids Count Data Book: 1998.* Baltimore: Author, 1998.

Claiborne, William. "A 'Life in Chaos' Shaped Young Shooter." *Washington Post* (March 2, 2000), pp. A1, A12.

Cohn, D'Vera. "Parents' Top Goal: Raising Thinkers," *Washington Post* (November 24, 1999), p. A8.

Coles, Adrienne D. "Crime Drops Since NYPD Takeover of School Security." *Education Week* (March 15, 2000), p. 6.

Crowson, Robert L., and Boyd, William Lowe. "Structure and Strategies: Toward an Understanding of Alternative Models for Coordinated Children's Services." In James G. Cibulka and William J. Kritek (eds.), *Coordination among Schools, Families, and Communities.* Albany, NY: State University of New York Press, 1996, pp. 137–170.

Elliott, Delbert S.; Williams, Kirk R.; and Hamburg, Beatrix. "An Integrated Approach to Violence Prevention." In Delbert S. Elliott, Beatrix Hamburg, and Kirk R. Williams (eds.), *Violence in American Schools.* Cambridge: Cambridge University Press, 1998, pp. 379–386.

Finn, Jeremy D. "Parental Engagement That Makes a Difference," *Educational Leadership,* vol. 55, no. 8 (May 1998), pp. 20–24.

Garbarino, James. "Educating Children in a Socially Toxic Environment," *Educational Leadership,* vol. 54, no. 7 (April 1997), pp. 12–16.

Gore, Mollie. "Drug Court for Youths Has Impact," *Richmond Times Dispatch* (October 19, 1999), p. A9.

Heath, Shirley Brice, and McLaughlin, Milbrey W. "The Best of Both Worlds: Connecting Schools and Community Youth Organizations for All-Day, All-Year Learning." In James G. Cibulka and William J. Kritek (eds.), *Coordination among Schools, Families, and Communities.* Albany, NY: State University of New York Press, 1996, pp. 69–93.

Hernandez, Tony. "Community Building in South Florida to Promote School Safety," *Education and Urban Society,* vol. 31, no. 3 (May 1999), pp. 368–374.

Hersch, Patricia. *A Tribe Apart.* New York: Ballantine Books, 1998.

Hildt, Barbara. "Amesbury, Massachusetts: A Community Violence Prevention Initiative." In Sarah Miller, Janine Brodine, and Terri Miller (eds.), *Safe by Design.* Seattle: Committee for Children, 1996, pp. 329–334.

Jacobson, Linda. "High-Quality Child Care Again Linked to Fewer Juvenile Arrests," *Education Week* (May 10, 2000), p. 6.

Jacobson, Linda. "Millions of School-Age Children Left on Their Own," *Education Week* (September 13, 2000), p. 3.

Laub, John H., and Lauritsen, Janet L. "The Interdependence of School Violence with Neighborhood and Family Conditions." In Delbert S. Elliott, Beatrix Hamburg, and Kirk R. Williams (eds.), *Violence in American Schools.* Cambridge: Cambridge University Press, 1998, pp. 127–155.

Loeber, Rolf, and Stouthamer-Loeber, Magda. "Juvenile Aggression at Home and at School." In Delbert S. Elliott, Beatrix Hamburg, and Kirk R. Williams (eds*.), Violence in American Schools.* Cambridge: Cambridge University Press, 1998, pp. 94–126.

Lorion, Raymond P. "Exposure to Urban Violence: Contamination of the School Environment." In Delbert S. Elliott, Beatrix Hamburg, and Kirk R. Williams (eds.), *Violence in American Schools.* Cambridge: Cambridge University Press, 1998, pp. 293–311.

McLaughlin, Milbrey W. *Community Counts.* Washington, DC: Public Education Network, 2000.

Maeroff, Gene I. *Altered Destinies.* New York: St. Martin's Griffin, 1998.

Perry, Cheryl L. *Creating Health Behavior Change.* Thousand Oaks, CA: Sage, 1999.

Popenoe, David. "The Family Condition of America: Cultural Change and Public Policy." In Henry J. Aaron, Thomas S. Mann, and Timothy Taylor (eds.), *Values and Public Policy.* Washington, DC: Brookings, 1994.

Portner, Jessica. "Columbine Report Underscores Need to Share Data with Police," *Education Week* (May 24, 2000), p. 5.

Portner, Jessica, and Richard, Alan. "Suits, Memorials Mark Columbine Anniversary," *Education Week* (April 26, 2000), p. 3.

Schorr, Lisbeth B. *Common Purpose.* New York: Doubleday, 1997.

Schulte, Brigid. "Montgomery Considers Putting Officers in Schools," *Washington Post* (April 12, 2000), p. B5.

Sherman, L. W.; Gottfredson, D.; McKenzie, D.; Eck, J.; Reuter, P.; and Bushway, S. *Preventing Crime: What Works, What Doesn't, and What's Promising.* Washington, DC: National Institute of Justice, 1997.

Smrekar, Claire. "The Kentucky Family Resource Centers: The Challenges of Remaking Family–School Interactions." In James G. Cibulka and William J. Kritek (eds.), *Coordination among Schools, Families, and Communities*. Albany, NY: State University of New York Press, 1996, pp. 3–26.

Soriano, Marcel; Soriano, Fernando I., and Jimenez, Evelia. "School Violence among Culturally Diverse Populations: Sociocultural and Institutional Considerations," *School Psychology Review*, vol. 23, no. 2 (1994), pp. 216–235.

Toby, Jackson, and Scrupski, Adam. "Coerced Community Service as a School Discipline Strategy." In Oliver C. Moles (ed.), *Student Discipline Strategies*. Albany, NY: State University of New York Press, 1990, pp. 267–282.

U.S. Department of Education. *A Guide to Safe Schools*. Washington, DC: Author, 1998.

Wuthnow, Robert. *Loose Connections*. Cambridge, MA: Harvard University Press, 1998.

Yankelovich, Daniel. "How Changes in the Economy Are Reshaping American Values." In Henry J. Aaron, Thomas E. Mann, and Timothy Taylor (eds.), *Values and Public Policy*. Washington, DC: Brookings, 1994, pp. 15–63.

SECTION III

School Safety: Questions and Reflections

A considerable body of knowledge about the causes of and cures for unsafe conditions in schools has accumulated over the past half century. Much of this knowledge is encompassed in the seven school safety standards and the various recommendations subsumed under each standard. Still, substantial gaps remain in our understanding of school safety. Other gaps, however, are a consequence of educators' lack of awareness of existing research, expert judgment, and legal opinion. Chapter 10 addresses some of the questions that educators ask regarding school safety and related matters. The concluding chapter reflects on what five decades of concern about school safety have taught us about our young people, our schools, and our society.

10 Questions about School Safety

MAJOR IDEAS IN CHAPTER 10

- Students have a right to privacy unless "reasonable suspicion" of criminal activity can be established.
- Specific criteria are needed to guide decisions to classify aggressive student acts as behavior disorders.
- Educators may be unable to prevent gang activity, but they can keep it from interfering with school operations.
- Schools can do a great deal to combat the negative effects of drugs and alcohol.
- Experience indicates that highly unsafe schools can be turned around.

Many issues related to school safety have been raised in the preceding chapters. In some cases, sufficient knowledge exists to permit a solid position to be taken on the issue. In other instances, the most that can be done is to point out different views and leave it up to the reader to decide on the best course of action. The present chapter addresses a variety of issues that have surfaced during the course of the book. Each issue is expressed in the form of a question that an educator, or other concerned citizen, might ask.

The chapter opens with several questions that relate to matters of law and education policy. They deal with drug testing, student searches, uniforms, and expulsions. The next section involves questions concerning specific safety threats, including aggressive behavior, drugs, alcohol, and gangs. The last set of questions concerns general safety issues, including the prospects for improving an unsafe school, how to target limited resources for school safety, and the special challenge posed by young adolescents.

Questions of Law and Policy

Should school policy require drug tests for students?

In the spring of 2000 the small town of Lockney, Texas, received national attention when the local school board enacted what, at the time, was one of the toughest drug testing policies in the United States (Yardley, 2000, p. A1). The policy required that all juniors and seniors take a mandatory drug test. Refusal to take the test resulted in the same punishment as failure to pass the test—an in-school suspension for first offenders.

Assisted by the American Civil Liberties Union, a Lockney parent challenged the policy, claiming that his son's Fourth Amendment rights prohibiting unreasonable searches had been violated. Did the Lockney school board overstep its bounds? Did local concern over increasing drug problems warrant mandatory drug testing for all students? Would random drug testing or drug tests for certain categories of students have been a more defensible policy?

Although the final verdict on drug testing in schools has yet to be heard, the measure can be better understood by referring to the 1995 U.S. Supreme Court decision in *Vernonia School District 47J v. Acton* (Imber & Van Geel, 2000, pp. 159–162). This case involved a policy in the Oregon school district of Vernonia that authorized random urinalysis drug testing of students participating in school-sponsored athletics. Drug use had become a significant problem in Vernonia, particularly with certain athletes. The district initially tried drug awareness classes, presentations to students by experts, and drug-sniffing dogs, but the problem persisted. District officials determined that the only way they could stem the tide of increasing drug use was to implement random testing. The policy was challenged after a student was barred from the high school football team for refusing to take a drug test.

In upholding Vernonia's policy, the Supreme Court declared that schools are charged with protecting the welfare of all students. In a 6 to 3 decision, the justices stated that random drug testing does not violate students' rights to privacy. The decision noted, however, the relevance of the circumstances faced by the Oregon district. Vernonia had tried other solutions to no avail. Random drug testing was warranted, they ruled, when reasonable suspicion existed that some students—in this case, athletes—might be using drugs. The Court registered its approval of the procedures followed by school officials, affording students privacy when collecting urine samples and protecting the confidentiality of test results.

Based on the Vernonia decision, drug testing policies appear to be defensible when they call for random testing of students for whom a reasonable suspicion of drug use exists. Furthermore, such testing should be regarded as a last resort, to be implemented only after the failure of less intrusive measures. It remains to be determined whether the courts will support the mandatory drug testing policy adopted in Lockney.

Drug testing of school district employees follows the general guidelines set down for student testing. Employees also have a right to privacy under the Fourth Amendment. Drug testing, therefore, is justified only when a reasonable suspicion of drug use exists or in cases in which the nature of the employee's responsibilities demand an unusual degree of caution. In the case of *Independent School District No. 1 of Tulsa County v. Logan,* for example, the Oklahoma Court of Appeals found that annual urinalysis drug testing of bus drivers was reasonable given the compelling safety issues associated with transporting students to and from school (Imber & Van

Geel, 2000, p. 321). Similar logic could dictate drug tests for driver education teachers and teachers who instruct students in the use of heavy machinery and dangerous equipment.

Under what circumstances should students be searched in school?

The courts consider drug tests to be a form of search, in that the procedure represents an invasion of an individual's privacy. What about other types of searches? Should school policies permit locker searches, automobile searches, searches of students' bookbags, and strip searches?

Schools are obliged to protect the rights of students in general as well as the rights of individual students. These two obligations may conflict when it comes to the conduct of student searches; thus school employees must understand the circumstances under which they are justified in setting aside an individual's right to privacy under the Fourth Amendment.

Based on *New Jersey v. T.L.O.*, a case involving a search of a student's purse that went to the U.S. Supreme Court in 1985, several criteria must be met so that a search by school employees is defensible (Dowling-Sendor, 1997, p. 18):

1. The search must be justified at its inception. In other words, reasonable suspicion that the search will reveal evidence of a violation must exist prior to beginning the search.
2. The search must be conducted in "a way that is reasonably related in scope to the facts that justified the search to begin with."

The second criterion requires that school employees take into consideration such matters as the age and gender of the student and the nature of the presumed violation *before* conducting the search. Conducting a strip search of a kindergarten student in order to locate a quarter that was reported stolen would not be warranted. The nature of the alleged offense does not merit the intrusiveness and possible traumatizing effects of the search.

In deciding when to conduct a search, school employees also must consider the background of the person being searched and the source of information leading to a search (Dunklee & Shoop, 1993, pp. 122–125). The courts are more likely to uphold the search of a student with a prior history of violations than a student with an unblemished record. Searches based on unsubstantiated rumor or reports from students of questionable character are less justifiable than those based on information from several reliable sources.

The key to deciding to conduct a search is the determination that *reasonable suspicion* of a violation exists. School employees, it should be noted, do not have to meet the same high standard as police officers, who are expected to operate on the basis of *probable cause.* Reasonable suspicion is not an absolute standard. What constitutes reasonable suspicion may vary depending on the seriousness of the situation.

When searching for an explosive device, for example, school employees would be accorded more latitude than when searching for stolen sneakers.

Guidelines governing the conduct of searches should take into account what is being searched as well as what is being sought. School employees are on firmer footing when searching a student's locker than they are when searching a student's automobile or backpack. The courts have reasoned that lockers are school property and that students understand when they are issued a lock that school authorities also possess a key or combination that allows them access. An automobile, on the other hand, is not school property. Unless contraband or weapons are inside the car within plain view, school employees are advised to avoid searching a vehicle. If reasonable suspicion exists that the car contains illegal or dangerous items, school employees should detain the student driver until either parents or law enforcement officers arrive (Dunklee & Shoop, 1993, p. 126).

The greatest caution must be exercised before school employees conduct a pat-down or strip search. Not only must reasonable suspicion be convincing, but the item or material being sought must pose an immediate danger to others or the probability must exist "that the contraband will be used, distributed, or destroyed if a search is not undertaken immediately" (Dunklee & Shoop, 1993, p. 130). When a Florida assistant principal discovered a bag of marijuana after searching a student whom he had spotted in a hallway with some other boys, the student was charged with delinquency in juvenile court ("Law Update," 1997). Eventually the Florida Court of Appeals heard the case and ruled against the school district. Simply seeing several students huddled in a hallway did not constitute reasonable suspicion, reasoned the justices. The assistant principal would have needed to see money being exchanged to justify the search that turned up the marijuana.

A final matter involves the use of drug-sniffing dogs. Dunklee and Shoop (1993, p. 132) note that the use of dogs to search inanimate objects such as classrooms and lockers is not regarded as a student search by the courts. They go on to warn, though, that the courts may regard the use of dogs to sniff students as a "highly intrusive search procedure requiring a high level of reasonable…suspicion of a student or students."

Should students be required to wear uniforms to school as a safety measure?

The campaign for school uniforms received an important boost in March 1996, when President Clinton endorsed the policy as a way to enhance school safety. Although some urban public schools had introduced uniforms in the eighties, Long Beach, California, in 1994, had become the first school system to mandate student uniforms in all elementary and middle schools. The results were very encouraging. Gang-related problems related to the wearing of "colors" and particular articles of clothing were reduced, along with school crime, discipline problems, and suspensions (White, 2000, p. 37). The Clinton endorsement of school uniforms derived, in part, from Long Beach's success.

What students wear to school has become a safety issue for several reasons. Gangs typically adopt certain types of clothing and colors so that members will be readily identifiable. Nonmembers found wearing gang gear may be subject to beatings or worse. In addition, students who wear expensive clothing, shoes, and jewelry become targets for theft. In some tragic cases, young people have been killed for these items. School authorities contend that provocative dress, such as short skirts and see-through blouses, undermines school decorum and places students at risk of taunts and assault. Concerns also are expressed that certain articles of clothing, such as baggy pants and large coats, allow students to conceal contraband and weapons more easily.

To control the disruptive effects of student attire, schools have two basic choices. They can require all students to wear the same uniform, or they can impose dress code regulations governing what students can and cannot wear to school. The latter allows students to choose what to wear to school as long as clothing meets certain criteria concerning modesty, cleanliness, and safety. The former policy is easier to enforce, because school employees do not have to spend time determining whether particular articles of clothing conform to stated guidelines. Questions, however, have been raised regarding the effectiveness of both types of policy. Various studies have failed to find consistently positive effects of dress codes and school uniforms (White, 2000). Even the encouraging results from Long Beach have been challenged on the grounds that uniforms were introduced at the same time as several other safety initiatives and educational reforms (Brunsma & Rockquemore, 1998). Consequently, it is difficult to separate the impact of uniforms from other changes.

Additional concerns have been raised about policies requiring all students to wear uniforms to school. Purchasing uniforms may pose an economic hardship for poor parents. School districts, therefore, must be prepared either to subsidize the purchase of uniforms for children from poor families or to permit them to opt out of the policy. Some civil rights advocates wonder whether dress codes and school uniforms infringe on students' rights to express themselves under the First Amendment. Imber and Van Geel (2000, p. 143) conclude that "school dress codes are constitutionally permissible when necessary to avoid distraction or disruption of the educational process." School authorities must be prepared, though, to offer evidence that what students wear to school has a deleterious effect on teaching, learning, and safety.

Should an expelled student be permitted to return to school?

The issue of expelling students from school as a consequence of violating school rules was addressed in Chapter 4. Evidence suggests that most school systems use expulsion as a consequence of last resort when dealing with the most serious infractions. The federal government requires that any school district receiving funds under the Gun-free Schools Act must expel students who bring firearms to school. Many states have mandated similar zero tolerance policies and mandatory expulsion for other offenses judged to pose a danger to staff and students.

One question that arises concerns whether expelled students should eventually be reinstated. A review of district policies reveals some variation with regard to the length of the expulsion period. In many districts, a student cannot apply to be reinstated for 365 days. In other districts, a student can seek readmission at the beginning of the school year following the year in which the expulsion occurred. This means that a student who was expelled in May could be reinstated in September. Expelled students are barred from returning to a regular public school forever in some school districts.

Because an education was determined to be a property right protected under the Fourteenth Amendment in *Goss v. Lopez,* the states have an obligation to provide an education for all young people, including those who are expelled from school or incarcerated. State laws generally do not specify, however, that expelled students must receive an education in a particular school or school system. Larger school systems sometimes permit an expelled student to return to a regular school, but not the one from which he was expelled. In other cases, alternative schools have been created especially for expelled students. Depending on the alternative school and local policy, students may complete their academic work and graduate from the alternative school or eventually return to a regular school, if they do well in the alternative setting. In 1989, Prince George's County, Maryland, took the controversial step of requiring expelled students to pay tuition if they desired to enter an alternative program. Tuition funds were used to underwrite the costs of operating the alternative programs.

The decision concerning whether to permit expelled students to return to a regular school should be based on a case-by-case analysis. Considerations should include the nature of the offense, whether any form of therapy or rehabilitation was undertaken by the student, an assessment of how well the student performed in the intervention, and whether options to regular schools are available. An expelled student who, in the judgment of school authorities and therapists, continues to pose a threat to the safety of others should not be returned to a regular school. These individuals' educational needs are best accommodated in a highly structured alternative program staffed by educators trained to handle difficult and dangerous young people. In some cases, homebound instruction may be preferable to assignment to an alternative program.

Questions Related to Specific Safety Problems

Under what circumstances should an aggressive or disruptive student be evaluated for a possible behavior disorder?

A day hardly passes in many schools without at least a few students becoming involved in a fight or disrupting class. There is little reason to evaluate every student who is charged with such misconduct for a possible behavior disorder. In some cases, however, school authorities may need to consider the possibility that a student's behavior is the result of psychological or medical problems requiring the assistance of specialists. What guidelines should be used in determining when students should undergo a formal assessment?

As a diagnostic category, "behavior disordered" is relatively recent. Coleman (1992, p. 22) explains that the preferred term for years was "emotionally disturbed." In the wake of Public Law 94-142, some states replaced this term with behavior disordered because it sounded less threatening and more compatible with the educational mission of the school. Presumably, teachers could observe and attempt to correct inappropriate *behavior. Emotions,* on the other hand, seemed to belong more in the domain of clinical psychology.

It should be noted that consensus regarding terminology in this area does not exist. Depending on the state, special education teachers may use behavior disordered or emotionally disturbed. "Conduct disorder" is frequently employed as a diagnostic category by mental health professionals working in residential treatment centers. Conduct disorders are indicated by the presence of multiple antisocial behaviors, such as fighting and physical cruelty, over an extended period of time. Walker, Colvin, and Ramsey (1995, p. 4) note that educators sometimes refer to conduct disorders and antisocial behavior as "social maladjustment." Representatives of law enforcement agencies and the courts may use the term "sociopathic" to describe behavior patterns that pose a danger to others.

Public Law 94-142 specified that "seriously emotionally disturbed" was a condition characterized by one or more of the following aspects (*Federal Register,* 1981):

- an inability to learn which cannot be explained by intellectual, sensory, or health factors
- an inability to build or maintain satisfactory interpersonal relationships with peers and teachers
- inappropriate types of behavior or feelings under normal circumstances
- a general pervasive mood of unhappiness or depression
- a tendency to develop physical symptoms or fears associated with personal or school problems

Serious behavior problems requiring clinical intervention may be divided into two general categories: internalizing behaviors and externalizing behaviors (Coleman, 1992, pp. 26–28). Internalizing behaviors, such as social withdrawal and apathy, generally pose no immediate safety problem for others. Externalizing behaviors, on the other hand, may place others at risk. These behaviors include defiance, disobedience, vandalism, aggression toward others, temper tantrums, and swearing. In the most extreme cases, young people lack the ability to distinguish right from wrong. They appear to have no conscience or respect for societal rules. These individuals may be referred to as psychopathic, sociopathic, or "solitary aggressive type" (Coleman, 1992, p. 159).

In determining whether aggressive behavior should be treated as disordered behavior, it is necessary to take into account its frequency and severity. When aggressive behavior has been present for a long period of time, when it results in serious harm to people and property, and when it is coupled with other externalizing behaviors, psychological assessment by trained personnel is justified. Teachers and administrators should be prepared to provide evidence of the frequency of behaviors and their effects on others.

To help resolve some of the confusion surrounding terminology and provide guidance concerning when to assess individuals manifesting problem behavior, the National Mental Health and Special Education Coalition created a working group to develop a new definition of behavioral disorder. The result of their efforts is the following statement (Forness and Knitzer, 1992, p. 13):

> The term emotional or behavioral disorder means a disability characterized by behavioral or emotional responses in school programs so different from appropriate age, cultural, or ethnic norms that they adversely affect educational performance, including academic, social, vocational or personal skills, and which:
> a) is more than a temporary, expected response to stressful events in the environment;
> b) is consistently exhibited in two different settings, at least one of which is school-related; and
> c) persists despite individualized interventions within the education program, unless, in the judgment of the team, the child's or youth's history indicates that such interventions would not be effective.

Labeling young people as seriously emotionally disturbed and behavior disordered, of course, can have negative consequences. The potential for misdiagnosis and the "self-fulfilling prophecy" effect is always present. To protect the interests of young people, guidelines have been established for evaluating students for special education services. As specified in Public Law 94-142, evaluations must involve non-discriminatory testing, parental participation, multiple criteria, team decisions, and test validity. Estimates of U.S. students who meet the criteria for behavior disordered range from less than 1% to more than 10% (Coleman, 1992, pp. 30–31).

Should drugs be used to control the behaviors of students with behavior disorders?

Deciding that a student should be labeled behavior disordered does not mean that the appropriate course of action is necessarily clear. Considerable controversy exists regarding the extent to which students who are seriously emotionally disturbed and behavior disordered should be medicated when they are in school.

Three main categories of drugs are used in conjunction with IEPs involving behavior disorders. Antipsychotic drugs (tranquilizers) are reserved for the most serious cases. They do not cure disorders, but they are helpful in controlling the symptoms of psychosis, including hallucinations and delusions. Coleman (1992, p. 54) reports that, when used in small doses, these drugs can relieve tension, anxiety, and agitation as well as control aggression and self-injurious behavior.

A second category of drug that has gained popularity with therapists in recent years is antidepressants. Although their use in educational settings is not widespread, antidepressants are occasionally prescribed for school phobia and extreme sadness. Stimulants, the third type of drug, are used to treat attention deficit disorder. There are indications that drugs such as Ritalin and Dexedrine can improve attention and reduce impulsivity in many young people.

Some child psychologists and physicians have raised serious questions about the use of drug therapy with young people. Breggin (2000, p. 61), a physician, has taken the extreme position of counseling parents *never* to permit their children to be placed on psychoactive drugs for the control of behavior or emotions. Not only does prescribing drugs send the wrong message to young people who we want to avoid drug dependency, but some evidence exists that drugs may have the opposite effect of that which we desire. Breggin (2000, pp. 127–146) notes that some of the boys involved in school shootings were taking drugs prescribed by physicians and psychologists. He points out that antidepressants can induce a manic reaction in which a young person feels invincible and godlike, feelings that can lead to violence. Interestingly, antidepressants also can cause depression, the very condition they are supposed to alleviate (Breggin, 2000, pp. 137–138). Stimulants do not escape Breggin's broadside. He refers to research that has traced violent and psychotic behavior to the use of stimulants such as Ritalin (Breggin, 2000, pp. 138–140).

There is no question that, despite its risks, drug therapy has an appeal for many people. Parents naturally want to see their children avoid getting into trouble in school. Educators want to reduce disorderly and dangerous behavior so that teaching and learning can take place. Prescribing antipsychotics, antidepressants, and stimulants for millions of students, however, is unlikely to provide long-term solutions to either unsafe schools or the psychological problems of young people. Drug therapy may be justified as a last resort in the most serious cases, but parents and educators must be apprised of the potential for harmful side effects.

What can schools do to reduce the harmful effects of drugs and alcohol?

Protecting young people from the negative effects of drugs and alcohol is not easy in a society that often glamorizes these substances. Young people frequently see adults, including their own parents, consuming alcoholic beverages in the course of relaxing and having a good time. They watch movies and television shows in which young people experiment with drugs in order to achieve heightened awareness and to cope with stress and anxiety. They read of admired athletes who take performance-enhancing drugs. Despite these impediments, there still is much schools can do to discourage students from using drugs and alcohol. Five strategies are particularly important:

1. Develop school cultures that discourage the use of drugs and alcohol.
2. Recognize when students might be using drugs and alcohol.
3. Provide instruction related to the harmful effects of drugs and alcohol and how to resist them.

4. Enforce school rules related to the possession, use, and distribution of drugs and alcohol.
5. Provide interventions and referrals for students involved in the abuse of drugs and alcohol.

In some schools, young people pick up the message that educators do not feel it is their responsibility to oversee drug and alcohol use. Other schools, meanwhile, are characterized by cultures that strongly oppose the use and distribution of dangerous substances. Young people are encouraged to develop sound health practices and play an active role in discouraging friends and siblings from using drugs and alcohol. School cultures that reinforce healthy behavior and warn against substance abuse have been found to have lower levels of drug problems than schools with cultures that do not take an active stand against such behavior (Gottfredson, 1997, p. 5-19).

A second responsibility of schools is to identify students who may be using drugs and alcohol. Educators must be alert to signs of drug and alcohol use, both at school and elsewhere. They should know the factors that can lead young people to experiment with controlled substances and recognize the signs and symptoms of drug and alcohol abuse. The latter include personality changes, changes in appearance, changes in behavior, and physical evidence. Table 10.1 contains a list of signs and symptoms. Any one of the signs and symptoms may be present in young persons who are not having drug and alcohol problems. The presence of multiple signs and symptoms, on the other hand, is more likely to suggest substance abuse.

Besides developing familiarity with the signs and symptoms of drug and alcohol use, educators need to help parents and students recognize these indicators. Students should be encouraged to report when classmates may be abusing drugs and alcohol. Students, understandably, are more likely to inform school authorities if their identity can be concealed. Several court cases indicate that school authorities are not compelled to disclose who provided them with information related to drugs and alcohol (Johnson, 1989).

Providing all students with instruction related to the harmful effects of drugs and alcohol is another important responsibility of all schools. Instruction should cover such issues as the consequences—physical, psychological, social and legal—of drug and alcohol abuse and how to handle situations in which there is pressure to use illegal substances. The latter often is referred to as "resistance training." Competency in self-control, stress management, social problem-solving, conflict resolution, and communications are additional useful goals of instruction. Gottfredson (1997, pp. 5-28 to 5-38) reported that instruction of the kind noted above can be an effective approach to curtailing substance abuse. Two instructional programs with demonstrated effectiveness for secondary students are ALERT (Ellickson & Bell, 1990) and Life-Skills Training (Botvin, Baker, Filazzola, & Botvin, 1990).

Enforcing school rules related to the possession, use, and distribution of drugs and alcohol is the fourth responsibility of schools that are committed to curtailing substance abuse. It is of little value to have rules if they are not enforced consistently. Many school systems in the United States operate with zero tolerance policies in mat-

TABLE 10.1   Signs and Symptoms of Drug and Alcohol Use

Personality Changes	Physical Changes	Behavioral Changes	Physical Evidence
■ Less caring and involvement at home ■ Lack of motivation ■ Frequent irritability ■ Periods of paranoia due to "dual life" (i.e., hiding substance abuse from family) ■ "I don't care" attitude ■ Unexplained mood swings alternating between depression and euphoria	■ Unkempt appearance ■ Weight loss, pale face, circles under eyes ■ Red eyes (or frequent use of eye drops) ■ Unexplained skin rashes, increased acne ■ Persistent cough, frequent colds, low resistance to illness ■ Changes in sleeping patterns ■ Changes in eating patterns	■ School attendance problems ■ Drop in grades/performance ■ Increased need for money ■ Quitting or getting fired from job ■ New friends with no last names, no contact with parents, lying, secretiveness ■ Inability to concentrate ■ Spending more time in room or away from home ■ Verbal and physical abuse toward parents, siblings, property ■ Tantrums over seemingly minor issues	■ Eye drops ■ Mouth wash or breath sprays ■ Cigarette rolling papers ■ Roach or alligator clips ■ Bongs, pipes, small screens, baggies, and "stash cans" ■ Seeds from marijuana plants ■ Drug insignia on clothing

Information in Table 10.1 came from "A Drug and Alcohol Awareness Handbook for Pelham Parents," 1999, prepared by Parents and Community Together (PACT) of Pelham, New York.

ters of drugs and alcohol. Consistent enforcement of these policies sends a potent message to young people thinking about bringing illegal substances to school.

Enforcing school rules related to controlled substances may entail periodic locker searches, drug testing, and "sweeps" by drug-sniffing dogs. The preceding discussion regarding student rights and privacy issues should be reviewed before adopting these measures. Surveillance cameras in isolated parts of the school can help to discourage students from transacting drug sales on campus. Some school systems provide a hot line so that students can provide school administrators with anonymous tips concerning drug deals, local parties where alcohol and drugs may be present, and classmates who are abusing these substances.

Blauvelt (1999, pp. 33–34) offers several guidelines concerning enforcement of rules related to drugs. When a school administrator comes across a suspicious substance, the individual should place it in a clean plastic bag and then place the bag in a clean envelope and seal it. The date and time when the substance was found should be indicated on the envelope along with where it was found and from whom it was received (if another person was involved). The police should be contacted and asked to pick up the envelope and run a test on its contents. When a police officer picks up the envelope, she should be asked to provide a written receipt.

Schools should be prepared to assist students who have been discovered to be abusing drugs and alcohol. Where zero tolerance policies are in place, such assistance, of course, may need to be provided outside of the regular school setting. Special counseling, behavior modification programs, and direct instruction can be useful, as can participation in a support group consisting of students with similar problems. Parents, too, may benefit from these interventions under certain circumstances. Alternative schools have proven to be effective settings for some young people in need of help overcoming substance abuse (Gottfredson, 1997, pp. 5-28).

Although schools alone may be unable to prevent all young people from experimenting with and abusing drugs and alcohol, they can play a vital role in community-based efforts to reduce these problems. The inability to control many of the factors that lead young people to use drugs and alcohol is not an acceptable reason for ignoring the problem.

What can schools do to combat the negative influence of gangs?

Gangs have long been a feature of U.S. social structure. There are indications that their influence, particularly in schools, is growing. A government report published in 1998 (U.S. Department of Education and U.S. Department of Justice, 1998, p. 34) indicated that the percentage of students reporting that street gangs were present at their schools rose from 15% in 1989 to 28% in 1995.

Gangs come in all shapes and sizes. Huff (1989), in studying Ohio gangs, identified three basic types of gangs. Informal hedonistic gangs concentrate primarily on partying and committing minor crimes, mostly against property. Instrumental gangs commit property crimes for economic reasons and engage in the sale of drugs. Predatory gangs are involved in violent crime. Gangs are a concern for educators because gang activity sometimes spills over onto campuses, resulting in fights, "get even" acts, and vandalism. Gang members, many of whom are no longer in school, also may recruit students and enlist them in efforts to distribute drugs and commit other crimes at school.

Efforts to eliminate gangs have not proven particularly effective (Sherman, 1997, pp. 3-10 to 3-19). Besides, educators alone are not in a position to take the lead in such endeavors. Educators, however, can work to reduce the underlying factors that lead to gang involvement and to discourage young people from turning to gangs as a way to resolve difficulties in their lives. Among the actions that schools can take to combat the negative influence of gangs are the following:

- Monitor students for indications of gang involvement
- Cooperate with local law enforcement in addressing gang-related problems
- Develop early intervention programs to deal with academic problems and anti-social behavior
- Support the development of after-school and weekend activities
- Promote mentoring programs

As in the case of drug and alcohol prevention efforts, there are various signs that suggest students may be involved in gangs. These signs include graffiti on school property, unusual attire, and fights involving groups of students. Educators need to be alert to such indicators. In some cases, students may not be actual gang members, but they may be emulating these individuals. In other instances, gang activities are occurring at school. By monitoring students for signs of gang involvement, educators can warn parents and the police as well as take a public stand against gang involvement. School officials should take immediate steps to remove graffiti and other symbols of gangs and to prohibit students from wearing gang-related attire to school.

If gangs have formed in a community, efforts to deal with them must involve local law enforcement agencies. Educators need to establish close ties with these agencies, informing them of suspicious activities at school and receiving advanced warnings of possible gang-related incidents in or around school. In the event that rival gangs become involved in a fight at school, the police should be contacted immediately and the appropriate crisis management plan put into effect. School personnel should not attempt to handle such incidents on their own.

The key to school-based efforts to deal with gangs is early intervention. Once adolescents have joined a gang, it is quite difficult to convince them to leave. Elementary school interventions should focus on assisting students who are experiencing academic problems and manifesting antisocial behavior. Antisocial behavior causes youngsters to be rejected by peers and teachers, thereby making them receptive to invitations from gangs. Many of the programs that have proven effective in preventing drug and alcohol use, such as training in resistance skills and effective problem solving, also may help young people cope with the lure of gang membership.

One school-based program that has shown promise in discouraging young people from becoming involved in gangs is Gang Resistance Education and Training (G.R.E.A.T.). Developed by the Phoenix Police Department, G.R.E.A.T. is a nine-week instructional program aimed at middle school students. Students learn about the impact of crime on victims and the community in general and how to meet their needs without joining a gang. Goal-setting is a key component of the training. A study that compared students who had and had not received G.R.E.A.T. instruction found that the former reported lower rates of delinquency and drug use (Gottfredson, 1997, pp. 5-39 to 5-40).

Because unstructured time opens the door to possible gang involvement, programs that offer young people interesting things to do after school, on weekends, and in the summer also may serve as antidotes to gang involvement (Sherman, 1997, pp. 3-26 to 3-28). Educators should create programs that use school facilities during nonschool hours and work with other groups to develop opportunities for involvement elsewhere in the community. Howell (1995, p. 95) concluded that

> Afterschool recreation programs can address the risk factors of alienation and association with delinquent and violent peers. Protective factors may include opportunities for involvement with prosocial youth and adults, skills for leisure activities, and bonding to prosocial others.

Some young people are drawn to gangs because they lack positive role models. To address this deficit, schools and communities can develop mentoring programs that place at-risk young people in contact with responsible and caring adults. There is substantial evidence that mentoring can be an effective intervention to prevent young people from joining gangs (Sherman, 1997, pp. 3-20 to 3-25). Mentors meet with their young charges several times each month as well as speaking with them over the phone on a regular basis. Young people share problems with mentors and join them in recreational activities.

The overall message for educators interested in reducing the harmful effects of gangs is identical to that for school-based efforts to confront drugs and alcohol. Though educators alone do not control the factors that give rise to gangs, it is crucial that they play an active role in discouraging gang involvement and providing constructive alternatives for young people.

Questions Related to General School Safety Issues

Is it possible to transform an unsafe school into a safe school?

Most schools in the United States are reasonably safe most of the time. There are schools, however, where students and staff members exist in a state of constant anxiety and fear. Bullying, disruption, and disrespect for authority are the norm. Effective teaching and learning are held hostage. Those who can escape to safer learning environments do so as soon as possible. In the late seventies, New York City's Samuel Gompers Vocational–Technical High School was just such a school. According to one account, "Alcohol, drugs, and fights in the halls were all commonplace. Assaults on teachers and fires in the classrooms were not uncommon" (Herbert, 1990, p. 99).

By the mid-eighties, Gompers had been transformed into a safe and successful high school. Student enrollment was up, crime and suspensions were down, and learning was taking place. Fear no longer roamed the halls. The school received national recognition as a "school of excellence." What accounted for this dramatic and relatively rapid turnaround?

In relating Gompers' story, Herbert (1990) identifies a variety of factors that helped to convert disorder into order. One key was a pragmatic principal who realized that students and staff members had to feel secure before teaching and learning could take place. He set to work apprehending students who routinely set off fire alarms. Coating alarms with indelible grease paint, he made a point of shaking students' hands until he identified the culprits. He also sent students home to change clothes when they wore expensive coats and gang attire to school. The schoolyard was reclaimed from groups of students who preferred hanging out to attending class. Serious crime, such as drug dealing and weapons possession, was dealt with swiftly and harshly. As they saw the school becoming safer, students and staff members gained confidence that they, too, could help make Gompers a good place to learn.

Once the student body and the faculty acknowledged that maintaining order was also their responsibility, and not just the administration's, efforts shifted to improving the curriculum and hiring new teachers. State-of-the-art electronics and computer programs were established, and weak teachers were replaced with well-trained young faculty. Students were selected for a consultative council that assisted administrators in handling such problems as attendance and hallway behavior. Pride supplanted fear as the prevailing feeling about the school.

Although inspiring, the Gompers' story is not unique. Gottfredson (1997, pp. 5-14 to 5-21) identifies a variety of studies that demonstrate the positive impact of schoolwide interventions. These initiatives vary, of course, in terms of particular strategies. Some involve behavior modification techniques, others rely on classroom management training, and still others stress consistent rule enforcement. In each case, though, the overall prescription for success is similar: safety first. Before effective teaching and learning can take place, students and staff members must feel safe and secure. Order is a prerequisite for, not a consequence of, good instruction.

To establish order, leadership is needed. Not just administrative leadership, but leadership by teachers and students. Individuals who insist on disrupting school and threatening people must be identified and dealt with. Training may be necessary so that students and staff members know how to handle challenging situations. Planning is important so that people understand what to do in an emergency. There are no shortcuts to safe schools. Planning and training require time. So does the cultivation of trust and feelings of safety. As the case of Samuel Gompers Vocational–Technical High School illustrates, however, patience and persistence have their rewards.

How should resources be targeted to make the biggest difference in school safety?

Educators know better than many professionals that we live in a world of limited resources. When it comes to making schools safer, they rarely are given a blank check to cover expenses. Assuming funds are limited, how can educators get the greatest benefit for their expenditures related to school safety?

This book has presented a variety of approaches to school safety, each involving certain costs. In some cases, the costs involve training for staff members and students. In other cases, special materials such as curriculum guides and workbooks must be purchased. Hiring school resource officers, hall monitors, special counselors, and other individuals to deal with safety-related responsibilities entails a considerable investment, as does making adjustments to school facilities and acquiring security technology such as surveillance cameras and metal detectors. Other expenditures may involve after-school programs and constructive alternatives to keep young people from getting into trouble. All of these cost items can contribute to school safety, but together they may be beyond the means of many schools.

Determining how to target scarce resources, of course, depends on the particular circumstances of a school. It is the judgment of the author that the most helpful strategy for relatively large middle schools and high schools—the schools where safety problems tend to be greatest—is to subdivide them into smaller units. The costs associated with downsizing a secondary school into houses, schools-within-a-school, or academies may include architectural fees, renovation expenses, stipends for teachers involved in planning activities, and salaries for additional personnel. The investment, though, is well worth it. Research suggests that smaller, less impersonal learning environments experience fewer behavior problems. Teachers get to know their students better and function as members of teams, assuming collective responsibility for the welfare of their students. Students feel a greater attachment to smaller learning units and participate in a wider range of activities.

In considering how best to invest funds for school safety, it is important to be guided by a comprehensive plan with specific goals. Goals should be based on actual data concerning safety concerns and student needs. Simply purchasing new security devices and sending teachers to school safety conferences are unlikely to yield benefits unless they are part of a coordinated series of initiatives aimed at addressing particular problems. To avoid wasting resources, a sensible first step should be to analyze school safety data and develop a comprehensive school safety plan. The plan, in turn, can guide subsequent expenditures.

It is important to remember that some of the most important keys to safe schools involve no cost at all. These include developing a clear set of expectations for student conduct and communicating them to students. Reinforcing positive values and treating students with care and respect entail no expense, but the potential dividends in terms of student well-being and school culture are inestimable.

What grade level poses the greatest challenge for educators concerned about school safety?

Although particular schools may experience problems in particular grades, eighth and ninth grades tend to be seen as the trouble spots in American education. Retention rates increase dramatically at the ninth grade, for example. Students who are retained at grade level for academic reasons are more likely to become discipline problems.

Eighth and ninth graders account for disproportionately high percentages of behavior referrals and suspensions. Academic work frequently plummets in these grades as young people deal with the challenges of adolescence and moving to high school (Duke, Bourdeaux, Epps, & Wilcox, 1998). Drug use becomes a major problem in the eighth grade, with more than one out of every five eighth graders trying marijuana and 17% experimenting with an illicit drug other than marijuana (Johnson, O'Malley, & Bachman, 1999, pp. 24–25). In *A Tribe Apart,* Hersch (1998, p. 134) cites a report by the Virginia Department of Education that captures the concerns surrounding eighth and ninth grades:

> "Incidents of weapons possession and referrals to substance abuse programs peak during the middle school years." The report says that "violent and unruly behavior" peak in eighth and ninth grades, that approximately 70 percent of weapons found in public schools statewide are found in middle schools.

When Austin, Texas, took a close look at its ninth graders, it found that fewer freshmen passed all of their courses than students in any other secondary grade (Paredes, 1991). Fewer than half of Austin's ninth graders passed all of their courses. With almost one out of every four ninth graders retained at grade level, the retention rate for ninth graders was more than three times as great as that for any other grade. Attendance for ninth graders dropped off dramatically, and disciplinary referrals exceeded any other grade.

Can anything be done to address the problems of eighth and ninth graders? Many educators feel that part of the problem, at least for ninth graders, stems from the transition from middle school to high school. It is hard to go from being "a big fish in a small pond" to being "a little fish in a big pond." To address the stresses of transition, school systems have tried a number of promising strategies. Intensive summer remediation programs have been developed for rising ninth graders with academic deficits. A growing number of high schools offer self-contained ninth-grade programs, some geared toward at-risk students and others designed for all ninth graders. Students in these transition programs take their core academic courses from ninth-grade teachers organized into teams. Modeled after middle school teams, these groups of teachers plan together for the same group of students. Because their classes are "blocked," they can rearrange time and group students to meet their academic and behavioral needs. A study of ninth-grade transition programs in Virginia found that most were perceived to have reduced discipline problems and enhanced students' psycho-social adjustment to high school (Duke, Bourdeaux, Epps, & Wilcox, 1998).

Some school systems have gone beyond teacher teams and block scheduling to create ninth-grade houses with their own assistant principal and guidance counselor. Physically separate from the rest of the high school, ninth-grade houses cut down on the problems that can arise when older students pick on and haze ninth graders. Several school systems, including Chicago, Illinois, and Alexandria, Virginia, have created separate schools for ninth graders. In other cases, such as Cincinnati, educators decided that the best way to deal with transition problems was to eliminate the transition. Secondary schools in these places house grades 7 to 12, thereby cutting out the need for students to switch schools at the end of the eighth grade.

To address the restlessness and disinterest in academics that characterize many eighth and ninth graders, some educators have created exciting new schools and programs based on physical challenges and problem-based learning. The Discovery program in Orange, Virginia, offers eighth graders an opportunity to meet academic requirements while preparing for an end-of-the-year wilderness survival training program with Outward Bound. In Franklin County, Virginia, students spend a semester at a regular middle school and a semester in a totally different environment, the Center for Applied Technology and Career Exploration (CATCE). Instead of traditional courses, CATCE students select six-week-long modules that require them to work in teams to solve practical problems such as how to clean up a polluted stream and how to collect evidence regarding a crime. CATCE and the Discovery program prove that school need not be boring for young adolescents. High-interest learning environments such as these report fewer behavior problems and better attendance.

Conclusion

The questions in this chapter certainly do not exhaust the safety-related queries that educators and concerned citizens might ask. They do represent, however, the types of questions with which educators and policy makers must grapple in the process of making schools safe for all students. Although there are no easy answers to the kinds of questions raised in the preceding pages, the responses suggest that there is ample cause for hope. School safety is not a matter of conjecture and lucky guesses. Much has been learned over the past half century about how to safeguard students and promote their well-being. Chapter 11 continues this theme by reviewing some of the lessons that have been learned on the road to school safety.

R E F E R E N C E S

Blauvelt, Peter D. *Making Schools Safe for Students.* Thousand Oaks, CA: Sage, 1999.

Botvin, G. J.; Baker, E.; Filazzola, A. D.; and Botvin, E. M. "A Cognitive-Behavioral Approach to Substance Abuse Prevention: One-Year Follow-up," *Addictive Behaviors,* vol. 15 (1990), pp. 47–63.

Breggin, Peter R. *Reclaiming Our Children.* Cambridge, MA: Perseus Books, 2000.

Brunsma, David L., and Rockquemore, Kerry A. "Effects of Student Uniforms on Attendance, Behavior Problems, Substance Use and Academic Achievement," *Journal of Educational Research,* vol. 92, no. 1 (1998), pp. 53–62.

Coleman, Margaret Cecil. *Behavior Disorders: Theory and Practice.* second edition. Boston: Allyn & Bacon, 1992.

Dowling-Sendor, Benjamin. "A Search of Last Resort," *The American School Board Journal* (November 1997), pp. 18–19.

Duke, Daniel L.; Bourdeaux, Jerry; Epps, Beverly; and Wilcox, Toni. "Ninth Grade Transition Programs in Virginia." A Policy Perspectives Paper from the Thomas Jefferson Center for Educational Design. Charlottesville, VA: University of Virginia, 1998.

Dunklee, Dennis R., and Shoop, Robert J. *A Primer for School Risk Management.* Boston: Allyn & Bacon, 1993.

Ellickson, P. L., and Bell, R. M. "Drug Prevention in Junior High: A Multi-Site Longitudinal Test," *Science,* vol. 247 (1990), pp. 1299–1305.

Federal Register. Washington, DC: U.S. Government Printing Office, January 16, 1981.

Forness, S. R., and Knitzer, J. "A New Proposed Definition and Terminology to Replace 'Serious Emotional Disturbance' in Individuals with Disabilities Education Act." *School Psychology Review,* vol. 21 (1992), pp. 12–20.

Gottfredson, Denise C. "School-Based Crime Prevention." In Lawrence W. Sherman, Denise Gottfredson, Doris MacKenzie, John Eck, Peter Reuter, and Shawn Bushway, (eds.), *Preventing Crime: What Works, What Doesn't, What's Promising.* College Park, MD: Department of Criminal Justice, University of Maryland, 1997, pp. 5-1 to 5-74.

Herbert, Victor. "Samuel Gompers Vocational–Technical High School: A Case Study of Collaborative School Improvement." In Oliver C. Moles (ed.), *Student Discipline Strategies.* Albany, NY: State University of New York Press, 1990, p. 99–105.

Hersch, Patricia. *A Tribe Apart.* New York: Ballantine Books, 1998.

Howell, James C. (ed.). *Guide for Implementing the Comprehensive Strategy for Serious, Violent, and Chronic Juvenile Offenders.* Washington, DC: Office of Juvenile Justice and Delinquency Prevention, 1995.

Huff, C. R. "Youth Gangs and Public Policy," *Crime and Delinquency,* vol. 35 (1989), pp. 524–537.

Imber, Michael, and Van Geel, Tyll. *Education Law,* second edition. Mahwah, NJ: Erlbaum, 2000.

Johnson, Lloyd D.; O'Malley, Patrick M.; and Bachman, Jerald G. *National Survey Results on Drug Use from the Monitoring the Future Study, 1975–1998.* Bethesda, MD: U.S. Department of Health and Human Services, 1999.

Johnson, T. Page. "Developments in School Law," vol. 5, no. 1 (July 1989). A newsletter published by the Virginia Association of Secondary School Principals.

"Law Update," *Education Week* (June 11, 1997), p. 12.

Paredes, V. "Caution: Hazardous Grade," Publication No. 90.26. Austin, TX: Austin Independent School District, 1991.

Sherman, Lawrence W. "Communities and Crime Prevention." In Lawrence W. Sherman, Denise Gottfredson, Doris MacKenzie, John Eck, Peter Reuter, and Shawn Bushway (eds.), *Preventing Crime: What Works, What Doesn't, What's Promising.* College Park, MD: Department of Criminology and Criminal Justice, University of Maryland, 1997, pp. 3-1 to 3-49.

U.S. Department of Education and U.S. Department of Justice. *Indicators of School Crime and Safety.* Washington, DC: Authors, 1998.

Walker, Hill M.; Colvin, Geoff; and Ramsey, Elizabeth. *Antisocial Behavior in School: Strategies and Best Practices.* Pacific Grove, CA: Brooks/Cole, 1995.

White, Kerry A. "Do School Uniforms Fit?" *The School Administrator,* vol. 57, no. 2 (February 2000), pp. 36–40.

Yardley, Jim. "Family in Texas Challenges Mandatory School Drug Test," *New York Times* (April 17, 2000), p. A1.

11 Lessons Learned on the Way to Safer Schools

MAJOR IDEAS IN CHAPTER 11

- School safety is a matter of cognition as well as control.
- How schools are organized and led can contribute to or reduce safety problems.
- How school safety problems are addressed reflects a great deal about the nature of our society.
- School safety problems are more likely to occur when the needs of young people are not met.
- A number of issues concerning school safety have yet to be resolved.

Just because some schools experience episodes of disruption and violence does not mean that advances in school safety have not been made. Although questions remain regarding how to handle certain safety problems, a clear sense of "best practice" is emerging among many educators and school safety specialists. Key dimensions of effective school safety initiatives have been identified by researchers. These dimensions helped frame the standards of school safety discussed in Section II. So, too, did professional judgment, public opinion, and legal decisions related to the treatment of young people and the operation of schools.

The quest for safe schools for all students has generated important insights, not only about effective policies, programs, and practices, but also about who we are as a society and how we make sense of school safety as a public concern. This chapter is a reflection on some of the less obvious lessons that have been learned on the road to safer schools.

Thinking about School Safety

Some of the most important lessons that have been learned about school safety are less concerned with what goes on in hallways than in heads. School safety is, to a substantial degree, a cognitive matter. We think about the nature of safety, how safety can and should be achieved, and how threats to safety can be explained. Improvements in school safety, therefore, may require changes in the way we think about it.

Lesson No. 1: Safety means different things to different people

Though obvious, it is necessary to reaffirm the fact that safety is a matter of perception. Perceptions, in turn, are highly influenced by experience. Someone who has experienced an assault is likely to think about safety differently from someone who has never been attacked. Those who know firsthand what it means to be victimized are less likely, for example, to take safety for granted. In schools serving poor students from high-crime neighborhoods, middle-class teachers with little personal experience of violence may find it difficult to comprehend what their students are thinking about as they sit in class. Someone who has never worried about what awaits them on the journey home or once they arrive may not appreciate the escalating anxiety that builds as the day goes on and intrudes on classroom learning. Someone who has never been abused by a family member may not understand why offers of help are met with distrust and wariness.

We have learned over the years that people's tolerance for certain behaviors varies considerably (Coleman, 1992, pp. 19–20). These variations reflect how they think about safety. One person may have a high tolerance for criticism and barbed humor, but another person is ready to fight at the drop of a sarcastic remark. It is not always easy to understand what factors in an individual's life conspire to produce a violent reaction. Our own perceptions frequently form a substantial barrier to understanding perceptions of others. Failure to understand, unfortunately, may only serve to exacerbate volatile situations.

Because school safety means different things to different people, it is prudent for educators to avoid assuming that consensus exists regarding such matters as the perceived level of safety in school or the best ways to combat safety threats. One violent incident, for example, may prompt some individuals to regard their school as unsafe. Others, because of their experiences, may treat fights and aggressive behavior as commonplace acts that do not necessitate great concern or unusual measures. Educators cannot turn back the clock and alter what students, staff members, and parents have experienced, nor can they easily dislodge inaccurate perceptions of school safety. What educators can do, though, is help people become aware of their different beliefs about safety and how best to achieve it.

Lesson No. 2: People confront threats to school safety with different mental models

How people think about matters such as school safety is highly influenced by what Senge (1990, pp. 174–204) calls "mental models." A mental model is a deeply held conviction about how the world works. Mental models range from simple generalizations, such as "some kids are just bad kids," to elaborate theories of human motivation. The power of mental models resides in the fact that they determine what we attend to. If we believe that unsafe schools are caused by a small number of "bad kids," we are unprepared to look for underlying conditions that contribute to violent and disruptive behavior.

Whether one reads books by experts or listens to citizens at public hearings on school safety, it is hard to ignore the variety of mental models that guide how people think about school safety. Chapter 2 presented six perspectives on, or ways to make sense of, school safety. Elliott, Hamburg, and Williams (1998, pp. 17–20) identify four theories that have guided research on school violence: social-ecological theory, life course theory, developmental theory, and public health theory. Coleman (1992, p. 20) reports that behavior disorders can be accounted for by five different conceptual models: behavioral, biophysical, psychodynamic, ecological, and sociological.

Highly formalized theories, conceptual models, and perspectives are more reflective of the thinking of researchers and experts than citizens in general. The mental models that characterize the thinking of nonexperts are apt to be less complex and more straightforward. Some people, for example, are convinced that public schools cannot be made safe for all students. Each violent incident, no matter how isolated, serves to confirm their cynicism. They expect the worst of their fellow man, and they are never disappointed. Believing that human nature is basically self-serving and aggressive, they approach life as if it were a matter of "survival of the fittest."

Other people possess mental models that recognize the possibility of safe schools. These individuals frequently express their beliefs with suppositions. "If only the troublemakers were removed, this school would be a safe place for everyone." The author once participated in a school improvement project at an urban junior high school. The faculty believed that, if a small number of disruptive students were placed in an alternative school, the remaining students would have a productive and problem-free educational experience. An alternative school was, in fact, created in an annex to the school, and the chronically disruptive students were assigned to it. Within three months, faculty members had identified a new group of disruptive students who stood between them and the goal of a peaceful and effective school.

Decades of initiatives designed to create safe schools have taught that the best mental models are not those based on a single solution to a complex problem. Because unsafe schools are the result of more than one cause, it is unlikely that "one best strategy" will transform them into safe schools. Multiple approaches are necessary. The first challenge for anyone committed to making schools safe for all students, therefore, is to provide opportunities for students, staff members, and parents to examine their mental models.

Lesson No. 3: Reflection is often a better response to safety problems than reaction

Teachers and school administrators contend on a daily basis with time constraints. There is never enough time to accomplish everything that needs to be done. Under such circumstances, reflection is a predictable victim. Educators complain that they spend a substantial percentage of their time reacting to situations that have little to do with teaching and learning. These situations often concern discipline problems and actual or potential safety threats.

If experience with school safety has taught any lesson, it is to beware of overly hasty reactions to problems. Most educators can recall at least one occasion when such a reaction made matters worse rather than better. Perhaps it was jumping to the conclusion that a student broke a rule, when, in fact, the individual was innocent. Or it could have been an ultimatum delivered in anger that left a student feeling alienated and misunderstood. Because educators are powerful role models for young people, it is crucial that they model circumspection and thoughtfulness when handling problems.

If busy educators are not mindful, they easily can slip into a mode of operation in which they wait until safety threats arise and then deal with them (James, 1994, p. 190). Such a reactive pattern of behavior means that little time is devoted to reflecting on the nature of school safety problems and what they might indicate about the unmet needs of young people and dysfunctional school practices. Reflection on such matters, in the long run, is a smart investment, not a waste of time. Only by reflecting on safety problems will educators be able to take the steps necessary to eliminate their causes.

Lesson No. 4: School safety is best regarded as a function of learning

Unsafe schools can be attributed to many factors—poverty, school size, racial and ethnic tension, neighborhood crime, gang activity, overcrowding, and so on. Of all the sources of threats to the well-being of students, though, ignorance may be the most serious. Many safety problems can be traced to lack of knowledge regarding how to handle difficult situations, when to avoid confrontations, and what to do in an emergency. People are not born knowing why rules exist or how to estimate the possible consequences of risky behavior. Young people do not spontaneously acquire strategies for resisting dangerous temptations and dealing with aggressive and abusive acts. They must learn how to conduct themselves in ways that reduce the likelihood of harm. Because the primary mission of schools is to promote learning that will allow young people to lead productive lives, it is entirely appropriate for schools to offer instruction related to personal safety.

The challenge for educators is to design environments in which students are likely to acquire the skills and knowledge to protect themselves and others. This learning cannot be assumed to occur at home. Chapter 3 stressed the importance of teaching students how they are expected to conduct themselves in school and the reasons for these expectations. Chapter 5 presented several ways that safety-related subjects could be approached by teachers. Measures included instruction in values and social skills. Chapter 6 emphasized the need to teach students how to communicate their safety concerns to school authorities. An important component of many intervention strategies for students who violate school rules is instruction in appropriate forms of behavior. Educators may not be able to guarantee that every student will take advantage of safety-related instruction, but they can make certain that such instruction is available and considered an integral part of the school's central mission.

Organizing for School Safety

The mission of the school is one key element of its organizational structure. As many of the recommendations in this book have indicated, how schools are structured helps account for their overall safety, or lack of it. Most threats to safety, of course, result from human action, but human action is influenced greatly by the nature of the organizations people inhabit. Schools may vary in terms of various aspects of organizational structure, including goals, rules, consequences for disobeying rules, roles of staff members, school size, decision making processes, and channels of communication. These characteristics help to determine what students and staff members do, or do not do, on a daily basis.

Senge (1990, pp. 17–26) observes that some organizations, like some people, are learning disabled. When organizations encourage staff members to focus only on their jobs and to disregard how their actions affect others, problems can arise. Another form of organizational learning disability derives from the tendency to focus on events rather than long-term processes. When an act of violence occurs in a school, for example, the temptation may be to zero in on the immediate cause of the act instead of trying to understand how it fits into a broader framework. Based on Senge's ideas, it can be assumed that schools do not become unsafe overnight. Schools that function as "learning organizations," to use his terminology, invest time and energy in trying to grasp the factors that cause them to be the way they are. The examination of research on school safety in this book reveals several lessons regarding the relationship between school organization and the well-being of young people.

Lesson No. 5: Safety problems are more likely to arise when school goals do not match the needs of students

Schools are expected to prepare young people to become productive adults. In the process of doing so, it is possible for educators to overlook the current needs of their students. The most pressing concerns in the lives of young people do not always revolve around academic work and future goals. Students contend with feelings of isolation and worries about being "different." They struggle to adjust to new environments, strive to develop an identity, try to make friends, assert their independence, and cope with fears and anxieties. When students sense that the concerns that matter most to them are not appreciated by their teachers, they can grow resentful and frustrated. Some are driven to harm themselves, and others strike out at the school, staff members, or classmates.

The first goal in preparing students to be productive adults is making certain they reach adulthood in a psychologically and physically healthy state. To accomplish this goal requires more than academic development. Schools must be designed in ways that encourage students to work together, develop constructive relationships with peers and adults, and acquire the skills necessary to handle various social interactions. Understanding the values and virtues on which a good society is based must be accorded as much importance as algebraic equations and good grammar. Research suggests that a key to reducing school violence is providing many opportunities for students to bond with their school and become actively involved in the educational process (Hawkins, Farrington, & Catalano, 1998, pp. 192–194).

Lesson No. 6: Safety problems are more likely to arise and intensify when communication channels fail to function effectively

A substantial portion of Section II dealt with the relationship between school safety and communications. Gottfredson (1997, pp. 5–14) reviewed various studies of school safety and found that schools "in which the administration and faculty communicate and work together to plan for change and solve problems have higher teacher morale and less disorder." School safety problems can be traced to expectations and rules that are not clearly conveyed to students, staff members who are too preoccupied to listen to the concerns of young people, and young people who are too upset to hear someone else's side of the story. It is an irony of many schools that communication goes on constantly, but it is often one-sided. Those who feel they are not heard develop negative feelings that can lead to withdrawal, resentment, and outbursts of anger.

Safe schools typically are characterized by a variety of opportunities for students, parents, and staff members to be heard. Good listening and regular feedback from all stakeholders are highly valued. Students are encouraged to share their fears, concerns, and suggestions for improving school safety. They receive training to enable them to resolve disputes peacefully and avoid saying things that could upset others. Staff members also receive such training so that they understand the connections between communication and safety.

Clear channels of communication are particularly critical during emergency situations. Chapter 7 covered a number of provisions related to communication in a crisis. Such times demand clear directions, ready access to critical information, rumor control, and the ability to convey calmness and the need for order. It is also vital that individuals know whom to contact to confirm that a crisis exists and to report injuries.

Lesson No. 7: Safety problems are less likely to occur when the well-being of students is considered to be every staff member's responsibility

Crucial elements of any organization are the designated roles that employees are expected to perform. Every role constitutes a set of expectations and responsibilities.

Those who work in schools fill a variety of roles, including classroom teacher, guidance counselor, administrator, teacher aide, school nurse, school resource officer, secretary, custodian, and cafeteria worker. When every employee's role includes responsibility for safeguarding students, the likelihood of safe schools for all students is increased.

Experience demonstrates that administrators alone cannot ensure that schools are orderly and peaceful places. School safety requires teachers and other staff members to enforce school rules, report students and colleagues who are having problems, and intervene when trouble is brewing. When staff members ignore or overlook problems that do not occur in their primary sphere of responsibility, students lose respect for the school as a rule-governed organization. In safe schools, safety is everybody's business.

School Safety and Leadership

Rules are no guarantee that students will behave appropriately. Nor are consequences for breaking rules. The formal mission statement of a school can proclaim a commitment to the well-being of young people, but such statements mean little if they are not internalized and valued. Leadership is that which enables organizational intentions to be translated into actions. Without capable and caring leadership, school safety initiatives may be no more than hollow gestures.

Lesson No. 8: The creation and maintenance of safe schools for all children requires capable and caring leadership

The preceding chapters have noted a variety of safety-related activities that depend on leadership. In some cases, such as the development and implementation of crisis management plans, the principal is expected to exercise leadership. When it comes to reinforcing appropriate behavior and instructing students about school rules, teacher leadership is essential. Student leadership also is necessary, particularly in resisting negative peer influence and reporting threats to school safety. To ensure that resources are available to support school safety efforts, community leadership is vital.

Of all the organizational challenges requiring leadership, three stand out: design, direction, and commitment. Safe schools, first of all, are the product of good educational and organizational design. Designing safe schools for all students involves an understanding of the role of time, space, expectations, relationships, roles, training, and culture. Leadership is needed to ensure that all the specialists who make up a school maintain a sense of the "big picture." It is always a temptation for staff members to think that their classroom or office is the only area that matters. In the absence of effective leadership, efforts to promote school safety can result in the creation of harsh and uninviting environments that repel young people. Poor design also can produce schools in which the absence of serious threats becomes an excuse for complacency and lack of preparedness.

Designs for safe schools are of little value, of course, if they cannot be taken from the drawing board and implemented. Effective leadership ensures that staff members understand what they must do to achieve a design. Guided by such leadership, people comprehend the direction in which they must head in order to reach the goal of safe schools for all students. Direction reduces uncertainty and ambiguity. People know, for example, what to do to reduce the likelihood of disorder and aggressive acts. When emergencies arise, they realize what has to be done and by whom. They grasp the importance of a comprehensive approach to school safety, one that encompasses both preventive strategies and interventions to handle problems when they do occur.

The third challenge of leadership is commitment. Good designs and a clear sense of direction are necessary, but insufficient to ensure safe schools. People must be committed to the goal of school safety in order to heed directions and implement designs. Inspiring commitment may pose the greatest challenge of all for school leaders because disagreements persist regarding the nature of safety and the best ways to achieve it. The preceding chapters described various controversies that illustrate these differences of opinion. Effective leadership, however, is able to help individuals transcend their differences for the sake of the common good.

School Safety As a Mirror of Society

In our efforts to create and maintain safe schools, we reveal much about the nature of our society. Although widespread agreement characterizes some aspects of our initiatives, other aspects exemplify our uncertainties and divisions. These uncertainties and divisions constitute the "unfinished agenda" of school safety.

Lesson No. 9: How we make sense of and handle school safety reflects a great deal about the nature of our society

Safety versus Risk.   Americans are, at some level, ambivalent about safety. Under certain circumstances, personal and public safety are highly valued. When crime goes unchecked and citizens feel vulnerable in their homes and workplaces, politicians and law enforcement agencies are expected to respond. At the same time, however, our society also embraces risk. We would not exist as a nation, in fact, if our forefathers had refused to take risks. Americans choose to engage in various dangerous activities, from extreme sports to martial arts. Those who invariably "play it safe" often are subject to ridicule.

If we are to create and maintain safe schools for all students, we must ask ourselves, "What level of risk do we desire?" Is it possible to value the risk entailed in athletics, entrepreneurial ventures, hunting, and adventure travel, while simultaneously rejecting the risk associated with experimentation with illegal substances and aggressive behavior? It is probably no coincidence that professional athletes increasingly are involved in violent and criminal incidents off the playing field.

Containing risk-taking to one sphere of life may be too challenging for many individuals.

Rights versus Responsibilities.   The debate over rights and responsibilities is primarily a matter of emphasis. No one suggests abolishing rights or ignoring responsibilities, but opinion divides regarding which should receive the most stress in schools. Some fear that overemphasizing the rights of students will undermine educators' efforts to maintain a disciplined environment. These people mourn the rise of legal challenges to school-based attempts to maintain order and promote safety.

Civil rights advocates, on the other hand, point out that many of the tactics used to create safe schools threaten the rights of young people. They question the Constitutional basis for drug testing, random searches, and examination of student records. They note that zero tolerance policies hold students to a tougher standard than that to which they would be subject in a court of law. Should the fear of unsafe schools justify the kind of curtailment of rights associated with times of war?

Crime versus Condition.   Another area of ambivalence involves the most appropriate way to think about serious and chronic behavior problems. Some people consider such conduct to be criminal in nature. They expect crimes to be punished. Others argue that repeated behavior problems involving a minor are symptomatic of psychological or medical conditions requiring treatment and understanding, not punishment. They criticize efforts to exclude students with behavior disorders from regular educational settings.

At what point should behavior that threatens the well-being of others—students and staff members alike—result in alternative placement, regardless of whether it is considered to be a medical problem? No thornier question confronts safety-conscious educators. Few teachers like to see young people with psychological problems removed from school, but they wonder whether retaining these individuals jeopardizes the opportunity to learn and the safety of other students. Are the rights of victims less important than the rights of victimizers?

Law versus Professional Judgment.   Students with serious emotional and behavioral problems who have been identified as eligible for special education services enjoy the protection of the law. The past half century has witnessed expanding influence over the operation of schools by lawmakers, lawyers, and the court system. Educators' concern over litigation and liability often leads them to think twice before disciplining students.

A number of people believe that the growth of education law is necessary to counteract possible discrimination and rights abuses by educators. They point to practices that result in harsher consequences for minority students and arbitrary disciplinary actions that deny young people due process. Others, however, note that safe schools are less likely to be achieved when educators' hands are tied by too many laws and regulations. A certain amount of discretion is essential if administrators and teachers are expected to maintain orderly learning environments. If educators cannot be trusted to exercise professional judgment in cases involving school safety, how can they be left to decide what is necessary to ensure that all students learn?

Safe Schools Can Be Achieved

Despite ambivalence regarding various issues related to school safety, the fact remains that most schools in the United States are reasonably safe and orderly places. This is not a coincidence. The decline in school violence and criminal activity in recent years is the result of the mobilization of public concern, the allocation of resources for school safety, the commitment of educators, and the creation of a knowledge base regarding school safety. Educators have clarified expectations for student behavior, developed comprehensive school safety plans, and obtained sophisticated training related to conflict and crisis management. Students, parents, and communities have been enlisted in the campaign for safe schools. That concerned citizens and conscientious educators can make a positive difference regarding the safety and well-being of young people is the most important lesson that we have learned.

Lesson No. 10: School safety can be achieved when schools and communities work together

There are many yardsticks by which the quality of a society can be judged. Perhaps one of the best measures of a society is its willingness to do whatever is necessary to safeguard the next generation. What we do to create and maintain safe learning environments for young people today will determine, to a great extent, the quality of our society tomorrow.

REFERENCES

Coleman, Margaret Cecil. *Behavior Disorders: Theory and Practice,* second edition. Boston: Allyn & Bacon, 1992.

Elliott, Delbert S.; Hamburg, Beatrix; and Williams, Kirk R. "Violence in American Schools: An Overview." In Delbert S. Elliott, Beatrix Hamburg, and Kirk R. Williams (eds.), *Violence in American Schools.* Cambridge: Cambridge University Press, 1998, pp. 3–28.

Gottfredson, Denise C. "School-Based Crime Prevention." In Lawrence W. Sherman, Denise Gottfredson, Doris MacKenzie, John Eck, Peter Reuter, and Shawn Bushway (eds.), *Preventing Crime: What Works, What Doesn't, What's Promising.* College Park, MD: Department of Criminology and Criminal Justice, University of Maryland, 1997, pp. 5-1 to 5-74.

Hawkins, J. David; Farrington, David P.; and Catalano, Richard F. "Reducing Violence through the Schools." In Delbert S. Elliott, Beatrix Hamburg, and Kirk R. Williams (eds.), *Violence in American Schools.* Cambridge: Cambridge University Press, 1998, pp. 188–216.

James, Bernard. "School Violence and the Law: the Search for Suitable Tools," *School Psychology Review,* vol. 23, no. 2 (1994), pp. 190–203.

Senge, Peter M. *The Fifth Discipline.* New York: Doubleday/Currency, 1990.

APPENDIX A

Standards for Safe Schools

Standard 1: Students know how they are supposed to behave at school and understand the reasons why.

Recommendation 1.1: Consider the various forms that behavioral guidelines may take and which forms are most appropriate for particular types of behavior, instructional purposes, and settings.

Recommendation 1.2: Make certain that school and classroom rules are reasonable and that they do not discriminate against any particular group.

Recommendation 1.3: Develop rules that are stated clearly and that are unlikely to be interpreted differently by different people.

Recommendation 1.4: Develop rules that are consistent with the Constitution and the mission of the school.

Recommendation 1.5: Develop rules related to illegal acts, classroom deportment, attendance, behavior outside of class, and academic work.

Recommendation 1.6: Periodically reassess rules to determine if revisions are necessary.

Recommendation 1.7: Instruct students about the meaning of school and classroom rules and help them understand why the rules are necessary.

Standard 2: Rules are enforced and consequences are administered humanely, fairly, and consistently.

Recommendation 2.1: Provide students accused of serious violations of school rules with a hearing and an opportunity to appeal a disciplinary decision.

Recommendation 2.2: Monitor rule enforcement efforts on a regular basis to ensure consistent interpretation of rules and application of consequences.

Recommendation 2.3: Clarify the purposes for which particular consequences are intended.

Recommendation 2.4: Ensure that consequences are legal, ethical, and consistent with the educational mission of the school.

Recommendation 2.5: Develop a range of consequences, including positive as well as negative, nonpunitive as well as punitive.

Recommendation 2.6: Evaluate the effectiveness of consequences on a regular basis and adjust or eliminate consequences that fail to produce desired effects.

Recommendation 2.7: Provide students who find it difficult to conform to expectations with access to alternative schools and programs.

Recommendation 2.8: Create a School Safety Team to develop and review responsibilities associated with school safety and rule enforcement.

Standard 3: Students feel valued and cared for.

Recommendation 3.1: Address issues of care and caregiving in the formal curriculum.

Recommendation 3.2: Provide opportunities for students and staff members to acquire and refine social skills.

Recommendation 3.3: Encourage staff, students, and parents to recognize and report signs of trouble.

Recommendation 3.4: Develop opportunities for students to play an active role in creating and maintaining caring school communities.

Recommendation 3.5: Provide a variety of opportunities for students to feel connected to school and expect students to take advantage of them.

Recommendation 3.6: Encourage students and staff to understand and accept student differences.

Recommendation 3.7: Develop clear policies concerning the handling of cases of abuse by students and staff members.

Recommendation 3.8: Conduct thorough background checks on all school employees.

Standard 4: A balance exists between efforts to promote appropriate conduct, discourage misconduct, and effectively handle misconduct when and if it does occur.

Recommendation 4.1: Develop a comprehensive school safety plan.

Recommendation 4.2: Include in the school safety plan school rules and expectations along with provisions for teaching them to students.

Recommendation 4.3: Include in the school safety plan provisions for a team-oriented approach at the school and grade levels.

Recommendation 4.4: Include in the school safety plan provisions for regular communication between students, parents, teachers, and administrators.

Recommendation 4.5: Include in the school safety plan provisions for proactive strategies, including efforts to help students academically.

Recommendation 4.6: Include in the school safety plan provisions for the systematic collection, management, and dissemination of data on school safety and student well-being.

Recommendation 4.7: Include in the school safety plan provisions for continuous staff development related to school safety.

Standard 5: School authorities anticipate and prepare for situations that could be disruptive or dangerous.

Recommendation 5.1: Develop plans to handle precrisis, crisis, and postcrisis situations.

Recommendation 5.2: Specify in each crisis management plan who should be contacted in the event of an emergency.

Recommendation 5.3: Specify in each plan the conditions under which the crisis management team should be convened.

Recommendation 5.4: Specify in each plan the duties of members of the crisis management team.

Recommendation 5.5: Specify in each plan the individuals and agencies that need to be contacted in the event of a crisis.

Recommendation 5.6: Specify in each plan what should be done when outside assistance is unavailable.

Recommendation 5.7: Make available to members of the crisis management team a variety of means of communicating with each other, various parts of the school, and sources of assistance outside the school.

Recommendation 5.8: Designate one member of the crisis management team to maintain an ongoing record of the crisis and the team's response.

Standard 6: The physical environment of the school has been designed to promote the safety and well-being of students.

Recommendation 6.1: Design schools with wide corridors free of lockers and other obstacles.

Recommendation 6.2: Provide disabled students with safe and ready access to all parts of the school.

Recommendation 6.3: Provide different routes into and out of school for bus riders and students who arrive by car or walk to school.

Recommendation 6.4: Design offices, classrooms, and workrooms with large windows or glazed walls and distribute them throughout the school at key locations.

Recommendation 6.5: Control access to school buildings and grounds by using a combination of direct supervision, limited points of entry, and security technology.

Recommendation 6.6: Design schools so that sections that are not used during nonschool hours can be closed to visitors.

Recommendation 6.7: Design school grounds to control access to pedestrian and vehicular traffic.

Recommendation 6.8: Build or subdivide schools so that students feel they are members of a personalized learning environment.

Standard 7: Parents and community members are involved in and committed to efforts to create and maintain safe schools.

Recommendation 7.1: Develop plans that address safety in school, at home, and in the community, and that involve educators, parents, and various community organizations.

Recommendation 7.2: Encourage parents individually and collectively to become involved in school and community safety initiatives.

Recommendation 7.3: Enlist community leaders in efforts to secure funds for and sponsor policies that promote school and community safety.

Recommendation 7.4: Develop guidelines governing the responsibilities of school resource officers and the circumstances under which law enforcement agencies become directly involved in school safety efforts.

Recommendation 7.5: Develop opportunities for young people to undertake meaningful activities in a supervised and safe setting after school, on weekends, and during the summer.

Recommendation 7.6: Include in collaborative school safety initiatives a component designed to strengthen families and support parents.

INDEX